THE LEGAL STATUS OF AIRCRAFT

THE LEGAL STATUS OF AIRCRAFT

PROEFSCHRIFT

TER VERKRIJGING VAN DE GRAAD VAN DOCTOR IN DE RECHTSGELEERDHEID AAN DE RIJKSUNIVERSITEIT TE LEIDEN, OP GEZAG VAN DE RECTOR MAGNIFICUS DR A. E. VAN ARKEL, HOOGLERAAR IN DE FACULTEIT DER WIS- EN NATUURKUNDE, TEGEN DE BEDENKINGEN VAN DE FACULTEIT DER RECHTSGELEERDHEID TE VERDEDIGEN OP WOENSDAG 13 JUNI, 1956 TE 14 UUR

DOOR

JAN PIET HONIG
GEBOREN TE NIEUWENDAM
IN 1914

'S-GRAVENHAGE
MARTINUS NIJHOFF
1956

ISBN 978-94-015-0391-4 ISBN 978-94-015-0987-9 (eBook)
DOI 10.1007/978-94-015-0987-9

Aan de nagedachtenis van mijn ouders

CONTENTS

LIST OF ABBREVIATIONS

CAA	Civil Aeronautics Administration
CJIA	Comité Juridique International de l'Aviation
CINA	Commission Internationale de la Navigation Aérienne
CITEJA	Comité International Technique d'Experts Juridiques Aériens
IATA	International Air Transport Association
ICAO	International Civil Aviation Organization
I.L.A.	International Law Association
I.L.O.	International Labour Office
J.A.L.C.	Journal of Air Law and Commerce
N.J.B.	Nederlands Juristenblad
PICAO	Provisional International Civil Aviation Organization
R.A.I.	Revue Aéronautique Internationale
Rec.	Recueil des Cours de l'Académie de Droit International à la Haye
R.D.A.	Revue de Droit Aérien
R.D.I.L.C.	Revue de Droit International et de Législation Comparée
R.D.I.P.	Revue de Droit International Privé
R.F.D.A.	Revue Française de Droit Aérien
R.G.A.	Revue Générale de l'Air
R.G.D.A.	Revue Générale de Droit Aérien
R.J.I.L.A.	Revue Juridique Internationale de Locomotion Aérienne

INTRODUCTION

I. Historical survey

The legal status of aircraft is a problem that has given rise to innumerable questions ever since the earliest years of aviation. But the majority of these questions only relate to certain aspects of the legal status of aircraft, and the problem as a whole has hardly been studied at all. The evolutionary process in the study of a number of facets of the problem is outlined below.

Nationality

The question of the nationality of aircraft has always received a lot of attention. As far as the principle is concerned, there can be little dispute on this point nowadays. The subject of the nationality of aircraft was discussed at the aviation conferences which led to the Paris Convention in 1919, the Ibero-American Convention in 1926, the Havana Convention in 1928 and the Chicago Convention in 1944.

According to Article 6 of the Paris Convention of 1919, an aircraft possesses the nationality of the State on whose register it is entered. The Ibero-American Convention of 1926 and the Pan-American Convention signed at Havana in 1928 start from the same principle.

The Chicago Convention of 1944 contains a whole chapter, Chapter III, devoted to the nationality of aircraft. In the Chicago Convention, which has superseded the convention concluded at Paris in 1919 and which includes rules of public law for international civil aviation, it is established that aircraft have the nationality of the State in which they are registered and that they cannot be validly registered in more than one State.

However, the Chicago Convention does not apply to one category of aircraft, namely State aircraft. The term "State aircraft" means police and customs aircraft, and of course military aircraft. Although there is not a single convention in regard to this category of aircraft, on the basis of existing international law it is assumed that such aircraft have the nationality of the State whose nationality marks they bear.

The Chicago Convention also contains a provision to the effect that the registration of aircraft in a certain State shall be made in accordance with the laws and regulations of that State. Each State can therefore decide for itself what requirements must be laid down with regard to the registration of an aircraft. One State may thus register aircraft belonging to aliens, whereas this may not be allowed in another State. It all depends on the national legislation.

Jurisdiction.

Besides the nationality of aircraft, another aspect of the legal status of aircraft has already occupied the attention of the aviation lawyers in the past. This is the jurisdiction of the State whose flag the aircraft carries, with respect to the conflict of laws on board the aircraft and the jurisdiction of other States in regard to such conflicts.

In contrast to the question of the nationality of aircraft, no solution has yet been found for this problem.

The jurisdiction problem was discussed at the meetings of the Comité Juridique de l'Aviation in 1912, 1921, 1922 and 1930.

The International Law Association has also taken a great interest in this problem and still continues to do so.

International Law Association

The problem of the legal status of aircraft, and the question of jurisdiction in particular, were studied by the International Law Association at its 31st conference in Buenos Aires in 1922, its 33rd conference at Stockholm in 1924, its 44th conference at Copenhagen in 1950 and its 45th conference at Lucerne in 1952.

The result of the Stockholm conference was a draft for a convention embodying rules with respect to the civil and criminal jurisdiction over aircraft. This draft has never been formally adopted but it has invariably served as a basis for further discussions. Since then the legal status of aircraft has always been maintained as an item on the agenda of the International Law Association.

In the year 1949, at the request of the International Law Association, Professor John C. Cooper prepared a study on the legal status of aircraft.[1]

During a meeting of the Air Law Committee of the International Law Association at London in April 1951, Professor Cooper was appointed as rapporteur in connection with a revision of the draft convention on the legal status of aircraft that had been drawn up at Stockholm in 1924. When the International Law Association met at Lucerne in 1952, he presented a report [2] dealing with the various questions which had to be answered before a revision of the draft could be undertaken.

At this meeting it was resolved that Professor Cooper should draw up a draft text for a convention on the legal status of aircraft and submit it to the Air Law Committee of the International Law Association.

International Civil Aviation Organization (ICAO)

The Legal Committee of the International Civil Aviation Organization has likewise put the question of the status of aircraft on its agenda. At the request of the Legal Committee a report on this subject [3] was submitted by Dr. Enrique Loaeza, the Mexican representative on the Council of the International Civil Aviation Organization. During its 9th session in 1953 the Legal Committee decided to give priority to the study of the problem of aerial collisions, but nevertheless the problem of the status of aircraft was retained as the second item on the agenda. The Legal Committee even went so far as to appoint a sub-committee to look into this subject. In this connection the Legal Committee wished to have special attention paid to the question of criminal and civil jurisdiction with respect to occurrences on board aircraft.

As is evident from the foregoing, the legal status of aircraft is a subject which has always enjoyed the interest of jurists concerned with air law.

---

[1] Cooper, "A Study on the Legal Status of Aircraft" (prepared for the Air Law Committee of the International Law Association), Sept. 1, 1949.

[2] Cooper, Report to the Air Law Committee of the International Law Association, May 23, 1952.

[3] Loaeza, Progress Report on the Legal Status of Aircraft. ICAO L. C. Working Draft 230, Dec. 20, 1950.

There are indications that in the near future this interest will begin to yield fruit – in the form of an international agreement. The main point in such an agreement will be the question of jurisdiction, since this frequently gives rise to difficulties in actual practice.

II. Chief problems

Following the above historical survey, the current problems relating to the legal status of aircraft are briefly explained below.

Sovereignty over the air space

The problem most closely connected with the legal status of aircraft is that of the freedom of the air.

According to Article 1 of the Chicago Convention of 1944, which has been ratified by practically all of the States concerned with aviation, other than the States behind the Iron Curtain, it is definitely established that the various States have complete and exclusive sovereignty over the air space above their territory.

It must be assumed that the air above the high seas, and also above regions which are not subject to the sovereignty of any State, is free. This is the only case in which it is possible to draw a comparison with the freedom of the seas, as the situation is fundamentally different in the case of air space above national territory.

Nationality of aircraft

The concept of the nationality of aircraft must be subjected to an examination, in view of the fact that it creates a certain relationship between the aircraft and a State.

Movable property sui generis

It will have to be established that the aircraft is not merely movable property but has a legal character sui generis. In the legislation of a number of States this finds expression in the method of acquiring ownership of an aircraft, which differs from that adopted for ordinary movable property, and in the fact that aircraft can be mortgaged.

Jurisdiction

It will be necessary to ascertain whether the law of the place or the law of the flag determines the legal status of aircraft. This problem crops up in the field of civil law as well as criminal law.

Consequences of the special legal status of aircraft

The consequences of the special legal status of aircraft will have to be investigated.

CHAPTER I

SOVEREIGNTY OVER THE AIR SPACE

THE CONCEPT OF AIR SPACE

In order to obtain a clear insight into the problems connected with sovereignty over the air space, it is advisable to determine what is meant by the term "air space."

The point at issue is whether the air space should be deemed to extend to infinity or whether it must be regarded as being limited.

If it is assumed that the air space extends to infinity, this implies that sovereignty over the air space likewise extends to infinity. Owing to the nature of things, however, a State exercises its sovereignty as high as its interests reach. The effective range of the sovereignty is therefore limited. The earth State will not extend the scope of its sovereignty to infinity but will only exercise it within a limited space. And, although the exercise of sovereignty may be limited, this does not necessarily mean that the sovereignty itself is also subject to restrictions. According to François,[1] on the other hand, the sovereignty of the State is simply the power to look after the national interests freely within the boundaries laid down by international law.

Sovereignty thus involves a limited territory over which it can be exercised, and in the present case this territory is the air space. An essential feature of sovereignty therefore is that the air space must be a limited territory and not one that extends to infinity.

Supposing that sovereignty does involve a limited territory, then it must also be possible to fix the boundary of that territory. If we recognize sovereignty over the air space, it follows that the air space must be a limited space.

[1] François, "Handboek van het Volkenrecht", Vol. I, p. 46.

But where is the boundary to be drawn? The most obvious solution is to let the air space coincide with the atmosphere round the earth. Danier [1] considers this "un espace relativement restraint." As may be seen from the following explanation, however, the delimitation of the atmosphere presents many difficulties.

The atmosphere is usually defined as consisting of four layers: the troposphere, the stratosphere, the ionosphere and the mesosphere. These layers gradually merge into one another until a zone is reached where the outermost layer, the mesosphere, merges into interplanetary space. The atmosphere is formed by gaseous air, the pressure of which is approximately one millionth of the weight of the earth. About three quarters of this is concentrated in the troposphere, slightly less than a quarter in the stratosphere, 1/3,000th in the ionosphere and 1/100,000,000,000th in the mesosphere. In the outermost layer of the atmosphere the air is therefore so rarefied that it is practically impossible to determine where the air completely disappears. For this reason the atmosphere does not form a clearly delimited space and consequently such a circumscription is useless from a legal standpoint. It might perhaps be decided by international agreement that the boundary of the air space should be drawn at an altitude where a specified atmospheric pressure is measured.

Of the writers who have occupied and are still occupying themselves with this question, two wish to fix another boundary for the air space.

Cooper [2] mentions the possibility of defining air space as "the space in which man-made or man-controlled flight might exist." The extent of the air space will then increase as technilogical progress continues. In Cooper's opinion, however, this would lead to "an impossible international legal position."

He points out that not a single State can exercise its sovereign rights "in outer space beyond the earth's attraction," adding that underneath there may also be a space where this is impracticable. Finally he suggests the following:

"Perhaps the territory of each State should be considered as

---

[1] Danier, "Les voyages interplanétaires et le droit", Revue Générale de l'Air, No. 6, 1952, p. 422.

[2] Cooper, Transport and Communications Review, Oct.-Dec. 1951, p. 3.

extending upward into space as far as then scientific progress enables the strongest State in the international community to control space above it."

The immediate comment on the above suggestion was that it is simply another way of saying that might is right.[1] It is strange that Cooper should think his first proposition would lead to an impossible international legal position, for his second proposition likewise suffers from the fault of vagueness and yet he considers it acceptable from a legal viewpoint. Notwithstanding this criticism, both of Cooper's suggestions are worth considering if no steps are taken to establish the boundary of the air space on a scientific basis.

Kroell [2] speaks of "une frontière céleste, c'est-à-dire celle entre la zone atmosphérique terrestre et l'espace interplanétaire". According to Kroell, such a frontier is formed by "la ligne où la valeur mathématique du champ de gravitation terrestre est nulle." He looks upon this as the frontier of the territory within which a State can enforce its standards.

However, it is practically impossible to establish Kroell's boundary of the air space (which is also mentioned by Cooper). How is one to determine the point where the gravitational attraction of the earth ceases? There is a distance where the gravitational attraction of the earth is counterbalanced by that of the sun and the moon. But this distance differs in relation to the sun and the moon. Furthermore, there is a difference at every point on the earth, and with the rotation of the earth this distance also varies from second to second at any given place on the earth.

The distance at which the gravitational attraction of the earth in relation to the sun is zero might well be calculated for a certain place on the earth's surface at a certain moment. The space inside an imaginary sphere enclosing the earth at that distance could then be designated as the air space. This would have to be internationally agreed upon. But a purely scientifically determined boundary, one which is fixed by nature, will never lead to a solution of practical value. A conference will be neces-

---

[1] Schachter, "Who owns the Universe?", Collier's, March 22, 1952, p. 71.

[2] Kroell, "Eléments créateurs d'un droit astronautique", Revue Générale de l'Air, No. 3–4, 1953, p. 233.

sary. There are also writers who merely specify a distance at random,[1] not like the distance of 1,500 metres chosen by Fauchille (as we shall see later), but of several hundred kilometres.

As already remarked, a State will naturally exercise its sovereignty as high as its interests reach. The fact that the State may not at present possess the necessary powers to exercise sovereignty in this space is immaterial. What Cooper rejects as "an impossible international legal position," viz. regarding the air space as the space in which air navigation is actually performed, appears to contain the germ of a solution. The space above the territory of a State, in which flight actually takes place, is then subject to the sovereignty of that State.

This solution too will give rise to great difficulties, as it will often be impossible to determine the State above whose territory certain events occur, but it will be easier to get this interpretation of the term "air space" internationally recognized than to agree upon a certain boundary.

Accordingly, the air space must not be deemed to extend to infinity. There is indeed a boundary, and this boundary ought to be drawn at the point beyond which the State no longer attaches importance to the exercise of sovereignty. Thus it is not a boundary fixed by nature but a boundary fixed by the national interest. If the interests of the different States are to be correctly weighed against one another, an international convention on the subject will be necessary.

HISTORY

Period prior to the Paris Convention of 1919

Since the beginning of aviation, which we can take at the start of this century, two theories have been put forward with regard to sovereignty over the air space, viz. the theory of the freedom of the air and the theory of the sovereignty of the States over the air space above their territory.

---

[1] Schachter, "Legal Aspects of Space Travel," Journal of the British Interplanetary Society, Jan. 1952, pp. 14–16.

Meyer, "Rechtliche Probleme des Weltraumflugs, Probleme aus der Astronautischen Grundlagenforschung", 1952.

Theory of the freedom of the air

As early as 1901 the French lawyer Fauchille published a treatise entitled "Le domaine aérien et le régime juridique des aérostats,"[1] in which he enunciated the maxim of "l'air est libre." This was the counterpart of the doctrine of the freedom of the seas propounded by Grotius in the year 1609, and it has become no less well-known.

Fauchille based his theory mainly on the proposition that it was impossible for a State to control the air space above the level up to which buildings can be erected.

In his opinion, however, the States were entitled to certain rights of self-preservation with respect to the air space above their territory.

Theories relating to the freedom of the air were subsequently developed by various other writers on the basis of the free air theory first formulated by Fauchille.[2]

These theories may be classified as follows:

1. Complete freedom of the whole air space;
2. Certain rights of self-preservation for the States concerned;
3. Complete freedom of the air above a certain height, underneath which
   (*a*) the States concerned should have certain rights of self-preservation;
   (*b*) the States concerned should have absolute sovereignty.

The theories mentioned under 3 are modelled on the three-mile zone of maritime law.

Fauchille soon inclined to the latter theories, which he expressed in the following terms:

"L'air est libre. Les Etats n'ont sur lui en temps de paix et en temps de guerre que les droits nécessaires à leur conservation. Ces droits sont relatifs à la repression de l'espionnage, à la police douanière et à la police sanitaire et aux nécessités de la défence."[3]

---

[1] Revue Générale de Droit International et Public, 1901, pp. 414 et seq.

[2] Lijcklama à Nijeholt, "La souveraineté aérienne", Revue Juridique Internationale de la Locomotion Aérienne, 1910, p. 236.
Hazeltine, "The Law of the Air", 1911, p. 45.
Nys, "Le régime juridique des aéronefs", Annales de l'Institut de Droit International, 1902.
Bonaparte, "Die Freiheit der Luft", 1914.
Meili, "Das Luftschiff und die Rechtswissenschaft", Berlin, 1909.

[3] Institut de Droit International, Annuaire, 1902, p. 32.

According to Fauchille's original view, the "droit de conservation" ought to allow the States to prohibit air traffic below an altitude of 1,500 metres. At that time it was technically impossible to make reliable photographs from a height of over 1,500 metres, so that the ban on flying at less than this height reduced the danger of espionage to negligible proportions.

After these writers several international organizations began to devote attention to the problem of sovereignty over the air space.

Institute of International Law. At its session in Ghent in 1906 [1] the Institute of International Law endorsed the view of Fauchille.

Since then, however, no other organization concerned with international air law has ever expressed itself in favour of the theory that "the air is free."

Fauchille also revised his opinion. In the report which he presented to the Institute of International Law in preparation for the sessions of this body at Paris in 1910 and at Madrid in 1911, he replaced the words "l'air est libre" by the words "la circulation aérienne est libre," [2] but he still qualified this by adding: "Néanmoins les Etats sous-jacents gardent des droits nécessaires à leur conservation, c'est-à-dire à leur propre sécurité et à celle des personnes et des biens de leur habitants."

Thus we have already reached the stage where the theory of the freedom of the air was to be abandoned. Fauchille leaves the question of sovereignty over the air space open and merely speaks of the use of the air space for air traffic.

The Institute of International Law adopted the new phrasing of Fauchille at its Madrid session in 1911.[3] The resolution passed by the Institute read as follows:

"La circulation aérienne internationale est libre sauf le droit pour les Etats sous-jacents de prendre certaines mesures, à déterminer, en vue de leur propre sécurité et de celle des personnes et des biens de leur habitants."

---

[1] Institut de Droit International, Annuaire, 1906, pp. 293 et seq., p. 305, pp. 327/328.

[2] Institut de Droit International, Annuaire, 1910, pp. 297 et seq.
Institut de Droit International, Annuaire, 1911, p. 107.

[3] Institut de Droit International, Annuaire, 1911, p. 346.

The Institute of International Law thus renounced the theory of the freedom of the air but did not go so far as to adopt the theory of sovereignty.

Comité Juridique International de l'Aviation. The Comité Juridique International de l'Aviation was founded in 1909 and held its first session in 1911.

It lost much of its importance after the formation of the International Commission for Air Navigation by the Paris Convention of 1919 and the Comité International Technique d'Experts Juridiques Aériens by the first international conference on private air law in 1925.

The original committee prepared a "Code de l'Air." Article 1 of this Code was worded in the same terms as the text of Fauchille (see above), which had meanwhile been adopted by the Institute of International Law [1]. The only difference is that the word "internationale" after "circulation aérienne" was dropped as being superfluous. At the fourth congress of the Comité Juridique in Monaco in 1921, Article 1 of the "Code de l'Air" was drafted as follows:

"La circulation aérienne est libre, sauf le droit pour l'Etat sous-jacent de prendre les mesures nécessaires en vue d'assurer sa sécurité et celle des personnes et des biens de ses habitants." [2]

Theory of sovereignty

International Law Association. The International Law Association did take the transitional step to the theory of sovereignty. At its sessions in Paris in 1921 and Madrid in 1913 the International Law Association occupied itself with the problem of sovereignty over the air space. The following text was drawn up at Madrid:

"It is the right of every State to enact such prohibitions, restrictions and regulations as it may think proper in the regard of the passage of aircraft through the air space above its territory and territorial waters; subject to this right of sub-jacent

---

[1] Comité Juridique International de l'Aviation, Compte Rendu du ler Congrès, pp. 64 et seq.

[2] Comité Juridique International de l'Aviation, Compte Rendu du 4me Congrès, Monaco, 1921, pp. 84, 88, 95, 180.

States, liberty of passage of aircraft ought to be accorded freely to the aircraft of every nation." [1]

Here we have the first step towards recognition of the sovereignty of each State over the air space above its territory.

Nevertheless the International Law Association still maintains that a State ought to allow other States free passage for their aircraft through the air space above its territory.

The legal character of the air space also came up for discussion at aviation conferences, where the principle of sovereignty over the air space was accepted right from the start.

The air navigation conference of 1910. The air navigation conference held at Paris in 1910 did not yield many positive results, but it was found that most of the delegations started from the principle of sovereignty over the air space – though recognizing the principle of liberty of passage of aircraft.[2]

Pan-American Aeronautic Federation. When the Pan-American Aeronautic Federation met at Santiago in 1926 it pronounced in favour of the sovereignty principle.

Scandinavian air conference of 1918. The question of sovereignty over the air space was also discussed at the first Scandinavian air conference held in Stockholm in 1918. This conference too supported the principle of sovereignty.

Congrès Juridique International pour la Locomotion Aérienne. The resolutions quoted below were adopted by this congress, which met at Verona in 1910:

"– que l'atmosphère dominant le territoire et la mer territoriale soit considérée comme une atmosphère territoriale assujettie à la souveraineté de l'Etat et que l'atmosphère dominant les territoires inoccupés et la mer libre soit considérée comme libre;

– que, dans l'espace territorial, le passage et la circulation des aéronefs soient libres, sauf les règles de police nécessaires et le régime juridique inhérent à la nationalité des aéronefs;

---

[1] International Law Association, 27th Report, Paris, 1912, pp. 213 et seq.; 28th Report, Madrid, 1913, pp. 533–545.

[2] P.V. Conférence Internationale de Navigation Aérienne, Paris, 1910.

– que les règles de la circulation des aéronefs dans l'espace libre soient établies par accords internationaux." [1]

The principle of sovereignty was thus accepted at all of the above-mentioned congresses.

There was a difference of opinion, however, in regard to the liberty of passage of aircraft.

The conclusion reached at Verona and Stockholm was that foreign aircraft ought to have liberty of passage, but the Pan-American Aeronautic Federation did not approve of this at all and thought that liberty of passage of aircraft in America should only be accorded to Americans.

It is therefore obvious from the foregoing that even before the conclusion of the Paris Convention the principle of the freedom of the air was abandoned in favour of the sovereignty principle.

In order to ascertain the reason for this, it is necessary to elucidate and analyze the arguments put forward in support of the two principles.

The principle of the freedom of the air is the Fauchille theory. He based this theory on the following arguments:

1. The impossibility of enforcing sovereignty over the air space. Fauchille expresses it as follows:
   "Il nous parait impossible d'isoler l'espace de l'air qui s'y trouve. La condition de l'air doit dès lors nécessairement se communiquer à celle de l'espace." [2]
   At the time when Fauchille advanced this argument it was quite acceptable, but now of course it no longer holds good. Present-day technology offers ample possibilities for effective control of the air space.
2. The analogy between the air space and the high seas. This is not a strong argument either. The importance of the air space above the territory of a State greatly exceeds any importance which the sea may have, no matter how great the latter may be. After all, a State without access to the sea is quite conceivable, while one cannot imagine a State without air space. Moreover, the high seas are separated from the territory of a maritime State by the three-mile zone. It is practically im-

[1] Lemoine, "Traité de Droit Aérien", p. 19.
[2] Revue Générale de Droit International et Public, 1901, p. 425.

possible to establish a similar zone for the air space. That has long been realized.[1]

3. The air is not susceptible of ownership.
   This is an unsound argument. It is purely a matter of private law and it is irrelevant as far as sovereignty over the air space is concerned.
   Fauchille simply takes Grotius's doctrine of the freedom of the seas and applies it to the air.[2] Later, however, Grotius reconsidered the matter and decided that sovereignty over the sea was indeed feasible – contrary to the theories which he had previously developed. The exercise of sovereignty over the air space is likewise feasible in every way. Mastery of the air space by means of an air fleet is now a generally established fact.

The principle of sovereignty over the air space is usually regarded as a corollary of the theory that the air space above the territory of a State is an integral part of that territory. Such a view is held by a number of writers.[3] It is the principle "cuius est solum eius est usque ad coelum." This rule of Roman law only applied to the part of the air space which used to be of interest, i.e. the air space up to the height to which buildings could be erected. But if this rule of civil law is transplanted to public law, it is understandable that a State should then claim sovereignty over the whole of the air space above its territory, in which case questions of security soon begin to play a part.[4] The air space has become too important for a State to neglect the sovereignty over it. It was therefore inevitable that the theory of sovereignty over the air space should find general acceptance. The interests

---

[1] Lijcklama, Revue Juridique Internationale de la Locomotion Aérienne, 1920, p. 264.

[2] Goedhuis, "Handboek voor Luchtrecht", p. 27.

[3] De la Pradelle, '"De l'Origine de la Maxime cujus solum, ejus coelum", R.G.D.A. 1932, pp. 294–302.
Zitelmann, "Luftschiffartrecht", p. 20.
Lijcklama, Revue Juridique Internationale de la Locomotion Aérienne, 1910, pp. 249, 264 et seq.
Hotchkiss, "Aviation Law", 132nd ed., 1938.
Cooper, "Roman Law and the Maxim of Cuius est Solum in International Air Law", McGill L. J. 23, 1952.
Kuhn, "The Beginning of an Aerial Law", 4 Am. J. Int. L. 109, 1910.
Hersey, "The International Law of Aerial Space", 6 Am. J. Int. L., p. 381, 1912.
Blackstone, "Commentaries on the Laws of England", Vol. II, p. 18

[4] Richards, "Sovereignty over the Air, "Oxford, 1912.

of military, police, sanitary and customs law made this necessary. The sovereignty of a State over the air space above its territory has therefore been accepted as a rule of international law.

In the light of the foregoing we must conclude that the principle of the freedom of the air is contestable from a theoretical standpoint and, what is much more important, it is impracticable from a governmental standpoint. The sovereignty principle is not only theoretically justifiable but, and this is the decisive point, it also coincided with the attitude which the various States had already adopted in actual practice.

The principle of sovereignty was therefore firmly established in the public law conventions relating to international civil aviation.

Paris Convention of 1919

Immediately after the signature of the armistice in 1918, which brought an end to the hostilities of the First World War, the aeronautical experts of the delegations to the Peace Conference began to draft rules and regulations for future international air traffic. The result was the "Convention relating to the regulation of aerial navigation," which was opened for signature on October 13, 1919. This Convention is nearly always referred to as the Paris Convention. It was ratified by the Netherlands in 1928.[1]

In Article 1 of the Paris Convention, the contracting States recognize that every power has complete and exclusive sovereignty over the air space above its territory.

The theory of sovereignty over the air space is thus established and consequently the air is not free. But this does not necessarily mean that air traffic is not to have liberty of passage. The question of liberty of passage was dealt with immediately after the sovereignty over the air space had been affirmed, as the latter is not absolute but can be restricted by treaty provisions.[2]

[1] Netherlands Statute Book, 226, 1928.

[2] Wagner, "Les Libertés de l'Air", Paris, 1948.
Scelle, "Preface, Les Libertés de l'Air", Paris, 1948.
van Kleffens, "Sovereignty in International Law".
Recueil des Cours de l'Académie de Droit International, 1953.
Rousseau, "L'Indépendence de l'Etat dans l'Ordre International", Recueil des Cours de l'Académie de Droit International, 1948 II.

Article 2 of the Paris Convention stipulates that in time of peace each contracting State shall accord freedom of innocent passage above its territory to the aircraft of the other contracting States, provided that the conditions laid down in the Convention are observed.

This right granted in Article 2 is a right of peaceful transit. It should be noted that there is no mention of a right to make landings. At least such a right is not expressly granted. However, the Convention proceeds on the assumption that such a right exists. The conditions under which foreign aircraft could land were those laid down in the national legislation. In this connection it must always be borne in mind that if the contracting States accord freedom of innocent passage this does not in any way imply that they accept the free air principle. They look upon this "innocent passage" as a right established by agreement, which can be revoked again. The restrictions imposed on air traffic by the Paris Convention may be divided into general and special restrictions.

General restrictions. Article 3 of the Paris Convention gives the possibility of a complete ban on air traffic, though only in certain areas. According to this Article, each contracting State can prohibit flying over certain areas of its territory for military reasons or in the interest of public safety. These prohibited areas must be designated without any distinction being made between aircraft of the State concerned and foreign aircraft. The latter is intended to ensure that no prohibited areas are so designated with the object of forming a barrier to air traffic.

In the first paragraph of Article 15 of the Paris Convention, aircraft of the contracting States are accorded the right to fly over the territory of another State without landing. However, such aircraft are bound to follow the routes fixed by the State concerned. According to the second paragraph of the same Article, an aircraft flying from the territory of one State to that of another State must land at a certain aerodrome if the latter State requires this.

Special restrictions. As far as scheduled air traffic is concerned, the third paragraph of Article 15 of the Paris Convention indicates that prior permission may be required for the operation of scheduled air services.

This provision is none too clear, since the grounds on which consent might be refused are not specified. On the other hand, it allows more latitude than Article 6 of the Chicago Convention of 1944, which will be discussed later. Most States insisted on prior permission before a scheduled air service could be established.

In Article 16 of the Paris Convention we find that each State is entitled to reserve the traffic between two points on its own territory for its national aircraft.

According to Article 32 of the Paris Convention a special authorization is required for the transit of military aircraft.

As appears from Article 33 of the Paris Convention, the cases in which police and customs aircraft may be granted permission to fly over the territory of a State will be determined in special arrangements between the States concerned.

As Goedhuis [1] puts it, however, it has been found that "in actual practice the right to make the establishment and operation of scheduled air services subject to prior permission has been used by the various States in such a way that there was nothing left of the principle of freedom of innocent passage."

Particularly in view of the attitude later adopted by the United Kingdom with regard to this question, the wording of Articles 1 and 2 proposed by the British delegation is rather remarkable.[2]

The British proposal made during the discussions on Article 1 of the Convention was to give the States complete sovereignty over the air space above their territory, subject to a proviso that the aircraft of one of the contracting States could fly freely into and over the territory of other contracting States on condition that they complied with the laws of the State over whose territory they flew.

On the basis of the British proposal, Article 2 of the Paris Convention should therefore have read as follows: "Each contracting State shall have the right to impose special restrictions by way of reservation or otherwise with respect to the public conveyance of persons and goods between two points on its

[1] Goedhuis, "Handboek voor het Luchtrecht", p. 52.

[2] P.V. Commission de l'Aéronautique, La Paix de Versailles.

territory, but such restrictions may not be imposed on a foreign aircraft where such aircraft is proceeding from one point to another within the territory of the contracting State either for the purpose (1) of landing the whole or part of its passengers or goods brought from abroad or (2) of taking on board the whole or part of its passengers or goods for a foreign destination, or (3) of carrying between the two points passengers holding tickets or goods consigned for through transit to or from some place outside the territory of the contracting State."

Had the proposal been accepted in that form, we should have obtained practically the same situation in international aviation with respect to the air as exists in international shipping with respect to the sea.

However, the text finally adopted at Paris allowed the States a completely free hand in fixing the conditions under which civil air traffic could be admitted.

The principles embodied in the Paris Convention are also to be found in the two conventions mentioned below.

Ibero-American Convention of 1926. The Ibero-American Convention was concluded in Madrid on November 1, 1926.[1] Its principles were the same as those of the Paris Convention. Since the principle of complete equality of status was inserted in the Paris Convention by the Protocol of 1929, the Ibero-American Convention no longer had any significance whatsoever after 1929, because its aim had been to counterbalance the preferential position of the then great Allied Powers, as laid down in the Paris Convention prior to amendment by the above Protocol.

Havana Convention of 1928. The Pan-American Convention signed at Havana on February 20, 1928, was likewise almost entirely in conformity with the principles of the Paris Convention. The name of this Convention, which was drafted on the initiative of the United States, is somewhat misleading. Apart from the U.S.A., Chile and Ecuador, only the Central American countries ratified the Havana Convention.[2]

---

[1] Ratified by Spain, Mexico, Paraguay, Dominican Republic and Costa Rica.

[2] Ratified by United States of America, Chile, Costa Rica, Dominican Republic, Ecuador, Guatemala, Haiti, Honduras, Mexico, Nicaragua, Panama.

An important difference from the Paris Convention is that, according to Article 21 of the Havana Convention, international air commerce between the contracting States is permitted without any restriction. No mention is made of prior permission for the operation of scheduled air services.

Until the year 1939, when the outbreak of World War II put an end to this, civil aviation in peacetime was subject to the rules laid down in the Conventions of Paris and Havana.

PRESENT SITUATION

Chicago Convention of December 7, 1944

On September 11, 1944, while the Second World War was still in progress, the Government of the United States of America sent an invitation to all the countries united in the struggle against the Axis Powers to attend a conference at Chicago, where new regulations for international civil aviation would be drawn up. At the same time a number of neutral States were invited to take part in the conference. With the exception of Russia and Saudi Arabia, all of the States in question accepted the invitation, so that on November 1, 1944, representatives of 54 States took their seats at the conference table.

According to the text of the invitation issued by the U.S. Government,[1] the objects of the conference were:

"I. (a) The establishment of provisional world route arrangements by general agreement to be reached at the Conference. These arrangements would form the basis for the prompt establishment of international air transport services by the appropriate countries.

(b) The countries participating in the conference would also be asked to agree to grant the landing and transit rights necessary for establishing the provisional route arrangements and air services referred to above.

II. The establishment of an Interim Council to act as the clearing house and advisory agency during the transitional period.

III. Agreement upon the principles to be followed in setting

[1] For text of invitation see "Proceedings of the International Civil Aviation Conference", Chicago, 1944, p. 11.

up a permanent international aeronautical body, and a multilateral aviation convention dealing with the fields of air transport, air navigation and aviation technical subjects."

One of the results of the conference was the Convention on International Civil Aviation concluded on December 7, 1944. This Convention supersedes the Paris Convention of 1919 and the Havana Convention of 1928. It has been ratified by practically every State which is actively engaged in aviation (including the Netherlands),[1] but not by the States behind the Iron Curtain.

The aim of those who drafted the Chicago Convention is stated in the following extract from the preamble to the Convention:

"..... the undersigned governments having agreed on certain principles and arrangements in order that international civil aviation may be developed in a safe and orderly manner and that international air transport services may be established on the basis of equality of opportunity and operated soundly and economically, have accordingly concluded this Convention to that end."

The conference also drew up the text of a Final Act, an Interim Agreement on International Civil Aviation, an International Air Services Transit Agreement and an International Air Transport Agreement. These agreements were ratified by the Netherlands Government.

Under the terms of the Chicago Convention, regulatory action can be taken not only in the field of air safety – which was the main purpose of the Paris Convention – but also in the political and economic fields. For this an international organization is necessary, and the Chicago Convention created such an organization. It consists of an Assembly, which is comparable to the International Commission for Air Navigation (CINA) instituted by the Paris Convention of 1919, an executive committee which meets in permanent session in the form of a Council, a Secretariat and a number of permanent committees. The organization as a whole is called the International Civil Aviation Organization (ICAO).

One of the cardinal points in drafting the Chicago Conven-

---

[1] Effective in the Netherlands, April 25, 1947 (Act of Feb. 28, 1947). Original text and Dutch translation published in Statute Book, June 3, 1947.

tion was the question of the freedom of the air. In fact the conference at Chicago was very nearly wrecked through the difficulties in connection with this subject.

The principle of complete and exclusive sovereignty of the States in regard to the air space above their territory was taken over from the Paris Convention without any curtailment. Article 1 of the Chicago Convention is thus almost identical to Article 1 of the Paris Convention. There was unanimous agreement on this principle and it did not give rise to any discussion at Chicago.

As far as the freedom of the air was concerned, however, sharply contrasting views were expressed at the conference in Chicago. Four proposals were submitted with respect to the freedom of the air.

Proposal of the United States of America [1]. The United States wanted the proposed convention to include the right of transit and the right to make landings without picking up or setting down passengers or goods. These two rights, which are mostly referred to below as the first and second freedoms of the air, were not to be subject to prior authorization. Commercial traffic had to be regulated by direct negotiations between the States concerned.

Proposal of the United Kingdom. [2] According to the British proposal, the development of air transport ought to take place under international control. The following rights were to be embodied in the proposed convention:

"*a.* the right of innocent passage through a State's air space;
b. the right to land for non-traffic purposes;
c. the right to disembark passengers, mails and freight destined from the country of origin of the aircraft;
d. the right to embark passengers, mails and freight destined for the country of origin of the aircraft.

The right to pick up and set down traffic to and from desti-

[1] "Proceedings of the International Civil Aviation Conference, Chicago, Illinois, November 1 – December 7, 1944, Vol. I."
U.S. Government Printing Office, Washington, 1948, p. 555.
[2] Ibid., p. 566.

nations which are not in the country of origin of the aircraft and the right to engage in the cabotage of another country would be a matter for negotiation."

The international authority to be established under the convention would be given certain powers to determine the permissible frequencies as well as to fix the fares and rates.

Proposal of Canada.[1] The Canadian proposal was fundamentally the same as that of the United Kingdom, but Canada wanted to give slightly greater powers to the international authority which was to be set up. The proposal speaks of an international authority "to ensure that, so far as possible, international air routes and services are divided fairly and equitably between the various member States."

Proposal of Australia and New Zealand.[2] Australia and New Zealand proposed the formation of an international air transport authority which would be entrusted with the operation of the main international air routes.

None of the proposals met with general acceptance. After a sort of combined proposal had been worked out, however, it was found that the United States and the United Kingdom were unable to reach agreement on the subject of the "fifth freedom" of the air. This fifth freedom may be defined as follows:

"The right of an airline to take on and discharge passengers at intermediate points along a through route traversing a number of countries."

Both States agreed that the above right must be restricted, but they disagreed as to the method of restricting it.

When the divergent views could not be reconciled, a compromise was sought in order to avoid a complete breakdown of the conference.

The United States then proposed that, besides the Convention, separate agreements on the freedom of the air should be drawn up. It was thought that the solution to the difficulties that had arisen could be found by drafting a Convention whereby each State obtains complete sovereignty over the air space above its

[1] Ibid., p. 570.
[2] Ibid., p. 457.

territory, and in which it is stipulated that no scheduled air service over or to a country may be started without the consent of that country. At the same time, however, two supplementary agreements would be drawn up, viz. the International Air Services Transit Agreement and the International Air Transport Agreement, thereby establishing a considerable measure of freedom in the air.

The extent to which this solution has been successful will be discussed later. In the meantime we shall examine the Convention.

The principle of sovereignty over the air space is laid down in the Chicago Convention in terms which are a faithful copy of the terms used in the Paris Convention. The rules of the Chicago Convention with respect to the freedom of the air likewise correspond to those of the Paris Convention of 1919, though the former are stricter and more detailed.

The "innocent passage" of Article 2 of the Paris Convention is only recognized by the Chicago Convention in the case of non-scheduled air traffic, and with certain restrictions, as we shall see later.

Restrictions on scheduled air traffic. The counterpart of Article 15 of the Paris Convention, whereby the establishment of scheduled air services *may* be subject to prior permission, is to be found in Article 6 of the Chicago Convention. According to this Article, no scheduled air service may be operated over or into the territory of a contracting State without special permission from that State. In contrast to the Paris Convention, the Chicago Convention expressly stipulates that special permission must be obtained. In actual practice, however, even under the Paris Convention it was always necessary to obtain permission. The door to freedom of scheduled air traffic, which had already been closed by the Paris Convention, was thus hermetically sealed by the Chicago Convention. On the other hand, the establishment of scheduled air services is of course much easier for the countries which ratified the International Air Services Transit Agreement and the International Air Transport Agreement, than was the case under the Paris Convention. Those States which merely ratified the Chicago Convention without adopting the two supplementary agreements have not advanced a single step towards the liberation of civil aviation since it first came into being.

Restrictions on non-scheduled air traffic. The situation is somewhat different in the case of non-scheduled air traffic. In the years preceding World War II non-scheduled air traffic was of no particular importance. The regulations applicable to aviation before 1944 made no distinction between scheduled and non-scheduled air traffic. As a general rule, however, the regulations governing scheduled air traffic – especially the provisions of the Paris Convention of 1919 – were also applied to non-scheduled air traffic. This meant that prior permission was also required for the performance of non-scheduled flights. In this respect the Chicago Convention is an improvement on the Paris Convention.

Unlike the Paris Convention, which did not deal with this subject, Article 5 of the Chicago Convention lays down regulations for non-scheduled air transport.

The text of the Article in question reads as follows:

"Each contracting State agrees that all aircraft of the other contracting States, being aircraft not engaged in scheduled international air services, shall have the right, subject to the observance of the terms of this convention, to make flights into or in transit non-stop across its territory and to make stops for non-traffic purposes without the necessity of obtaining prior permission, and subject to the right of the State flown over to require landing. Each contracting State nevertheless reserves the right, for reasons of safety of flight, to require aircraft desiring to proceed over regions which are inaccessible or without adequate air navigation facilities to follow prescribed routes, or to obtain special permission for such flights.

Each aircraft, if engaged in the carriage of passengers, cargo or mail for remuneration or hire on other than scheduled international air services, shall also, subject to the provisions of Article 7, have the privilege of taking or discharging passengers, cargo or mail, subject to the right of any State where such embarkation or discharge takes place to impose such regulations, conditions or limitations as it may consider desirable."

This establishes the principle of freedom of international air traffic, at least as far as non-scheduled air traffic is concerned.

On reading the first part of Article 5 which contains the rules governing the operation of non-scheduled flights, we see that such flights can be made without the necessity of obtaining prior permission, except "for reasons of safety of flight." Our joy is short-lived, however, when we see that this only applies to transit flights and landings when no passengers or goods are embarked or discharged. Such landings are referred to as technical landings.

But in the second part of Article 5 it is stated that landings where passengers and goods are embarked or discharged (i.e. commercial landings) shall be subject to such restrictions as the State in which the landing takes place considers desirable.

It is only natural that an article worded in these terms should have given rise to considerable difficulties of interpretation, and it still does so. Some States apply this article with very little regard for the promising beginning of the article. On investigating the origin of Article 5 we find that it represents the outcome of two articles proposed by the United States of America at the Chicago conference. In these articles it was stipulated that non-scheduled flights could be operated *"without the necessity of obtaining prior permission."* [1] This principle has been maintained in the final text of the Chicago Convention; only aircraft desiring to proceed over regions which are inaccessible or without adequate air navigation facilities need to obtain special permission for such flights. The fact that the article in question is entitled "Right of non-scheduled flight" plainly confirms the intention to give expression to this principle.

The Netherlands logically interprets Article 5 in the sense that no matter what restrictions may be imposed on the performance of non-scheduled flights, there is no need to obtain prior permission.

After all, according to the first part of Article 5 an aircraft making a non-scheduled flight is entitled to fly over the territory of another State and to make technical landings without the necessity of obtaining prior permission. But the second part of Article 5 says that an aircraft can *also* make commercial landings provided that it complies with the applicable regu-

---

[1] Goedhuis, "Pacta sunt servanda", 1952.

lations. The word "also" implies that the aircraft has the right specified in the first part of the article, namely to land without prior permission, and also the right to make commercial landings subject to certain conditions. The primary right is to be allowed to land without prior permission. In the second part of the article this right is not withdrawn for commercial landings but extended to cover them. On account of the difficulties that had arisen, the Council of the International Civil Aviation Organization directed the Secretariat of this organization to prepare an analysis of Article 5 of the Chicago Convention. This analysis largely corresponded to the interpretation given above.[1] The analysis of the Secretariat was subsequently discussed by one of the permanent committees of ICAO, the Air Transport Committee. During the discussion in the Air Transport Committee the analysis was subjected to a great deal of criticism. The majority of the members of the Air Transport Committee appeared to be unable to agree with the view of the Secretariat that prior permission was not required for the flights referred to in the second part of Article 5. The Secretariat was instructed to revise its analysis and bring it into line with the views of the majority of the members of the Air Transport Committee. The redraft which the Secretariat then produced contains the following phrase:

"the right of the State to impose regulations, conditions, or limitations is unqualified." [2]

The words appearing in the original analysis, viz.:

"the Secretariat believes that it was the intention of those who drafted and adopted this article that carriers covered by the article should enjoy this privilege without the necessity of obtaining prior permission" have disappeared. [3]

This development in regard to the interpretation of Article 5 is extremely disappointing. From the history of the article and from the text finally adopted, it is clearly correct to take the view that no prior permission is required for a non-scheduled flight.

On analyzing international practice with regard to the appli-

[1] ICAO Doc. 6894–AT/694, Aug. 26, 1949, pp. 5–12.
[2] ICAO Doc. AT/WP/206, Feb. 27, 1951.
[3] Goedhuis, "Pacta sunt servanda".
Goudsmit, "Het Internationale Ongeregelde Luchtvervoer en artikel 5 van het Verdrag van Chicago", 1953.

cation of Article 5, it is found that most of the States violate the spirit of this article. They fall into three distinct groups:

a. States which admit non-scheduled air traffic (both commercial and non-commercial) without prior permission. This group includes the Netherlands.

b. States which insist on prior permission even though they recognize the fact that Article 5 is not intended to create the possibility of requiring prior permission for non-scheduled air traffic. This group includes the United Kingdom.

c. States which act on the assumption that Article 5 entitles them to require prior permission for non-scheduled air traffic. This group includes the United States. [1]

The views of most writers agree with the standpoint adopted by the Netherlands, [2] but there are also writers who have expressed views to the contrary.[3]

Accordingly, not much has come of the intention of Article 5 to clear the way for free international non-scheduled air traffic. In order to achieve a considerable measure of freedom as far as scheduled air traffic is concerned, the proposal of the United States that the freedoms of air traffic should be incorporated in two supplementary agreements was accepted at the Chicago conference.

Two agreements establishing the rights to fly over and to make landings in the territory of the contracting States were concluded at the same time as the Chicago Convention. They are the above-mentioned International Air Services Transit Agreement and the International Air Transport Agreement. The rights reciprocally granted to one another by the signatory States are known as the Five Freedoms, viz.: –

1. Freedom of peaceful transit.
2. Freedom of non-traffic stops (for fuel, repairs, etc.).
3. Freedom to take traffic from the homeland to any country.
4. Freedom to bring traffic from any country to the homeland.

---

[1] ICAO Doc. 6894–AT/694, Aug. 26, 1949.
ICAO Doc. 7008–AT/702, June 27, 1950.
ICAO W.P. 10–EC/5, March 23, 1953.

[2] Riese, "Luftrecht", p. 136.
Oppikofer, "Aktuelle Probleme des Luftrechts", Zeitschrift für Schweizerisches Recht, 1946, p. 192.
Lacour et Riese, "Précis de Droit Aérien", Paris, 1951, p. 92.

[3] Cooper, "The Right to Fly", p. 173.

5. Freedom to pick up and discharge traffic at intermediate points.

The two Agreements apply exclusively to scheduled air traffic.

International Air Services Transit Agreement

The first and second freedoms are embodied in the International Air Services Transit Agreement.

As mentioned earlier, at the start of the conference in Chicago the United States suggested that these two freedoms should be included in the Convention itself, but this was only agreed to in the case of non-scheduled air services.

Up till now the Transit Agreement has been signed by 41 States. It forms a supplement to the Chicago Convention and it can only be ratified by signatories of this Convention.

Without these two freedoms international air traffic is impossible. To that extent the Transit Agreement is naturally of great importance. But these two freedoms should really only be the first steps on the road leading to complete freedom of the air. This was fully realized during the Chicago Conference and so another agreement which went much further was drawn up besides the Transit Agreement, viz. the International Air Transport Agreement.

International Air Transport Agreement

The International Air Transport Agreement is also known as the "Five Freedoms Agreement," because it contains all the five freedoms mentioned earlier. It is clear that freedom of the air depends on acceptance of this agreement. Although the Air Transport Agreement is more restricted than international practice with regard to merchant shipping, international air transport would have been greatly benefited by general ratification of this Agreement. For a moment it seemed that the Air Transport Agreement was a step in the right direction, i.e. along the road to complete freedom of the air. However, the agreement was ratified by very few States. The number of signatories has never exceeded fifteen, and of these the United States, Sweden and the

Netherlands were the only countries actively engaged in international air transport.

The denunciation of the Air Transport Agreement by the United States in 1946 was its deathblow. This seems strange, because it was the United States that proposed the Air Transport Agreement at the Chicago conference. In order to explain the reason we shall give a very brief outline of U.S. air policy since the beginning of civil aviation.

From 1919 until 1935 the United States advocated the freedom of the air. As we have seen above, the U.S.A. signed the Havana Convention of 1928, which, in contrast to the Paris Convention of 1919, did not make the operation of scheduled air services subject to prior permission. After 1935 the United States switched over to a policy of restricting freedom of the air on security grounds and for protectionistic motives.

During World War II the United States again revised its attitude, this time in favour of the freedom of the air.

On the point of winning a world war and fully aware that it had a great material advantage over its Allies, the U.S.A. considered that freedom of the air was the surest guarantee of being able to play a dominant role in post-war international air transport. Strangely enough, the proposal first put forward by the United States at the Chicago conference in regard to the freedom of the air did not go beyond freedom for non-commercial traffic. Commercial traffic would have to form the subject of direct negotiations between the States concerned. Later, however, the U.S.A. proposed the Five Freedoms Agreement. Why was it that this country now reversed its policy and withdrew from the agreement?

The U.S.A. itself tried to justify this action by asserting that the Air Transport Agreement had not shown any viability. It is true that the agreement found little acceptance, but there is good reason to doubt whether this was the real reason for denouncing the agreement. From what was said in the U.S. Senate during the discussion of the Chicago Convention, for example, it is clearly apparent that there was strong opposition to the Air Transport Agreement in the United States and that the ratification of the Chicago Convention would be seriously jeopardized if the Air Transport Agreement was not dropped. This is illustrated by a few passages from the speeches made by two Senators on this subject. Addressing the Senate on July 25, 1946, Senator McCarran spoke as follows:[1]

"Mr. President, as long as the United States was an adherent to the five freedoms agreement, I felt – and I know that other members of this body held the same view – that the convention on international civil aviation, which is now before us, ... held dangers so great that it would be my duty to oppose it ...... However, Mr. President, I am so greatly relieved that we have pulled out of the five freedoms agreement that I shall not now oppose the treaty."

On the same date Senator Brewster remarked:

"The five freedoms were the things that gave away America's air to the world. Fifty-four nations could come here and do about as they pleased."

These last words in particular reveal the true reason for the denunciation of the Air Transport Agreement by the United States, namely the real or imaginary threat to the predominance of the United States in civil aviation. The United States thus reverted to its protectionist air policy of the years immediately preceding World War II. Shortly before the denunciation of the Air Transport Agreement came into effect, the United States turned its back on the principle of freedom of the air. At a meeting on the islands of Bermuda in February, 1946, the United States concluded an agreement with the United Kingdom.[2]

This "Bermuda Agreement" has become a model for a long series of bilateral air agreements between the various States. Such agreements refer to certain routes which may be flown and airports where landings may be made, besides specifying the frequency of the flights and the capacity to be provided. Quite apart from the transition from a multilateral to a bilateral agreement, this represents a considerable departure from the principles of the Air Transport Agreement.

Further restrictions on the freedom of the air

Under the terms of Article 7 of the Chicago Convention, as was

[1] Congressional Record, July 25, 1946.

[2] Air Services Agreement between the United States of America and the United Kingdom of Great Britain and Northern Ireland, Bermuda, February 11, 1946.

the case with Article 16(1) of the Paris Convention, the air traffic within the territory of a State is reserved for the aircraft of that State.

Article 9 of the Chicago Convention prohibits foreign aircraft from flying over prohibited areas designated as such by the State concerned. This article is comparable to Article 3 of the Paris Convention, but with the difference that foreign aircraft are merely prohibited from flying over such areas, whereas Article 3 of the Paris Convention stipulated that this restriction should apply equally to foreign and national aircraft. In order to ensure that the international scheduled air services of the State concerned would not be placed in a privileged position vis-à-vis foreign air services, however, the ban on flying over prohibited areas was also declared applicable to national aircraft engaged in scheduled services.

According to Article 10 of the Chicago Convention, an aircraft entering the air space above a contracting State is obliged to land at a certain airport if so required by that State (for the purpose of customs and other examinations). This corresponds to Article 15(e) of the Paris Convention.

The Chicago Convention only applies to civil aircraft and is not applicable to State aircraft. The latter are not permitted to fly over or to land on the territory of another State without a special authorization.

With regard to the application by the various States of the provisions of the Chicago Convention which restrict the freedom of the air, it must be remarked that – as was the case with the Paris Convention – these make the freedom of the air almost illusory.

CONCLUSION

On the basis of the evolutionary process outlined above we come to the conclusion that the principle of the sovereignty of each State *over the air space above its territory* is firmly anchored in international air law. The air space above the territory of the various States must be looked upon as the territorial zone of the sea. Just as sovereignty extends over the territorial waters, the sovereignty of a State extends to the territorial air space. This territorial air space is the whole column of air above the territory of a State. In modern air transport it is unthinkable to delimit a zone, as Fauchille wanted to do, in this space. Sovereignty over the territorial air space must be regarded as inviolable. It is not to be expected that this principle will again be forsaken.

But the sovereignty of the States only extends to the air space above their territory. The air above the high seas, and also above territory which is not subject to the dominion of any State, is free.

A comparison between air and sea is therefore quite feasible. There are territorial waters and there is territorial air space, over which sovereignty is exercised by the States concerned. There is freedom of the sea outside the territorial waters and there is freedom of the air outside territorial air space. The doctrine of the freedom of the high seas is based on a general legal conviction. It has become an international rule of law. We must make a similar assumption with respect to the air outside the territorial air space. In the course of history the doctrine of the freedom of the seas has been attacked on more than one occasion. In this connection we need only refer to England's claim to maritime sovereignty at the beginning of the 17th century. Sir Leoline Jenkins boldly stated:

"So long an arm has God given to this vice-regent the King of Great Britain; why not claim the whole, including north and south poles."

This is history, however, and as far as the air space is concerned, it does not seem essential that a process of evolution like that of the freedom of the seas should have to be gone through in order to arrive at the above-mentioned rule of international law.

In principle, therefore, there is no difference between the free sea and the free air.

The main difference lies in the measures taken by the States to prevent foreign aircraft flying to and from their territory; this course of action differs considerably from that adopted with respect to world merchant shipping. Accordingly, the liberalization of air traffic will not be achieved by discarding the sovereignty principle but by treating air traffic in the same way as merchant shipping, and it is in this direction that a solution must be sought.

CHAPTER II

NATIONALITY OF AIRCRAFT

INTRODUCTION

The aircraft

Before we can go further into the problems surrounding the legal status of aircraft, we must consider what is meant by "aircraft." For this purpose we shall examine the definitions of aircraft in international and national law.

International law

Paris Convention of 1919. In Annex A to the Paris Convention of 1919 we find the following definition of the term "aircraft": Any machine that can derive support in the atmosphere from the reactions of the air.

Annex A also indicates which categories of machines must be classified as aircraft, viz.: aeroplanes, airships, gliders, free balloons, captive balloons and kites. The definition therefore covers lighter-than-air as well as heavier-than-air aircraft.

Chicago Convention of 1944. The definition contained in Annex A to the Paris Convention is repeated in Annex 6 to the Chicago Convention of 1944. Neither in the Chicago Convention nor in the Paris Convention is the definition of the term "aircraft" included in the Convention itself.

National law

France. In the French Aviation Law of May 31, 1924, we read that:

"sont qualifiés aéronefs pour l'application de la présente loi tous les appareils capable de s'élever ou de circuler dans les airs."

United States of America. The following definition is given in the Civil Aeronautics Act:

"any contrivance now known or hereafter invented, used or designed for navigation or flight in the air."

The Netherlands. In Dutch legislation the term "aircraft" is defined in Article 1 of the Air Traffic Regulations (L.V.R.) and in Article 770h of the Netherlands Code of Civil Procedure in exactly the same way as in the Paris and Chicago Conventions, viz.:

"any machine that can derive support in the atmosphere from the reactions of the air."

We find the same definition in Article 1 of the Regulations for State Control or Air Navigation (R.T.L.), except that it does not include captive balloons, kites and gliders. The Dutch Aviation Act does not contain any definition of the term "aircraft", but Article 1 of this Act gives a limitative list of the machines which must be regarded as aircraft, viz. aeroplanes, airships, free balloons, captive balloons and kites. This means that a glider is not an aircraft within the meaning of the Aviation Act.

Conclusion

The above definitions are very broad and they are also intended as such. The requirement of having a connection with air traffic is definitely not laid down. This is logical because air law is not exclusively transport law.[1] Otherwise a comparatively narrow definition might suffice. Air law, however, must specify which objects capable of flight are subject to the rules of air law, and this must be taken into account in a general definition. It is very doubtful whether it is really desirable to give a scientific definition of the term "aircraft." The private law conventions in the field of aviation do not define aircraft at all.[2] The legal experts who drafted these conventions preferred to let jurisprudence determine the cases in which aircraft are involved. The draw-

---

[1] Riese, "Luftrecht", p. 187.

[2] Convention for the unification of certain rules relating to carriage by air, Warsaw, 1929.

Convention on liability for damage caused by aircraft to third parties on the surface, Rome, 1952.

Convention on recognition of rights in aircraft, Geneva, 1948.

back of the definitions cited above is that they cover categories which they are certainly not meant to. For this reason the system followed in the Dutch Aviation Act, whereby a list is given of the categories of machines to be regarded as aircraft, has much to commend it.

State and civil aircraft

Just as maritime law makes a distinction with respect to ships, air law distinguishes between State and civil aircraft. Fauchille [1] made such a distinction with regard to balloons as early as 1902. In the air navigation regulations which he drafted for the Institute of International Law in that year he speaks of public and private balloons. This classification of Fauchille is purely legal, being based on the distinction between public and private law, so that it is not a technical distinction. In a later draft which he prepared for the Institute of International Law in 1910 [2] Fauchille adopted the same classification, but this time he subdivided the public balloons into military balloons and civil State balloons. In 1908 the Swiss jurist Meili made a still greater differentiation: [3] he classified aircraft as State aircraft, military aircraft, public service aircraft and private aircraft.

International air navigation conference of 1910

The draft convention prepared at the air navigation conference in Paris in 1910 largely adhered to Fauchille's classification, though with a still further subdivision.[4] Public aircraft were defined as:

"les aéronefs affectés au service d'un Etat et se trouvant sous les ordres d'un fonctionnaire dûment commissionné de cet Etat."

The draft also divided public aircraft into the following categories:

"*a.* aéronefs militaires, c.-à.-d. ceux qui, se trouvant au service militaire, sont placés sous les ordres d'un commandant portant l'uniforme et ont à bord un certificat établissant leur caractère militaire;

[1] Annuaire de l'Institut de Droit International, 1902, p. 25.

[2] Ibid., 1910, p. 305.

[3] Meili, "Das Luftschiff im internen Recht und Völkerrecht," p. 11.

[4] Conférence internationale de navigation aérienne, Paris, 1910, procès-verbaux des séances et annexes.

b. aéronefs de police, c.-à.-d. ceux qui sont chargés notamment du service de la sûreté publique, de la police sanitaire ou de la police douanière; (et qui) doivent être dirigés par un fonctionnaire de l'Etat dûment commissionné."

Comité Juridique International de l'Aviation

The "Code de l'Air" drawn up by the Comité Juridique International de l'Aviation likewise made a distinction between public and private aircraft.[1]

The difference between State and civil aircraft was laid down in the Paris Convention of 1919.

International Law

Paris Convention of 1919. The Paris Convention of 1919 made a distinction between State and civil aircraft. State aircraft were subdivided into military aircraft and aircraft exclusively employed in State service. The relevant Article 30 of the Paris Convention reads as follows:

"The following shall be deemed to be State aircraft:

(*a*) Military aircraft;

(*b*) Aircraft exclusively employed in State service, such as posts, customs, police.

Every other aircraft shall be deemed to be a private aircraft.

All State aircraft other than military, customs and police aircraft shall be treated as private aircraft and as such shall be subject to all the provisions of the present Convention".

The criterion for this classification is whether the aircraft are intended for public service or not.

The curious feature is that according to the above rules, aircraft which only carry mail are classed as State aircraft, but from the second part of the article it appears that they must be treated as civil aircraft.[2]

Military aircraft. The Paris Convention devoted a separate article to military aircraft, viz. Article 31. This Article states that "Every aircraft commanded by a person in military service

---

[1] Ier Congrès International de la législation aérienne du Comité Juridique International de l'Aviation.

[2] L. W. F. H. Omta, "Immuniteit van Staatsschepen en -ladingen en van Staatsluchtvaartuigen", Amsterdam, 1938.

detailed for the purpose shall be deemed to be a military aircraft."

The above wording has been severely criticized.[1] It must be remarked, however, that it is by no means easy to give an accurate definition of the term "military aircraft." As Goedhuis rightly argues, however, it is incorrect that the military character of an aircraft should be determined by a personal criterion, while the nature of the aircraft itself is ignored. The difficulty encountered in defining the term "military aircraft" lies mainly in the fact that civil aircraft can also be used for military purposes. Zondag [2] deals with the question of military aircraft at considerable length in his thesis. He discusses the various different factors which determine the military character of the aircraft. He puts the proprietary relationship first, though he himself admits that this does not form a particularly good criterion for determining the military character of the aircraft. He then refers to the employment for war purposes as a standard for determining the military character of the aircraft. As indicated above, however, aircraft intended purely for civil purposes can also be used for war purposes. The criterion of military command, which he describes as being a decisive factor with respect to the military character of the aircraft, is the solution chosen in the Paris Convention. This is open to the objections already mentioned. The additional requirement of being attached to the armed forces, which he describes as a criterion, does not make much difference to the foregoing.

A number of writers [3] take as a standard the fact that the aircraft carries military markings, but it does not seem right that the character of an aircraft should be determined by its markings. Lastly we come to the question of use for military purposes as a criterion for the military character of aircraft, as laid down in a draft convention of the Harvard Research concerning "Rights and Duties of Neutral States in Naval and Aerial War." [4] This is the criterion adopted in the Chicago Convention of 1944.

---

[1] Goedhuis, "Handboek voor het Luchtrecht", p. 62.
Zondag, "Neutraliteit in de Lucht", p. 17.

[2] Zondag, "Neutraliteit in de lucht", 1940, p. 10.

[3] Klein, "Staatsschiffe und Staatsluftfahrzeuge in Völkerrecht", p. 26.
Catellani, Le Droit Aérien, (trad. le Droit Aérien, Paris, 1912).

[4] American Journal of International Law, July 1934.

Chicago Convention of 1944. The provisions of the Chicago Convention dealing with State and civil aircraft are much less detailed than those of the Paris Convention.

In Article 3(a) of the Chicago Convention it is stated that the Convention only applies to *civil aircraft* and not to State aircraft.

Article 3(b) indicates what is meant by "State aircraft." The Article reads as follows:

"Aircraft used in military, customs and police services shall be deemed to be State aircraft."

The use of an aircraft in these services stamps it as a State aircraft. The strange construction with regard to aircraft used for the transport of mail has – quite rightly – not been copied from the Paris Convention.

The drawback of Article 3 is that it does not indicate whether there is still a third category of aircraft besides civil aircraft and State aircraft, or whether all aircraft not deemed to be State aircraft are classed as civil aircraft, or vice versa. Nor is it clear whether Article 3(b) gives an exhaustive definition of the term "State aircraft." Another strange thing is that whereas Article 3(a) of the Convention says that it is not applicable to State aircraft, Paragraphs c and d of the same Article give rules for State aircraft. Paragraph c, for instance, reads:

"No State aircraft of a contracting State shall fly over the territory of another State or land thereon without authorization by special agreement or otherwise, and in accordance with the terms thereof."

If the above-mentioned authorization is granted, this implies that certain rules such as Articles 9 and 12 of the Convention will undoubtedly be applicable. But that is contradicted by Paragraph a, according to which the Convention only applies to civil aircraft and is not applicable to State aircraft. This point will have to be looked into in the event of the Chicago Convention being revised.

Military aircraft. Unlike the Paris Convention, the Chicago Convention does not include any special provisions relating to military aircraft. Under the terms of Article 3(b) of the Chicago Convention, military aircraft are aircraft used in military services. This criterion is based neither on the technical character of the aircraft nor on its external markings. The use made of the aircraft is deemed to be the sole decisive factor. This is a better construction than that of the Paris Convention, in which the military command served as a criterion for the military character in the case of military aircraft. Although objections can likewise be raised against the above criterion of the Chicago Convention, in view of the fact that military aircraft can be used for non-military purposes without losing their military character, at any rate it is the most serviceable of the criteria so far mentioned.

National law

The Netherlands. In Dutch law we do not find any definition of the term "State aircraft." According to Article 52(m) of the Aviation Act, rules for the admission of military as well as police and customs aircraft are to be given by Order in Council. The relevant Order was indeed issued in 1931.[1] Article 1 of this decree gives the following definition of *foreign* military aircraft:

"All aircraft of foreign nationality commanded by a person in foreign military service."

It is easy to trace the origin of the above definition: it is the definition contained in Article 31 of the Paris Convention. Consequently the earlier criticism of that Article also applies here.[2] In the Regulations for State Control of Air Navigation, Article 1(b) states that these regulations apply to aircraft which do not belong to the Dutch Navy or Army.

As far as *Dutch* aircraft are concerned, we shall therefore have to refer to Article 3 of the Chicago Convention in order to establish their military character.

Conclusion

The question whether an aircraft can be described as a State aircraft depends on the use that is made of the aircraft in question. But this still leaves difficult problems, as in the case of a military aircraft carrying non-military passengers.

If the Air Force charters aircraft from a civil airline, it may happen that these aircraft continue to bear civil markings. In

[1] Decree of April 29, 1931, S. 179.

[2] Goedhuis, "Handboek voor het Luchtrecht", p. 62.

that event the aircraft commander will have to be provided with documentary evidence of the military character of the aircraft.

Another point that is not clear is the status of aircraft which have been built for military purposes but are used to give demonstrations by the factory which built the aircraft. In such cases the contract will have to be the deciding factor. Each case in which the above-mentioned difficulties arise must be judged on its own merits.

NATIONALITY

HISTORY

Period prior to the Paris Convention of 1919

The question of the nationality of aircraft has been discussed at considerable length since the beginning of this century. There are two opposing views on the subject, viz. the view of those who favour the analogy with ships [1] and the view of those who want to have aircraft treated in the same way as motor cars, etc.[2]

Supporters of the first view hold that there must be a special relationship between the aircraft and its country of origin, expressed by conferring on the aircraft the nationality of that country.

Supporters of the latter view consider it sufficient if the aircraft can be identified by a certain distinctive mark.

A. Theory of the nationality of aircraft

The treatise of Fauchille entitled "Le domaine aérien et le régime juridique des aérostats," [3] which has already been referred to in Chapter I, presupposes the nationality of aircraft.

Although Fauchille advocated the free air theory, he acknowledged that the States concerned ought to have certain rights of self-preservation. This in itself made a distinction be-

[1] Ibid., p. 65.
Cooper, "The Legal Status of Aircraft", p. 61.

[2] Riese, "Luftrecht, "pp. 201 et seq.
Mandl, "La Nationalité des Aéronefs n'est qu'une dénomination erronée", Droit Aérien, 1931, p. 161.

[3] Revue Générale de Droit International et Public, 1901, p. 414.

tween national and foreign aircraft. The aircraft had to have a national protector.

As early as 1908 Daus [1] declared that an aircraft flying above the high seas must be regarded as part of the territory of its country of origin.

In the same year Kuhn [2] expressed the view that it might be advisable to introduce government supervision of aircraft, which would entail registration of all aircraft, as well as the granting of a nationality, which would be symbolized in the carrying of the flag.

In 1909 it was postulated by Zitelmann,[3] just as Daus had done the year before, that aircraft above the high seas must be treated as parts of the territory of their States, at least if statutory provision had been made with respect to the possession of nationality and the carrying of the national flag.

It was also in 1909 that Meurer [4] advanced the theory that the airworthiness of aircraft ought to be officially established. Each aircraft ought to have a name and a number and be entered on a public register.

The problem of the nationality of aircraft now began to appear on the agenda of the various organizations which occupied themselves with international air law.

Institute of International Law. In Fauchille's report to the Institute of International Law, which was mentioned in Chapter I in connection with sovereignty over the air space, he states that every aircraft should have a nationality.[5] The nationality of the aircraft must be determined by the nationality of the owner. Each aircraft ought to be entered on a register kept either by the State to which the aircraft belongs or the country in which the owner is domiciled.

During the session of the Institute of International Law at Paris in 1910, when the aforesaid report of Fauchille was dis-

[1] Daus, "Die Luftschiffahrt in staats- und völkerrechtlicher Hinsicht, 1908, p. 16.

[2] Kuhn, "Aerial Navigation in its Relation to International Law", Proceedings of American Political Science Association, 5th Annual Meeting, 1908, p. 85.

[3] Zitelmann, "Luftschiffahrtrecht", Zeitschrift für internationales privat- und öffentliches Recht, Vol. 19, 1909, pp. 458–496.

[4] Meurer, "Luftschiffahrtrecht", Zeitschrift für internationales privat- und öffentliches Recht, 1909, pp. 21–27.

[5] Institut de Droit International, Annuaire, 1910, pp. 297 et seq.

cussed, Von Bar [1] submitted a proposal to the effect that aircraft must be regarded as forming part of the territory of the State in which they were registered, at any rate so long as they were airborne.

Comité Juridique International de l'Aviation. In the "Code de l'Air" drafted by the Comité Juridique International de l'Aviation in 1910, the second chapter was partly devoted to the nationality of aircraft.[2] Aircraft were to be registered and have a nationality.

During its first meeting at Paris in 1911 the Comité Juridique accepted the principle that every aircraft should have a nationality, but only one nationality.[3] The aircraft would have the same nationality as its owner, who must have it entered in a public register.

The subject of nationality of aircraft was also discussed at various aviation conferences as well as by the above organizations.

Congrès Juridique International pour la Locomotion Aérienne (Verona, 1910). One of the principal subjects dealt with by this Congress was the ownership of aircraft. It was agreed that aircraft ought to have a nationality. The conditions for granting nationality must be the same in all States, namely that aircraft should have the nationality of their owner. The aircraft would have to be entered on a public register.[4]

International air navigation conference of 1910. The international air navigation conference held at Paris in 1910 yielded practically no positive results, but the decisions and discussions of this conference have undoubtedly influenced the subsequent national and international legislation.

In a draft for an international air agreement drawn up at the conference, the first chapter was devoted to the nationality and registration of aircraft.[5]

---

[1] Ibid., p. 317.
[2] Revue Juridique Internationale de la Locomotion Aérienne, Vol. 1, 1910, p. 45.
[3] Ibid., pp. 201–202.
[4] Ibid., p. 181.
[5] Conférence Internationale de Navigation Aérienne, Paris, 1910, Proces-verbaux des séances et annexes, Imprimerie Nationale, pp. 188–205.

Article 2 of the draft stated that this only applied to aircraft possessing the nationality of the contracting States.

Article 3 stipulated that the nationality of the aircraft should be based on the nationality of its owner, this being determined by the law of each contracting State.

Article 4 specifies that once an aircraft possesses the nationality of a State, it cannot acquire the nationality of any other State.

At this conference we first encounter opposition to the idea of granting aircraft a nationality of their own.

B. Theory of the analogy between aircraft and automobile.

The delegations of Switzerland and the Netherlands [1] proposed that aircraft should be placed under the same regime as motor cars, so that it was only necessary to provide for their identification.

The conference decided in favour of granting nationality to aircraft, but there were still some writers who did not approve.[2] Riese speaks of the so-called nationality of aircraft; according to him, only natural persons have a nationality in the proper sense of the word. In his opinion the law of the flag for merchant vessels had misled many writers on air law into regarding aircraft as airborne territory. Riese considers that the legal status of aircraft is identical to that of an automobile. However, the matter did not go any further. Those who advocated the principle of granting a nationality to aircraft had won their case even before statutory regulations came into force, as may be seen from the following explanation.

The problem of the nationality of aircraft is very closely connected with the principle of sovereignty over the air space. As soon as this principle had been adopted, different treatment was accorded to foreign and national aircraft. The national aircraft were entitled to protection under certain circumstances, while at the same time a State became responsible to other States for its own aircraft. This is formulated as follows in the report drawn up by Fauchille for the Paris Conference of 1910: [3]

[1] Ibid., p. 73.

[2] Riese, "Luftrecht", p. 201.
Mandl, "Droit Aérien", 1931, p. 161.

[3] Conférence Internationale de Navigation Aérienne, Parijs, 1910, op. cit. p. 74.

"La responsabilité et le droit de protection, réunis dans les mains d'un seul et même Etat, constituent entre cet Etat et l'aéronef un lien analogue à celui qui existe entre le navire et l'Etat dont il porte le pavillon, et qu'on appelle la nationalité du navire."

The recognition of the nationality of a ship was necessitated mainly by the prolonged sojourn as an isolated community on the high seas. Such a community had to be subject to certain rules. Although the same thing applies to aircraft, it is not so imperative, because the travelling time is much shorter. The nationality of an aircraft begins to assume importance when the aircraft enters the air space over which sovereignty is exercised by its own or another State.

It is clear that when a situation arises whereby aircraft enjoy the protection of the State of origin and the latter also accepts responsibility to other States for the conduct of the aircraft, identification alone is no longer sufficient.

The principle of the nationality of aircraft was therefore laid down in the ensuing international and national legislation.

International law

Paris Convention of 1919. The fact that the Paris Convention recognized the sovereignty of the States in the air space above their territory implied that regulations governing the nationality of aircraft must follow. The second chapter of the Convention is therefore devoted to the nationality of aircraft.

According to Article 6 of the Convention, aircraft possessed the nationality of the State where they had been registered. There was no argument about this principle.

Article 7, as drafted in 1919, prescribed that an aircraft could not be entered on the national register unless it wholly belonged to subjects of the State in which the register was kept.

In 1929, however, Article 7 was amended in conformity with the Havana Convention of 1928, in such a way that the nationality of the owner of the aircraft was no longer the deciding factor with respect to registration of the aircraft. The requirements for registration were to be laid down in the national legislation. The result of this was that one country could impose much stricter regulations than another country with regard to the granting of its nationality to an aircraft. This applied particularly in the case of aircraft belonging to corporate bodies. Otherwise it did not really make much difference. As far as aircraft owned by the State were concerned, the matter was simple – they possessed the nationality of the State to which they belonged. For aircraft which were not State property, in actual practice it was always the nationality of the owner which determined the nationality of the aircraft, as had originally been laid down in the Convention.

Article 8 of the Convention stipulated that an aircraft could be validly registered in more than one State.

International Law Association. The Paris Convention was discussed during the meeting of the International Law Association at Portsmouth in 1920.[1] Professor H. D. Hazeltine observed that the analogy between the nationality of an aircraft and that of a ship had been adopted in the Paris Convention. At the same time he pointed out that the provisions relating to the registration of aircraft were obviously derived from maritime law.[2]

A Dutch jurist, Miss I. Lijcklama à Nijeholt, threw light on this subject.[3] In her report she again emphasized the desirability of laying down equal requirements for the granting of nationality to ships and aircraft. This seems rather surprising, in view of the attitude of the Dutch delegation at the air navigation conference in Paris in 1910. On that occasion the representatives of the Netherlands had advocated that aircraft ought to be regarded as automobiles and only needed to be identifiable.[4]

In the Ibero-American Convention of 1926 as well as in the Havana Convention, it was likewise stated that every aircraft possessed the nationality of the State in which it had been registered. The Havana Convention of 1928 provided that each State must decide for itself what requirements should be laid down for granting the nationality of that State to an aircraft. This Convention never included the requirement that the nationality of the owner should be the decisive factor.

---

[1] International Law Association, Report of 29th Conference, 1920, p. 396.
[2] Ibid., p. 396.
[3] Ibid., p. 417.
[4] Conférence Internationale de Navigation Aérienne, Paris, 1910, op. cit. p. 73.

The principle of the nationality of the aircraft was also recognized in the Hague Air Rules of 1923,[1] a set of rules for aerial warfare, though these have never been embodied in an international convention. The nationality principle was likewise adopted in a study by the Harvard Research in International Law entitled "Rights and duties of neutral States in naval and aerial war."[2]

PRESENT SITUATION

Chicago Convention of 1944

The Chicago Convention of 1944 gives an even more definite character to the nationality of aircraft than the Paris Convention of 1919.

Chapter III of the Chicago Convention, which deals with the nationality of aircraft, corresponds to Chapter II of the Paris Convention.

In Article 12, a very far-reaching obligation is imposed on the States which have ratified the Chicago Convention or have adhered to it. The text of this article reads as follows:

"Each contracting State undertakes to adopt measures to insure that every aircraft flying over or maneuvering within its territory and that every aircraft carrying its nationality mark, wherever such aircraft may be, shall comply with the rules and regulations relating to the flight and maneuver of aircraft there in force.

"Such contracting State undertakes to keep its own regulations in those respects uniform, to the greatest possible extent, with those established from time to time under this Convention.

"Over the high seas, the rules in force shall be those established under this Convention.

"Each contracting State undertakes to insure the prosecution of all persons violating the regulations applicable."

The State whose nationality an aircraft possesses must therefore see to it that this aircraft complies with rules of the air laid down by other States. The responsibility for guarding against violations of the rules of the air is borne not only by the State

[1] Spaight, "Air Power and War Rights", pp. 498–508.
[2] American Journal of International Law, Vol. 33, 1939, p. 167.

flown over but also by the State whose flag the aircraft carries, under the terms of this article. This unusual construction can be traced back to the origin of Article 12, which is to be found in Article 25 of the Paris Convention, viz.:

"Each contracting State undertakes to adopt measures to ensure that every aircraft flying above the limits of its territory and that every aircraft wherever it may be, carrying its nationality mark, shall comply with the regulations contained in Annex D.

"Each of the contracting States undertakes to ensure the prosecution and punishment of all persons contravening these regulations.

The difference between Article 25 of the Paris Convention and Article 12 of the Chicago Convention, however, lies in the fact that according to Article 25 of the Paris Convention it was only necessary to take steps to ensure compliance with the regulations contained in the relevant Annex.

The following brief explanation of the different character of the annexes to the Conventions of Paris and Chicago may serve to clarify this.

Like the Chicago Convention, the Paris Convention was intended to secure international uniformity in the field of flight technical regulations. For this purpose the Paris Convention was supplemented with a number of Annexes.

These Annexes were definitely of a flight technical character. Their object was to give effect to the principles expressed in the various articles of the Convention.

The International Commission for Air Navigation (CINA), the international aviation authority instituted by the Paris Convention, had legislative power with respect to modification of these Annexes. If a modification of an Annex was approved by the International Commission for Air Navigation with a three-fourths majority, it merely had to be notified to the contracting States which ratified the Paris Convention in order to become effective.

The Chicago Convention has a somewhat different system. According to Article 37 of the Chicago Convention, the contracting States undertake to collaborate in securing the highest practicable degree of uniformity in flight technical regulations. To this end, international standards and recommended practices are published by the International Civil Aviation Organization

(ICAO), which was established by the Chicago Convention. In contrast to the Paris Convention, where the annexes were drawn up and adopted by the contracting States at the same time as the Convention, under the terms of the Chicago Convention ICAO was merely instructed to adopt and amend from time to time the aforesaid standards and recommended practices. This is done in the form of Annexes to the Convention. Compliance with the standards laid down in the Annexes by the contracting States is considered essential in the interests of safety and regularity of international air traffic, while the adoption of the recommended practices is considered desirable. But now we come to the difference as compared with the arrangement under the Paris Convention. ICAO has no legislative power. According to Article 38 of the Chicago Convention, the contracting States are not obliged to accept the provisions of the Annexes, but they undertake to include these provisions in their legislation subject to such modifications as they may find necessary. In that event, however, they are obliged to give notice of these modifications to ICAO.

Almost complete uniformity of the flight technical regulations of the contracting States was thus achieved under the Paris Convention (though special arrangements were still feasible in the case of Annex D, etc.), while under the Chicago Convention there is a much greater possibility of important differences. After all, the Annexes to the Paris Convention weie law, subject to the admissibility of special arrangements in certain cases, whereas those of the Chicago Convention are not.

It was therefore impossible to copy the exact wording of Article 25 of the Paris Convention in Article 12 of the Chicago Convention because there was no question of compliance with the regulations laid down in the relevant Annex on the subject of air traffic, since the Chicago Convention does not impose any obligation on the States to adopt the said Annex. Instead of aircraft complying with the regulations of an Annex, according to Article 12 of the Chicago Convention they must comply with "the rules and regulations there in force." This means that a contracting State is obliged to prosecute in the event of its own aircraft violating foreign air traffic regulations.

Under Article 17 of the Chicago Convention, aircraft have the nationality of the State in which they are registered. The conditions of registration are to be those of the national laws, and hence the registration of an aircraft determines its nationality.

The Chicago Convention thus continues along the lines of the Paris Convention of 1929, whereby it was left to each State to lay down conditions under which it was willing to enter an aircraft on its national register. However, this liberal attitude was not upheld in the International Air Services Transit Agreement and the International Air Transport Agreement, which were intended to supplement the Chicago Convention. These agreements both contain the following provision.:

"Each contracting State reserves the right to withhold or revoke a certificate or permit to an air transport enterprise of another State in any case where it is not satisfied that substantial ownership and effective control are vested *in nationals* of a contracting State, or in case of failure of such air transport enterprise to comply with the laws of the State over which it operates, or to perform its obligations under this Agreement."

From this it appears that importance is still attached to the fact that an aircraft actually belongs to nationals of the State whose registration marks it bears. The origin of the conditions laid down with respect to registration of aircraft is to be found in maritime law.[1] In the case of merchant ships, the protection of the flag was considered so important that the States wished to reserve this protection for ships belonging to their own nationals. The same consideration applies in the case of aircraft. On the other hand, States which permitted foreign aircraft to enter their territory, to land there and to take off again, also wanted to make sure that such aircraft belonged to subjects of the State whose nationality marks they bore.

From the fact that the Chicago Convention again introduces the requirement of national ownership in a roundabout way (via the Air Services Transit Agreement and the Air Transport Agreement), it is evident that this argument has not yet lost its force.

In actual practice, however, it has proved to be necessary – under certain circumstances – to operate air services with aircraft which do not belong to the operator of the air service in question.

[1] Goedhuis, "Handboek voor Luchtrecht", p. 63.

International Air Transport Association

The International Air Transport Association (IATA), an organization whose members include nearly all important airlines operating scheduled air services, has devoted attention to this problem.[1] The study of the following two problems was decided upon in a resolution adopted by IATA:

a. establishment of an international aircraft register with the purpose that aircraft thus registered may freely be used by airlines of the contracting States;

b. elimination of any legislation of the contracting States which prevents aircraft which are not owned by one of the nationals of a State from being registered in the registers of such State."

In view of the historical development of the aircraft nationality principle, an international register replacing the national register seems to be an impossibility. If the proposal put forward by Australia and New Zealand at the conference in Chicago [2] had found acceptance (this was a proposal to internationalize the operation of the main air routes), an international register of aircraft would have been the logical outcome.

At present there are a number of objections to this. The purpose of the international register is that aircraft entered in it can be put into service by the airlines of the contracting States without any further formalities.

International registration would entail that the supervision of the airworthiness of the registered aircraft would also have to be on an international basis. In other words, it would have to be exercised by an international authority.

Admittedly the States which have ratified the Chicago Convention co-operate within the framework of ICAO, but this is without prejudice to the sovereignty of these States. Thus an international authority of the kind referred to above does not exist and would have to be created. The issue of licences for the members of the crew of the aircraft would also have to be done by an international authority. In addition, arrangements would have to be made with regard to the rights to make commercial landings in the various countries. These objections are almost insuperable,

---

[1] Fifth Annual General Meeting of I.A.T.A., The Hague, September 1949.

[2] Proceedings of the International Civil Aviation Conference, Chicago, 1944, p. 457.

particularly the last one. After all, the operation of scheduled air services is largely dependent on the conclusion of bilateral agreements whereby the national aircraft of both parties obtain certain reciprocal rights. But if there is only an international register, a separate arrangement would still have to be made in connection with these rights which are only to be granted to aircraft of a certain nationality. This would lead to continuation of the national register besides the international register. The international register would only serve a limited purpose, while the national registration would remain in existence. In that event the aircraft would be registered twice.

An advantage of this would be that if the aircraft were temporarily used by an airline of another State, transfer of registration would be unnecessary; notification to the international register and the nationality register might suffice. As a result of this notification, the aircraft would come under the supervision of the authorities in the State of the user, and throughout the period of use it would not enjoy the protection of the State of origin, even though it was still entered in the nationality register. However, the aircraft could take advantage of the landing and commercial rights obtained by the State of the operating airline.

In this way it would be possible to avoid the payment of customs duties and other taxes, the necessity of obtaining permission from the authorities concerned, and other obstacles encountered in the transfer of an aircraft from one register to another. This method may perhaps be correct from a theoretical standpoint but there are numerous practical drawbacks attaching to it. The exact delimitation of the scope of the two registrations would give rise to considerable difficulties. Realizing this, IATA pointed out that an alternative way to facilitate exchange of aircraft would be the removal from the various national legislations of the provisions which prevent the registration of aircraft belonging to aliens in the national register of aircraft. It would then be necessary to permit the registration of aircraft belonging to a foreign airline in the national register when they are in use by a national airline.

In this case the problem thus becomes one of national law instead of international law.

National law

There are only a few States [1] whose national legislation allows aircraft belonging to subjects of a foreign State to be entered in the national register of aircraft. From this it is obvious that, just as in the case of merchant ships, the national character is still the primary consideration in the registration of aircraft. The Netherlands is one of the countries making such an exception in its legislation.

The Netherlands. Article 6 of the Dutch Aviation Act of 1926 stipulates that an aircraft performing air navigation must bear nationality and registration marks. This provision is based on Article 10 of the Paris Convention but it is likewise in conformity with Article 20 of the Chicago Convention.

Article 12 of the Aviation Act prescribes that a register is to be kept in the Netherlands for the registration of aircraft on behalf of the Minister of Transport. The practical application of this, including the conditions which an aircraft must satisfy if it is to be eligible for registration in the Netherlands, is laid down in the Regulations for State Control of Air Navigation (R.T.L.). The conditions governing the registration of an aircraft in the Dutch register of aircraft, which determines the nationality of the aircraft, have been drafted on the lines of the regulations governing the registration of merchant ships.

Article 311 of the Dutch Commercial Code gives detailed regulations indicating which ships are Dutch ships and can therefore be entered in the Dutch register of shipping. The gist of these nationality regulations is that the ships must either belong entirely to Dutch nationals or else at least two-thirds must be owned by Dutch nationals and the remainder by persons resident in the Kingdom of the Netherlands, while in any case the principal place of business of the shipping company must be established in the Netherlands.

The rules for the registration of aircraft, as given in the aforesaid Regulations for State Control of Air Navigation, have obviously been inspired by Article 311 of the Commercial Code, but the original text drafted in 1928 [2] did not impose such strict

[1] ICAO Doc. C.W.P./382, Aug. 18, 1949.

[2] Dutch Regulations for State Control of Air Navigation, Decree of Dec. 6, 1928, S–454.

requirements with respect to the Dutch character of the aircraft as those laid down for ships. When the R.T.L. was last amended in 1953 [1] this was carried a stage further.

In 1928 the Minister of Transport was already allowed some latitude in regard to the registration of aircraft not belonging to Dutch nationals. According to Article 3 of the R.T.L., aircraft were eligible for registration in the Dutch register of aircraft if they belonged to:

1. the State or a public body in the State;
2. Dutch citizens resident in the State;
3. corporate associations and limited liability companies formed in accordance with Dutch law and established in the Kingdom of the Netherlands, the managing official thereof being a Dutch citizen resident in the State. If the management consists of several persons, the chairman and at least two-thirds of the members must be Dutch citizens resident in the State.

The above conditions are all a more or less weak copy of those applicable in maritime law.

However, the Minister of Transport can also permit the registration of aircraft belonging to:

1. Dutch citizens who are not resident in the State;
2. persons resident in the State who are not Dutch citizens;
3. corporate associations and limited liability companies formed in accordance with Dutch law and established in the Kingdom of the Netherlands, which do not fulfil or do not entirely fulfil the requirements specified in the first paragraph of Article 3 of the R.T.L. with regard to the management.

The first steps along the road leading to abandonment of the principle that an aircraft must be national property (i.e. owned by nationals of the State concerned) in order to be entered in the national register, were therefore taken by the Dutch legislators at the very outset. This course was continued when the R.T.L. was amended in August 1953, because the need had been felt in the Netherlands to be able to charter aircraft which belonged to alien or foreign corporations and which could be entered on the national register of aircraft.

Owing to the fact that a foreign aircraft chartered in this

[1] Decree of Aug. 27, 1953, S–451.

manner cannot be entered on the Dutch register of aircraft, it must still bear foreign nationality and registration marks, the crew must hold foreign licences, and countless foreign rules and regulations must be observed on board the aircraft. In order to eliminate these drawbacks, a new paragraph has been added to Article 3 of the R.T.L., viz.:

Par. 6. So long as a Dutch citizen resident in the State, or a corporate body according to Dutch law, is the holder of an aircraft owned by an alien not resident in the State or by a corporate body according to foreign law, the registration of such an aircraft may be permitted by or on behalf of the Minister.

In view of the special character of such registration, it seemed advisable that in this case the obligations which must otherwise be fulfilled by the owner of the aircraft or by the person in whose name the aircraft is registered should be imposed on the holder of the aircraft.

Prior to August 1953, Article 4 of the Regulations for State Control of Air Navigation contained special conditions attaching to the registration of a transport aircraft.

In conformity with the Annexes to the Chicago Convention, however, aircraft are no longer registered as transport aircraft, sports aircraft, etc., and so these conditions could be done away with. Article 4 was therefore amended to read as follows:

"If registration is permitted under the term of Article 3(6), the obligations which the present regulations impose on an owner of an aircraft or on the person in whose name the aircraft is registered, must be fulfilled by the person who is stated to be the holder of an aircraft in the register of aircraft."

In its national legislation the Netherlands has thus met the wishes of the International Air Transport Association. Aircraft belonging to citizens of a foreign State can be entered in the Dutch register of aircraft. It is true that the consent of the Minister is required, but in principle the possibility exists. If the national airline therefore wishes to make use of an aircraft of a foreign airline for a long or short period, this aircraft can be transferred to the national register of aircraft. In that event it can be flown by a crew of the national airline without giving rise to any difficulties. Supervision of the airworthiness and further control of the aircraft is carried out by the national civil aviation authorities. If the aircraft had still been registered in the country of the owner, this would not have been possible without the consent of the country in question.

An amendment of the law was not strictly necessary to accomplish all this, since the transfer of an aircraft to another register is always feasible if title to the aircraft is transferred at the same time. The aircraft concerned, for example, might be sold to the user subject to a right of repurchase, but such a solution seems undesirable. Numerous complications may arise with regard to security, import and export licences, foreign exchange licences, etc. However, as long as the example of the Netherlands is not followed by a large number of States, the latter legal procedure will still be adopted.

CONCLUSION

It is evident from the foregoing that the requirements for national recognition of an aircraft are derived from maritime law. The importance of granting nationality to aircraft is not the same as in the case of a ship. The recognition of the nationality of the ship was mainly necessitated by the sojourn as an independent community on the high seas, whereas in the case of an aircraft its nationality is primarily of importance in connection with the sovereignty which the various States exercise in the air space above their territory. After all, commercial aviation is almost entirely dependent on bilateral air agreements. It is therefore of the greatest importance that a relationship should be established between the aircraft and a certain State. This is done by granting it a nationality.

The aircraft is then entitled to protection by the State whose flag it carries, while on the other hand this State accepts certain responsibilities in regard to the aircraft.

The nationality of the aircraft finds expression in its registration on the national register of aircraft.[1] Such registration does not create a nationality but is evidence of nationality. Originally the Paris Convention stipulated that only aircraft belonging

[1] de Planta, "Principes de droit international privé applicables aux actes accomplis et aux faits commis à bord d'un aéronef", Geneve, 1955.

to nationals of a certain State could be entered on the aircraft register of that State. This was altered in 1929 and it was left to the various States to determine the conditions on which they would enter aircraft on their national register. The Chicago Convention adopted this same principle. However, most States do not allow registration of aircraft owned wholly or partly by aliens. The Netherlands is one of the few countries which does so – for practical reasons. Airlines may want to charter aircraft abroad in order to be able to cope with an unexpected increase of traffic or unexpected setbacks due to losses (this applies particularly in the Netherlands, where there is only one airline). The airlines will wish to operate such aircraft as their own aircraft, for which purpose they must be entered on the national register.

This is now feasible in the Netherlands. In other countries a practical solution has been found in the form of fiduciary transfer to title.

It is obvious that aircraft require a nationality in order to take part in international air transport.

CHAPTER III

RIGHTS IN AIRCRAFT

A. AIRCRAFT AS MOVABLE PROPERTY

There is no doubt that aircraft are movable property. But the regulations which are applicable to movable property do not all apply to aircraft. In spite of aircraft being movable property, their legal status differs in many respects from that of ordinary movables. As explained in the previous chapter, aircraft possess a nationality, and consequently each State has to keep a public register for the registration of aircraft. The fact of being entered on this register determines the nationality of the aircraft. That is laid down in public international law (Chicago Convention of 1944). Practically all of the States engaged in aviation have therefore recognized this exceptional status of aircraft as movable property.

In private law there are also rules for aircraft which form important exceptions to the general rules in force for ordinary movable property.

Private international air law, however, lags far behind public international law in this field. In the Final Act of the Chicago Convention of 1944,[1] we find the following recommendation:

"Considering:

That the sale of aircraft to be used in international operations will render it desirable for the various governments to reach a common undeιstanding on the legal questions involved in the transfer of title;

The International Civil Aviation Conference recommends:

That the various governments represented at this International Civil Aviation Conference give consideration to the early calling

[1] International Civil Aviation Conference, Final Act and related documents. United States Government Printing Office.

of an international conference on private international air law for the purpose of adopting a convention dealing with the transfer of title to aircraft and that such private air law conference include in the bases of discussions:

(*a*) The existing draft convention relating to mortgages, other real securities, and aerial privileges, and

(*b*) The existing draft convention on the ownership of aircraft and the aeronautic register,

both of which were adopted by the Comité International Technique d'Experts Juridiques Aériens (CITEJA) in 1931."

This recommendation has led to a convention which will be discussed later, viz. the Convention on the International Recognition of Rights in Aircraft, concluded at Geneva on June 19, 1948.[1] As we shall see, this convention makes it obligatory for the contracting States to recognize a number of rights which place the aircraft in a unique category of movable property. Amongst other things the Convention makes provision for mortgages on aircraft.

Only a few countries have so far ratified the Convention.[2] However, in many countries (including the Netherlands) steps are now being taken to bring the national legislation into line with the Convention, after which more ratifications will undoubtedly follow.

Furthermore, a number of States have already included special rules concerning aircraft in their legislation. It is therefore natural to regard aircraft as movable property *sui generis*, as several writers in the field of air law have done.[3]

On examining the relevant national legislation on this subject in various countries, we find that the position is as follows.

1. France

The "Loi relative à la navigation aérienne" (May 31, 1924) contains the following provisions:

---

[1] Convention on the International Recognition of Rights in Aircraft, Geneva, June 18, 1948.

[2] U.S.A., Pakistan, Brazil, Norway, Sweden and Chile (without reservations); Mexico (with reservation).

[3] Shawcross and Beaumont, "Air Law", p. 14;
McNair, "Law of the Air," p. 107;
Lemoine, "Traité de Droit Aérien", p. 174;
Cooper, "A study of the Legal Status of Aircraft", 1949, p. 56.

"*Art. 12* Les aéronefs constituent des *biens meubles* pour l'application des règles posées par le code civil. Toutefois la cession de propriété doit être constatée par écrit et ne produit d'effet à l'égard des tiers que par l'inscription au registre d'immatriculation.

Toute mutation de propriété par décès et tout jugement translatif, constitutif ou éclaratif de propriété doit être inscrit sur le registre à la requète du nouveau propriétaire."

Although aircraft answer to the definition given in Article 528 of the Civil Code, the French legislature has thus laid down exceptions to the normal rules applicable to movable property. It is definitely established that aircraft are movable property, but separate rules apply with regard to alienation and acquisition of title. We shall revert to these rules when discussing the method of acquiring title to aircraft.

"*Art. 14.* Les aéronefs sont susceptibles d'hypothèque. L'hypothèque est inscrite au registre d'immatriculation. La loi du 5 juillet 1917, sur l'hypothèque fluviale, est déclarée applicable à l'hypothèque des aéronefs, le fonctionnaire chargé de la tenue du registre d'immatriculation étant substitué au greffier du tribunal de commerce pour l'application de cette loi."

According to this article, aircraft can be mortgaged. The provisions of the law of July 5, 1917, relating to the "hypothèque fluviale" are declared applicable to aircraft. We shall revert to this as well when discussing mortgages on aircraft.

"*Art. 57.* La loi du 29 avril 1916 sur l'assistance et le sauvetage maritime est applicable aux aéronefs en péril en mer et aux pilotes des aéronefs, qui peuvent prêter assistance aux personnes en péril."

"*Art.* 58. Toute personne qui trouve une épave d'aéronef doit en faire la déclaration à l'autorité municipale dans les quarante-huit heures de la découverte.

Toute contravention à cette disposition est punie des peines prévues par l'article 475, par. 12, du code pénal. Toutefois, les règles relatives aux épaves maritimes s'appliquent seules aux épaves d'aéronefs trouvées en mer ou sur le littoral maritime."

Here too we have special regulations applying to aircraft. Reference is made to maritime law, just as in the case of mortgages.

To sum up, it is apparent that in France aircraft differ from ordinary movable property not only because they have a nationality and are subject to recordation in a register kept for purposes of private law, but also because separate regulations apply to the acquisition of title and alienation, the rule that possession implies full title does not apply to aircraft, they can be mortgaged and, lastly, special regulations apply with regard to attachment. This will be dealt with in more detail at a later stage. In the meantime, however, it may be remarked that – according to the foregoing – aircraft must undoubtedly be regarded as movable property sui generis under French law. It should be borne in mind that this special regime for aircraft only applies to French aircraft, due to the fact that the special rules relating to aircraft are based entirely on the recordation of these aircraft, and only French aircraft can be recorded in France.

2. *Italy*

The "Code de la Navigation" which came into force on April 21, 1942, includes the following provision:

"*Art. 861.* En l'absence de dispositions contraires, les aéromobiles sont soumis aux règles relatives aux *biens meubles.*" [1]

The principle that the aircraft is essentially movable property is clearly established in the above article. Articles 864 and 865 of the "Code de la Navigation" contain rules which differ from those in force for ordinary movable property. All deeds relating to the creation, transfer or cancellation of a right of property or other right in rem must be executed in writing, otherwise they are null and void, while the recordation of such deeds has constitutive effect. We shall revert to these points when discussing the method of acquiring title to aircraft.

As is the case in French law, aircraft can be mortgaged under Italian law. The register of aircraft serves a dual purpose in Italy as well as in France since it has a function in both public law and private law.

In the "Code de la Navigation" we also find that the same regulations apply to the lifting of sunken ships and sunken aircraft (Art. 73), while Arts. 489–497 and 981–992 give identical regulations with respect to assistance and salvage of ships and aircraft.

[1] Translation from Revue Française de Droit Aérien, 1949, 1–4.

Like French legislation, Italian legislation thus contains special provisions for aircraft, entirely different from those applicable to ordinary movable property.

Assuming that aircraft possess a nationality, they differ from ordinary movable property on account of the fact that they are recorded in a private register, are subject to special regulations with regard to the creation, transfer or cancellation of rights of property and other rights in rem, can be mortgaged and are assimilated with ships in various respects.

In the light of the foregoing, it is clear that aircraft are likewise regarded as movable property sui generis under Italian law.

3. The Anglo-Saxon countries.

United Kingdom. British law does not contain any statutory provisions concerning the legal character of aircraft, but according to common law the aircraft is a chattel.[1]

Just as in French and Italian law, we have an assimilation of aircraft and ships with respect to assistance and salvage. This is evident from Article 51 of the Civil Aviation Act of 1949. The assimilation of ships with aircraft, however, does not extend beyond the field of assistance and salvage.

The British register of aircraft is only used for purposes of public law. It does not have any function whatsoever in regard to private transactions. So far as the transfer of title is concerned, aircraft are not subject to special rules. In this case the rules applying to ordinary chattels are applicable without any difference. Aircraft can be the object of a chattel mortgage, but this is also possible for other chattels.

Contrary to French and Italian law, therefore, British law has practically no special provisions on the status of aircraft where rights in rem are concerned.

As far as public law is concerned, however, there are important variances from the rules applicable to ordinary movable property. There are certain statutory provisions relating to the construction and the use of aircraft, they possess a nationality and they are entered in the national public register of aircraft.

In view of the foregoing, Shawcross and Beaumont conclude: [2]

[1] Shawcross and Beaumont, "Air Law", p. 467.

[2] Ibid., p. 14

"There seems to be no doubt that an aircraft is *sui generis*, and whilst sharing some of the characteristics of both, it cannot be classified either as a ship or vessel or as an automobile."

This view is shared by other writers.[1]

It can therefore be stated that in the United Kingdom the aircraft is also looked upon as movable property sui generis.

United States of America. In the United States, Section 501 of the Civil Aeronautics Act of 1938 provides for the registration of aircraft, while according to Section 503 of this Act all rights in aircraft must be recorded in a record kept by the Civil Aeronautics Administrator – at least if they are to be valid against third parties.

Like ordinary movable property, aircraft can be the subject of a chattel mortgage. In the same way legal forms such as the bill of sale, contract of conditional sale, lease and equipment trust do not apply exclusively to aircraft but also to other movable property. No special regulations in this connection have been laid down with regard to aircraft. As mentioned above, however, such agreements are not valid against third parties unless they have been noted in a record kept by the Civil Aeronautics Administrator.

Registration under the terms of Section 501 of the Civil Aeronautics Act, 1938, gives the aircraft American nationality.

Although American legislation does not go so far as the French and Italian legislation, the regulations applicable to aircraft in the United States differ from those in force for ordinary movables, with the result that aircraft definitely possess the character of movable property sui generis.

4. The Netherlands

Article 565 of the Dutch Civil Code leaves no doubt about aircraft being movable property.

Pursuant to the Dutch Aviation Act, however, a register of aircraft is kept in the Netherlands – at the office of the Department of Civil Aviation, The Hague. It is a public register and aircraft entered on this register are Dutch aircraft. The fact of

---

[1] Spaight, "Aircraft in Peace and the Law".
McNair, "Law of the Air".

being entered on the register thus determines the Dutch nationality of the aircraft.

This means that as far as public law is concerned, in the Netherlands we find the same difference between an aircraft and ordinary movable property as in practically all the national legislations, viz. aircraft have a nationality.

With regard to private law, Article 770 (h–k) of the Dutch Code of Civil Procedure contains special rules relating to the precautionary arrest of aircraft. These rules are taken from the relevant international convention signed at Rome in 1933.[1]

In addition, aircraft are assimilated with ships as regards assistance and salvage. In Article 571 of the Dutch Commercial Code, the seventh title of this Code dealing with assistance and salvage of ships is declared applicable to an aircraft or its occupants when assistance is rendered on the water.

In the Netherlands too we are therefore justified in speaking of aircraft as movable property sui generis.

There will be still more justification for this if the Aircraft Recordation Bill is passed by the Dutch Parliament. The bill in question is intended to adapt Dutch legislation to the Convention on the International Recognition of Rights in Aircraft, which was signed at Geneva on June 19, 1948. All sorts of special regulations will then apply to aircraft. In the first place, aircraft will be capable of being mortgaged but exempt from liens. Furthermore, the position with regard to rights in aircraft will differ considerably from the law applicable to other objects of property. The charter of a recorded aircraft for example, will confer on the charterer a right in rem, while an agreement whereby the holder of a recorded aircraft is entitled to acquire ownership of the aircraft under the terms of a purchase agreement on payment of a certain amount or on fulfilment of a certain condition will also give this holder a right in rem.

According to the Aircraft Recordation Bill, it will no longer be possible to exercise the right of retention and the right of recovery in regard to aircraft. Article 2014 of the Dutch Civil Code will likewise cease to apply to recorded aircraft. The bill also provides that if anyone obtains a recorded aircraft in good

[1] Convention for the unification of certain rules relating tot the precautionary arrest of aircraft)Rome, May 29, 1933).

faith and in virtue of a lawful title, he acquires ownership of it by way of prescription through possession for a period of one year. This short-term acquisitive prescription is included on account of the comparatively short useful life of aircraft. The bill makes the sale of aircraft to a foreign buyer subject to the approval of the holders of rights in rem over the aircraft. It is also stipulated that attachments laid on aircraft shall cease in the event of bankruptcy.

Needless to say, the enactment of this bill will give aircraft the character of movable property sui generis to a much greater extent than is already the case.

B. ACQUISITION OF TITLE TO AIRCRAFT

I. International Law

The Comité International Technique d'Experts Juridiques Aériens (CITEJA) has already endeavoured to secure international uniformity of legislation with respect to the method of acquiring title to aircraft.

CITEJA was set up pursuant to a resolution of the first conference in the field of private international air law, which was held at Paris in 1925. The conference was called in order to discuss a draft for a convention on international air transport, from which the Warsaw Convention emerged in 1929.[1] At that conference it was decided to appoint a commission for the study – on an international level – of the various problems arising in the field of air law. This commission became the Comité International Technique d'Experts Juridiques Aérien (CITEJA). It was resolved that CITEJA should be composed of experts nominated by the different States. CITEJA carried out the preparatory work in connection with the above-mentioned Warsaw Convention and a number of other conventions, [2] besides making a study of

[1] Convention for the unification of certain rules relating to international carriage by air (Warsaw Convention of October 12, 1929).

[2] Convention for the unification of certain rules relating to damage caused by aircraft to third parties on the surface (Rome Convention of May 29, 1933).

Convention for the unification of certain rules relating to the precautionary arrest of aircraft (Rome, May 29, 1933).

Convention on assistance and salvage of aircraft at sea (Brussels, 1938).

various subjects concerned with air law, including the acquisition of title to aircraft. CITEJA was abolished in 1947, when its duties were taken over by the Legal Committee of the International Civil Aviation Organization.[1] In 1929 the Italian member of CITEJA, Giannini, submitted a draft for an international convention on "la propriété et le registre aéronautique."[2] This draft was discussed by the "première commission" of CITEJA under the chairmanship of Giannini.[3]

The first problem encountered by the commission was that of the nationality of aircraft. It was decided to adhere to the provisions of the Paris Convention, as amended by the Protocol of June 7, 1929, whereby registration in the nationality register of one of the contracting States should be effected in accordance with the regulations of that State.

The commission also considered it important to indicate what ought to be regarded as an aircraft within the meaning of the draft convention. The following definition of the term "aircraft" was therefore included in Article 1:

"Est considéré comme aéronef aux effets de la présente Convention tout appareil susceptible de transporter par air des personnes ou des choses."

Thus the commission did not venture to formulate a scientific definition. In any case the definition quoted is quite serviceable for the purposes of the draft convention, viz. to regulate the recordation and transfer of title to aircraft.

In Article 1 it was likewise stipulated that with a view to the establishment of ownership and rights in rem, the aircraft must be entered on a record kept by the competent authority of the State in which the aircraft is registered as to nationality. The text reads as follows:

"En vue de la constatation de la propriété et des droits réels, tout aéronef doit être inscrit sur un registre tenu par l'autorité compétente de l'Etat où il est inscrit au registre d'immatriculation."

---

[1] CITEJA is discussed in:
Lemoine, "Traité de Droit Aérien," pp. 48–50.
Riese, "Luftrecht", pp. 34, 36 and 51.
Smirnoff, "Le CITEJA", Paris, 1936.
Sudre, "Le CITEJA", R.G.A., 1946.

[2] CITEJA, Session of May 1929.

[3] CITEJA, Doc. Nos. 32 and 50.

The draft therefore makes it obligatory for the contracting States to keep a record for purposes of civil law.

Article 2 of the draft guards against double recordation of the aircraft.

Article 3 provides solutions for three recordation difficulties in connection with:

1. aircraft in course of construction;
2. aircraft built for sale but not yet delivered;
3. aircraft sold to non-residents.

In order to preclude the necessity of these aircraft being entered on the record of the country in which they have been built or are located and subsequently recorded in the country to which they are definitely transferred, Article 3 provides for temporary recordation.

The Article is worded as follows:

"Les aéronefs en construction ou destinés à la vente avant d'être mis en service ou acquis par des ressortissants d'autres pays, pourront être inscrits à titre provisoire, dans le registre, prévu à l'article ler, du pays dans lequel ils sont inscrits ou dans lequel ils se trouvent, jusqu'au moment où ils seront inscrits dans le registre de l'Etat où ils doivent être inscrits à titre définitif."

It is left to the State to establish a separate record for these provisional entries or to have them recorded in the same book as the definite recordations.

Article 4 of the draft stipulates that the record must contain the name of the owner of the aircraft. In this article it is also stipulated that for the benefit of a person who has obtained any right in an aircraft in good faith, the recordation establishes the right of the owner – unless proof to the contrary is submitted.

In Article 5 it is stated that the transfer or title and the establishment of rights in rem are only valid with effect from the date of entry on the record.

Articles 4 and 5 read as follows:

"Article 4: Le registre porte l'indication du nom du propriétaire de l'aéronef. Cette inscription au registre fait foi, du droit du propriétaire inscrit à l'égard de ceux qui ont acquis de bonne foi des droits sur l'aéronef.

Article 5: Les transferts de propriété entre vifs, les constitutions et cessions de droits réels et d'hypothèques ainsi que les renonciations à ces droits, ne produisent d'effets qu'à dater l'inscription au registre."

In view of Article 4 of the draft, this means that the positive system is adopted and the creditors are thus given the greatest possible security.

Article 5 states that the entry in the record has constitutive effect. The establishment of the right in rem is not perfect until it is recorded. As we shall see later, the majority of the members of CITEJA were unwilling to accept this last principle, and it has therefore been omitted from the draft finally adopted by CITEJA.[1]

The problem of whether the aircraft must be regarded as movable or immovable property is not touched upon in the draft.

Article 6 of the draft lays down rules concerning the spare parts of the aircraft, the article being formulated in the following terms:

"Sont considérés comme faisant partie intégrante des aéronefs les moteurs, les outils et, en général, tous les biens destinés à l'usage permanent des aéronefs, indiqués dans l'inventaire ou d'autres documents, même s'ils sont temporairement séparés, sous réserve des droits des tiers acquéreurs de bonne foi."

Difficulties also arose in connection with the record. The point at issue was whether the existing public register could also be used for purposes of private law, or whether a new record ought to be established exclusively for the latter purposes.

The draft does not solve this problem. According to Article 7, it is left to the national legislature to decide whether the existing public register is to be utilized or whether a new record is to be instituted. There is no doubt, however, that there must be a record which can fulfil the function referred to in Article 1. This record must also be public.

At the session of CITEJA in October 1931 Giannini submitted a revised draft.[2]

Article 1 of this draft, as originally presented by Giannini, reads as follows:

"Les Hautes Parties Contractantes s'engagent à établir dans leurs lois nationales que tout aéronef immatriculé dans une des

[1] CITEJA, Doc. No. 162.
[2] CITEJA, Doc. No. 108, September 1931.

H.P.C. soit inscrit sur un registre tenu en vue de la constatation de la propriété et des droits réels du dit Etat.

Le dit registre peut être celui de l'immatriculation de l'aéronef ou un registre distinct. Dans ce dernier cas une concordance sera établi entre les deux registres."

The Czechoslovakian delegation pointed out that according to Article 1 of the draft the public registration must precede the recordation.[1] But since the entry on the public register depends on the nationality of the owner, the recordation ought to come first.

The Italian delegation objected to the words "constatation de la propriété" and wanted to substitute "l'inscription de la propriété." [2]

If, as is the case in many States, the public registration is to depend on the nationality of the owner of the aircraft, the first step is to determine who the owner is. Recordation is necessary to determine the name of the owner in the event of transfer of title, but this recordation can only take place after the public registration. Here we have a vicious circle.

However, a solution could be found if the provisions of the second paragraph of Article 9 of the draft, which deals with the consequences of recordation of rights of property and other rights in rem, were declared applicable to aircraft which had already been recorded. (This paragraph will be discussed later).

As far as the substitution of another word in place of "constatation" is concerned, it may be remarked that naturally there is always a possibility that the person recorded as the owner is not really the owner. In that case the word "constatation" is indeed too strong. On the other hand, it may be argued that the purpose of the record is to establish the ownership, the consequences of which are to be found in Article 9 of the draft. This argument was not sufficiently convincing to secure maintenance of the word "constatation." The Italian proposal was accepted and the words 'l'inscription de la propriété" were inserted in the text ultimately approved by CITEJA.[3]

Article 2 of the revised draft gave rise to prolonged discussions.

---

[1] CITEJA, Doc. No. 128, October 1931.

[2] Ibid.

[3] CITEJA, Doc. No. 162.

It lays down detailed rules for the transfer of an aircraft from the record of one State to the record of another State.

The text of paragraphs 1 and 2 reads as follows:

"Un aéronef inscrit dans un pays d'une des H.P.C. ne peut être inscrit sur le registre d'une autre H.P.C. sans que le propriétaire justifie avoir effectué la radiation de l'inscription primitive.

Au cas où l'aéronef est grévé de charges réelles inscrites au registre, l'inscription au nouveau registre sera subordonnée à la preuve que les créanciers ont été payés ou ont consenti au transfert de l'inscription. Dans ce dernier cas les charges réelles seront inscrites sur le nouveau registre sous la seule justification des inscriptions existantes sur le registre précédent."

Some practical objections against the above regulations were put forward during the discussions in CITEJA.[1]

Paragraph 2 makes provision for two cases, viz. the case where the creditors have been paid and the case where the creditors are unpaid. If a mortgagee has been paid, for example, the owner of the aircraft must arrange for cancellation of the record of the mortgage. If the mortgage is not deleted from the record because the mortgagee has not been paid, the latter must give his consent to any recordation of the aircraft in a record in another country.

In the first case there is the difficulty of finding out whether the creditors have been paid. For instance, what evidence must one produce to the Italian keeper of the record if creditors in Germany have been paid?

It will also be very difficult to prove in actual practice that all the creditors consent to the transfer of the aircraft.

Article 2 merely regulates "l'inscription au nouveau registre." It does not state that transfer of the aircraft in the same country – i.e. where there is no necessity for entry in a new record – cannot take place without the creditors consent.

Article 2 of the draft also gives detailed instructions as to the way in which recordation and cancellation must be effected in the records. Much of this article is copied from Article 15 of the "Convention Fluviale." [2]

---

[1] CITEJA Doc. No. 128.

[2] Convention concernant l'immatriculation des bateaux de navigation intérieure de 9 décembre 1930; ratified by the Netherlands, Act. of June 24, 1939.

In Article 3 of the draft, provision is made for the establishment of a record for aircraft under construction.

This article has been greatly simplified in comparison with Article 3 of Giannini's first draft.[1]

Article 4 is almost identical to Article 6 of the first draft.[2] The regulations given in Articles 5, 6, 7 and 8 are purely administrative.

The main point of the draft lies in Article 9, which has already been referred to above.

In the text that Giannini submitted to CITEJA,[3] Article 9 was worded as follows:

"1) L'inscription au registre fait foi du droit du propriétaire inscrit à l'égard de ceux qui ont acquis de bonne foi des droits sur l'aéronef.

2) Le transfert de propriété entre vifs, les institutions et cessions des droits réels et d'hypothèques, ainsi que les renonciations à ces droits ne produisent d'effets qu'à dater de l'inscription au registre."

The above text furnishes protection for persons who, acting in good faith, have acquired rights of property or any other right in aircraft from the person who was entitled to grant such rights according to the record. This principle was accepted by CITEJA, but it was finally expressed in the following terms:

"2) Celui qui a acquis de bonne foi la propriété ou un droit réel de la personne inscrite au registre comme titulaire de ce droit ne peut pas se voir opposer le défaut de droit de son auteur".[4]

According to the text of Giannini's draft, the recordation also has constitutive effect in regard to the transfer of title to the aircraft and the establishment of rights therein. Between the parties the validity of these legal formalities likewise depends on the recordation of the aircraft. There was great opposition to this in CITEJA, the chief spokesman being the German delegate Richter.[5] Although Giannini received support from the French delegation led by Ripert, the majority of CITEJA voted against the constitutive effect of the recordation of the aircraft.

---

[1] CITEJA Doc. No. 50, October 1930.
[2] Ibid., p. 117.
[3] CITEJA Doc. No. 128.
[4] CITEJA Doc. No. 162.
[5] Ibid.

It was decided that the recordation should have declarative effect. The transfer of title between parties does not depend on the recordation of the aircraft, but if this transfer is to be valid against third parties it must be recorded. This principle was formulated as follows:

"1) Tous transferts de propriété entre vifs, constitutions, cessions de droits réels et renonciations à ces droits ne sont valables à l'égard *des tiers* que par leur inscription au registre et ne produisent effect qu'à la date de cette inscription."

However, no further action was taken and no convention has been concluded on the basis of the above draft.

In this connection it must be mentioned that a convention for the unification of certain rules relating to the *precautionary* arrest of aircraft was signed at Rome in 1933,[1] but the question of attachment under an execution has not yet been regulated.

A convention on the international recognition of rights in aircraft was adopted at Geneva in 1948.[2] Under the terms of this convention, which will be discussed later, the contracting States undertake to recognize rights in aircraft which have been recorded in these States, provided that such rights are validly constituted.

The object of the convention is to safeguard creditors holding rights in rem. Admittedly it also has the object of protecting the owner, but very little attention is devoted to this. Accordingly, the Geneva Convention will not be discussed here in that connection.

We shall now briefly consider a number of national legislations on the subject of acquisition of title to aircraft.

II. National Law

1. France

According to Article 12 of the "Loi relative à la navigation aérienne" (May 31, 1924) a written document is required for the transfer of title to an aircraft:

"*Art. 12* Les aéronefs constituent des biens meubles pour l'ap-

[1] Ratified by the Netherlands on April 28, 1938; the provisions were incorporated into Dutch legislation as Art. 770 (h–k) of the Code of Civil Procedure.

[2] Convention on the International Recognition of Rights in Aircraft, Geneva, June 18, 1948.

plication des règles posées par le code civil. Toutefois, la cession de propriété *doit être constatée par écrit* et ne produit d'effet à l'égard des tiers que par l'inscription au registre d'immatriculation.

Toute mutation de propriété par décès et tout jugement translatif, constitutif ou éclaratif de propriété doit être inscrit sur le registre à la requête du nouveau propriétaire."

No requirements are laid down with respect to the form of the aforesaid document. Lemoine [1] is of the opinion that a simple exchange of letters and telegrams is sufficient. With a view to the entry in the register, however, it is essential that the document should clearly indicate which aircraft is involved.[2] He bases this theory on the fact that in the words of the law, the transfer of title "doit être constaté par écrit." For the transfer of title itself, mutual consent is all that is needed. The document is nothing more than a piece of evidence, without which no entry can be made on the register, and the transfer of title is not valid against third parties unless it is recorded in the register.

But the regulations laid down by the Law of 1924 are not without imperfections. According to this Law, recordation must also take place in case of acquisition of title by inheritance and by judicial decree. The second paragraph of Article 12 states this without any qualification. The sanction contained in the first paragraph, whereby the transfer of title is not legally valid against third parties in the event of non-recordation, is not included in the second paragraph. In French legal writings, however, it is assumed that – just as in the case of sale – if the transfer of title is not recorded it has no legal consequence vis-à-vis third parties.[3]

The logical conclusion to be drawn from the foregoing is that the rule of "possession vaut titre" applicable to normal movables does not apply to aircraft. For this reason Article 11 of the Law of 1924 contains the following provision:

"*Art. 11* Le registre d'immatriculation indique le nom et le domicile du propriétaire de l'aéronef, la catégorie de l'appareil,

---

[1] Lemoine, "Traité de Droit Aérien", p. 179.
[2] Le Goff, "Traité théorique et pratique de Droit Aérien", p. 521.
[3] Lemoine, "Traité de Droit Aérien", p. 181.
Planiol et Ripert, "Traité Pratique de Droit Civil Français", III, p. 687.

son nom ou son numéro d'ordre. *L'inscription au registre vaut titre.*"

In other words, Article 2279 of the French Civil Code is rendered inoperative as far as aircraft are concerned. If the validity of his title is contested, the holder will not be able to rely exclusively on his right of possession. Revindication by the owner or the recorded creditor is possible for a period of thirty years. In this connection the question arises whether acquisition of title to an aircraft through prescription is feasible.[1] The same difficulty occurs with ships. In actual practice the question of prescriptive acquisition of title to aircraft is of no interest, in view of the comparatively short useful life of an aircraft. Lemoine refers to maritime law, whereby acquisition of title through prescription is possible according to current doctrine. By analogy, a thirty-year term of limitation would also apply to aircraft.

On the basis of Article 11 the majority of the French writers conclude that recordation is sufficient to establish title to the aircraft, at least vis-à-vis third parties.[2]

We thus come to the final conclusion that Articles 11 and 12 of the Law of 1924 are not concerned with the relationship between two parties but vis-à-vis third parties. The recordation does not have any constitutive effect with respect to the transfer of title.

2. *Italy*

The legislation of this country bears a certain resemblance to French law on the points under discussion. Italy is another country in which the statutory rules applying to ordinary movable property differ from those applicable to aircraft. Just as in France, the registers of aircraft in Italy are valid for purposes of private law.

Articles 864 and 865 of the "Codice della navigazione"[3] are devoted to the transfer of title to aircraft. The text of these Articles reads as follows:

"Art. 864 (Forme des actes relatifs à la propriété des avions).

---

[1] Lemoine, "Traité de Droit Aérien," p. 182 .

[2] Planiol et Rippert, "Traité Pratique de Droit Civil Français", III, p. 687.
Ripert, "Droit Maritime", I, p. 424.
Lemoine, "Traité de Droit Aérien, " p. 182.

[3] French translation published in Revue Française de Droit Aérien, No. 2, April–June 1949.

Les actes constitutifs, translatifs ou extinctifs de propriété ou autres droits réels concernant tout ou partie d'un avion doivent, à peine de nullité, être passés par écrit. Ces actes doivent, à l'étranger, être reçus par l'autorité consulaire.

Les dispositions de l'alinéa précédent ne sont pas applicables au planeurs.

Art. 865 (Publicité des actes relatifs à la propriété des avions). En vue de produire les effets prévus par la Code Civil, les actes constitutifs, translatifs ou extinctifs de propriété ou autres droits réels concernant tout ou partie d'un avion sont rendus publics par voie de transcription sur le registre aéronautique national et d'inscription sur le certificat d'immatriculation ou, s'il s'agit de planeurs, par voie de transcription sur le registre matricule de l'Union Aéronautique Royale Nationale . Tout autres actes ou demandes pour lesquels la transcription est requise par le Code Civil doivent être rendus publics dans les mêmes formes."

The above Articles reveal an important difference from the French legislation. Not only must all legal transactions whereby a right of property is created, transferred or cancelled, be confirmed in writing, but in order to have legal validity they must also be entered in the register. Under French law, registration of the transfer of the aircraft is only necessary in order to make it valid against third parties, but in Italy recordation is also necessary to legalize the transfer of title from one party to another. In this case therefore the recordation has constitutive effect.

In the event of discrepancies between the nationality register and the record, the latter takes precedence.

3. Spain

Under the Spanish law of December 27, 1947 title is transferred by the recordation of a conveyance. The system of publicity functions in the same way as with immovable property.[1] The recordation has constitutive effect in addition to being conclusive evidence.

4. Anglo-Saxon countries

United Kingdom. The rules applicable to normal movable property

[1] Gay de Montella, "La personalité de l'aéronef et la publicité aéronautique en droit espagnol", Revue Française de Droit Aérien, No. 2, April–June 1949, p. 137.

also apply to the transfer of title to aircraft. There are no special regulations on this subject in the United Kingdom. During the period from September 1939 until August 1945, however, it was illegal to sell an aircraft without the permission of the Air Ministry.[1]

The British register of aircraft is purely a public register. It does not serve any function whatsoever with respect to the transfer of title to aircraft and the establishment of rights in rem over aircraft. Since the rules for movable property are applicable to the transfer of title, the ownership of aircraft is transferred by mutual consent of parties. A bill of sale is not needed.

The conclusion to be drawn from the foregoing is that this subject has received very little attention from the British legislature.

United States of America. Under the terms of Section 503 of the Civil Aeronautics Act of 1938,[2] the purchase and sale of aircraft and the establishment of rights in rem over aircraft must be registered by the Recordation Division of the Civil Aeronautics Administration in Washington. Not until this recordation has taken place are the above rights valid against third parties. The relevant clauses of Section 503 (abridged) read as follows:

a. The Administrator shall establish and maintain a system for the *recording* of each and all of the following:

(1) Any conveyance which effects the title to, or any interest in, any civil aircraft of the United States;

c. No conveyance the *recording* of which is provided for by section 503(a) (1) shall be valid in respect of such aircraft, aircraft engine or engines, propellers, appliances, or spare parts against any person other than the person by whom the conveyance or other instrument is made or given, his heir or devisee, or any person having actual notice thereof, until such conveyance or instrument is filed for recordation in the office of the Administrator."

In order to avoid confusion, the American legislation refers to the filing in public law as "registration" and the filing in private law as "recordation". It must be borne in mind that various states of the U.S.A. also require recordation of conveyance, etc.,

---

[1] Shawcross and Beaumont "Air Law", p. 467.
[2] Amended in 1942, 1947 and 1948.

in their local register. Legal opinion differs as to the correctness of this.[1]

Furthermore, it is possible to record rights in aircraft engines of more than 750 h.p. as well as in the aircraft itself.

An important point is that the rules concerning the recordation of rights in rem over aircraft are incorporated in the Civil Aeronautics Act of 1938, so that there is uniformity of legislation in this field. With regard to other material rights, however, the rules vary in the different states.

5. The Netherlands

Dutch legislation does not contain any provisions concerning the acquisition of title to aircraft other than the normal rules for transfer of title to movable property. Delivery of an aircraft is therefore effected merely by handing it over, except in cases where the party acquiring the aircraft already has possession of it pursuant to Article 667 of the Dutch Civil Code. On the basis of Article 639 of the Dutch Civil Code, it must be assumed that such delivery of an aircraft results in transfer of ownership when it has taken place in consequence of a title of transfer originating from the party who had the right to dispose of the property.

There is a Dutch register of aircraft but this has no significance in private law.

A considerable change will be brought about, however, if the Aircraft Recordation Bill is passed by the Dutch Parliament. This bill, which we have mentioned earlier in the present chapter,[2] is intended to adapt Dutch legislation to the "Convention on the International Recognition of Rights in Aircraft "signed at Geneva on June 18, 1948.

In accordance with the above bill, a public register will be kept for the recordation of Dutch aircraft, legal rights in rem over these aircraft may be recorded in the said register. The bill also stipulates that the delivery of an aircraft recorded in the aforesaid register shall be effected by the recordation of a relevant deed in this register.

As in the case of ships, the recordation of aircraft is not com-

---

[1] Taylor, "A practical Reconciliation of State and Federal Control" 12 Journal of Air Law and Commerce 232, 1941.

[2] See page 70.

pulsory. A minimum weight requirement for recordation will be specified by Order in Council.

Besides the above-mentioned general rule laid down in Article 639 of the Dutch Civil Code, the special regulations contained in Article 2014 of the Dutch Civil Code are at present applicable to aircraft. When the Aircraft Recordation Bill is enacted, however, Article 2014 will no longer apply to recorded aircraft.

C. MORTGAGES ON AIRCRAFT

International law

History

Long before the Second World War it was generally agreed that international regulations ought to be established for the protection of those who hold a mortgage or other right in rem over an aircraft. This subject has appeared on the agenda of CITEJA ever since that body was set up in 1925. In addition to the draft convention on the ownership of aircraft and aeronautical registers [1] – which has already been discussed – a second draft convention relating to mortgages on aircraft [2] was drawn up by CITEJA. The latter draft was also adopted at the Paris session of CITEJA in 1931, but it never reached the stage of being put before a diplomatic conference.

At the International Civil Aviation Conference in Chicago in 1944 the attention of the newly founded International Civil Aviation Organization (ICAO) – at that time still called the Provisional International Civil Aviation Organization (PICAO) – was drawn to the two draft conventions adopted by CITEJA in 1931 on the subject of mortgages and registers. The Legal Commission of PICAO combined both drafts in a single new draft and sent it to CITEJA for consideration. Shortly afterwards CITEJA was replaced by the Legal Committee of ICAO. During its first meeting at Brussels in 1947 the Legal Committee prepared a completely revised draft,[3] which was put before the meeting of ICAO at Geneva in June 1948. An Ad Hoc Committee

---

[1] CITEJA Doc. Nos. 50 and 162.
[2] CITEJA Doc. No. 73.
[3] ICAO Doc. 4635–L.C./71, Sept. 5, 1947.

was appointed to study the draft,[1] after which it was submitted to the General Assembly for approval and was unanimously adopted.[2]

The official name of this convention is the Convention on the International Recognition of Rights in Aircraft. It was drawn up in English, French and Spanish, each text being of equal authenticity, and it was published by ICAO on October 1, 1950.

General comments on the Convention

Object. The object of the Convention is to make it easier for airlines to obtain credit by giving the lenders a security. The original intention was to promote legal security on the transfer of title to aircraft,[3] but in the final text of the Convention this aim was relegated into the background. The Convention mainly endeavours to secure international recognition of those standards of security which prevail in the United States of America with respect to the financing and granting of credit to civil aviation. The question of *transfer* of title to aircraft is not mentioned at all.

Method. In order to accomplish the above object the framers of the Convention adopted a method which differs considerably from that followed by CITEJA. The latter aimed at the maximum unification of law and only left to the rules of conflicts of law the settlement of points which could not possibly be brought within the scope of the unification rule. The jurists who drafted the Convention, on the other hand, contented themselves in principle with laying down rules on conflict of laws. All real security rights which may be applicable to aircraft are listed as fully as possible in the Convention, in order to ensure international recognition of these rights.

The articles of the Convention

Rights recognized

Article I

Under the terms of the Convention, the contracting States are

[1] ICAO Doc. 5722.

[2] The Convention was signed by 27 States, including the Netherlands; so far it has been ratified by the U.S.A., Pakistan, Brazil, Norway, Sweden and Chile (without reservations), and by Mexixo (with reservation).

[3] CITEJA Doc. 468.

only obliged to recognize the rights specified in Article I. Other rights may also be recognized under the national laws of the States, but such rights must not take priority over those referred to in Article I. The contracting States undertake to recognize:
(*a*) rights of property in aircraft. This relates to the full ownership of the aircraft, as well as the rights of any person who has reserved ownership of the aircraft as security.

Wilberforce[1] raises the question of whether it is worth including rights of property here. He comes to the conclusion that this is definitely the case, since it guarantees international recognition of such rights.

Admittedly the frame of the Convention did not want to lay down a unification rule for rights of property in aircraft, but they have given a rule of conflicts of law: according to the Convention, rights of property must be validly constituted and recorded in conformity with the law of the State in which the aircraft was registered as to nationality.

Even before the Convention was signed a great many writers [2] in the field of air law expressed views in favour of this rule, though there were also some writers [3] who advocated the "lex rei sitae."

However, it is only logical that the law of the State in which the aircraft is registered as to nationality should be declared applicable. After all, the aircraft is primarily an international means of transport, with the result that it repeatedly comes within the jurisdiction of other States. If the lex rei sitae were to be applicable, the aircraft would constantly be subject to different systems of law; this is avoided by accepting the law of the State of registry.

---

[1] Wilberforce, "The international recognition of rights in aircraft", International Law Quarterly, 1948.

[2] Arminjon: "Précis de droit international privé", Paris, 1934.

Niboyet: "Traité de droit international privé français", 6 vol. Paris T.V.: La territorialité, 1947.

Coquoz: "Les perspectives d'avenir du droit privé international aérien", 1938 pp. 29–33.

Wolff: "Das Internationale Privatrecht Deutschlands", Göttingen-Heidelberg, 1949, p. 149.

[3] De Visscher: "Les Conflicts de Lois en matière de Droit Aérine", Académie de Droit International, Recueil des Cours 1934, p. 305.

Milch: "Die Luftfahrzeughypothek," Berlin, 1930, p. 45.

Calkins: "Creation and International Recognition of Title and Security Rights in Aircraft", Journal of Air Law and Commerce, 1948, p. 160.

In the case of ships, the application of the law of the flag is justified for two reasons. The first is the reason referred to above in connection with aircraft, namely the great mobility of seagoing vessels. The second is the existence of private registers of shipping in practically every country. As we have seen, this is still far from being the case with respect to aircraft. The Convention does not make it mandatory for the contracting States to keep a record of aircraft for purposes of private law but the assumption is that this will be done. Wider ratification of the Convention will therefore undoubtedly lead to the establishment of such records in the various States. Both of the reasons which have led to adoption of the law of the flag for shipping will then apply to aircraft too, thus further justifying the choice of the law of the State of registry in the Convention.

In a number of cases reference to the law of the State of registry of the aircraft will not furnish a solution, since the law of the State of registry on conflicts of law will be applicable and consequently it is quite possible that ultimately the lex rei sitae may be applied. Since the Convention also omits to specify what is meant by the valid constitution and regular recordation of rights, difficulties may arise in deciding whether certain legal questions are covered by this constitution and recordation. It is therefore to be hoped that as a result of the Convention the various States will revise their national legislation on this subject, so that more uniformity of law will ensue.

(b) rights to acquire aircraft by purchase coupled with possession of the aircraft. Here we have an Anglo-Saxon legal construction. An option of this nature is not regarded as a right in rem in the Netherlands. Special legislation will have to be enacted to provide the possibility of creating such rights under Dutch law. Wilberforce [1] is of the opinion that the inclusion of these rights in the Convention is both illogical and superfluous. According to him it will be practically impossible for an owner-creditor to sell the aircraft without the knowledge of the holder-debtor – who is in possession of the aircraft – and thus to make the debtor's rights illusory. But Wilberforce forgets that the creditor might be able to establish a right in rem over the aircraft and

[1] Wilberforce, "The international recognition of rights in aircraft", International Law Quarterly, 1948.

thus put the purchaser-debtor at a disadvantage.[1] The inclusion of these rights in Article I of the Convention offers an adequate safeguaıd against this.

(c) *rights to possession of aircraft under leases of six months or more.* For European lawyers this is also an unfamiliar legal construction. The American origin is obvious. The English text speaks of "rights to possession of aircraft," so that the emphasis must apparently fall on protection of rights to possession, in contrast to the "rights to acquire aircraft" mentioned under *b.*[2] In this case a lease is fully recognized as a right in rem. Here too Dutch law must be amended in such a way that a lease of an aircraft will be regarded as a right in rem.

(d) *mortgages, hypothèques and similar rights in aircraft which are contractually created as security for payment of an indebtedness.* Mortgages and hypothèques are specifically mentioned, but for the rest there is merely a reference to "similar rights." Nothing is said about *statutory* and *judicial* mortgages. In order to obviate any possible doubt in regard to these rights, the words "mortgage" and "hypothèque" are left untranslated in the French and English texts, respectively.

The above rights are thus recognized by all the States that have ratified the Convention. The list covers practically all known real securities. Individual mention was necessary because no international definition could be found to cover all these rights.

Conditions for recognition of the rights

Two conditions are laid down for the recognition of the Convention rights, viz. such rights must have been "constituted in accordance with the law of the contracting State in which the aircraft was registered as to nationality at the time of their constitution," and they must also be "regularly recorded in a public record of the contracting State in which the aircraft is registered as to nationality."

The rights have to be recognized if these two conditions are fulfilled. If this is not the case, recognition of the rights is left to the discretion of the State concerned. Since the drafters of the

---

[1] Rijks, "Het Verdrag van Genève", 1952, p. 112.
[2] Hofstetter, "L'hypothèque aérienne", Lausanne, 1950, p. 222.

Convention had agreed not to lay down any unification rules, the above-mentioned conditions are logical and understandable. After all, it was necessary to stipulate which law should apply in deciding whether the rights were validly constituted. As explained earlier (in connection with rights of property), the law of the State of registry was selected for this purpose on undoubtedly correct grounds. Furthermore, recognition was made conditional upon recordation of the rights.

Although the framers of the Convention thus had two clearly defined principles in mind, the text is not absolutely clear. This vagueness is probably due to the fact that an attempt is made to cope with the difficulty which arises when an aircraft is transferred to another register during the period between the constitution of the right concerned and the recognition thereof. The position is confused because the laws of two States may be applicable in succession. It would have been better to declare that only the law of the State in which the right was recorded should be applicable.

The regularity of the successive recordings in the different contracting States, however, is determined in accordance with the law of the State where the aircraft was registered as to nationality at the time of each recording.

Consequences of the recognition of the rights
Article II
The second paragraph of Article II of the Convention reads as follows:

"Except as otherwise provided in this Convention, the effects of the recording of any right mentioned in Article I, par. 1, with regard to third parties shall be determined according to the law of the contracting State where it is recorded."

In conformity with the system adopted in drafting the Convention this article merely gives a rule of conflicts of law (Paragraph 3):

"A contracting State may prohibit the recording of any right which cannot validly be constituted according to its national law."

The intention of those who drafted the Convention, however, was that this could only be done pursuant to a statutory regulation,[1] so that the decision does not rest with the official who keeps the record.

Maintenance of the records

Article III

The Convention does not create an obligation to establish a public record for purposes of private law. But nevertheless the Convention clearly assumes that such a record shall be established: in Article II of the Convention it is stated that all recordings relating to the same aircraft must appear in the same record, while Article III of the Convention makes it obligatory to show on every aircraft's certificate of registration the address of the authority responsible for maintaining the record. Moreover, anyone is entitled to receive from the authority responsible for maintaining the record duly certified copies or extracts of the particulars recorded. Such copies or extracts constitute prima facie evidence of the contents of the record.

If the law of a contracting State provides that the filing of a document for recording has the same effect as the recording itself, this filing shall have the same legal consequences for the purposes of the Convention as the recording itself.

Lastly, the authority responsible foı maintaining the record can make a reasonable charge for its services.

Privileges

Article IV

This Article contains rules with respect to privileged rights, i.e. rights which take priority over the rights specified in Article I. The article mentions two categories of claims which rank above all other rights in and claims on aircraft, viz.:

"(*a*) compensation due for salvage of the aircraft, or

(*b*) extraordinary expenses indispensable for the preservation of the aircraft."

The salvage of the aircraft covers salvage on land as well as at sea.[2]

It should be noted that recognition of the two privileges is only prescribed in cases where such claims are indeed given

[1] ICAO Doc. 5722, p. 231.

[2] ICAO Doc. 5722, p. 136.

priority by the State within whose territory the salvage takes place or the expenses are incurred. This is another consequence of the endeavour to encroach on the national legislation as little as possible.

But these are not the only claims to which the Convention grants priority. When injury or damage is caused to persons or property on the surface of the contracting State where the sale in execution takes place, by an aircraft subject to a mortgage, the national law of this contracting State may provide in case of seizure of such aircraft that the persons who have suffered injury or damage shall be granted priority for 20% of the sale price of the aircraft. The costs incurred in the course of the execution proceedings take precedence over all other claims.

In Article XII of the Convention it is stated that nothing in the Convention shall prejudice the right of the contracting States to enforce against an aircraft its national laws relating to immigration, customs or air navigation. At first sight this article appears to lie within the field of public law, but its purpose was to empower the contracting States to collect fines in respect of breaches of the aforesaid national laws without making allowance for the rights specified in the Convention.[1] From a practical standpoint this is also a privilege, but the Convention is by no means systematic in its provisions relating to privileges.

The rights specified in Article IV do not have to be recorded in order to be enforceable. At the same time, however, Article IV expressly prohibits the contracting States from recognizing the said rights after expiry of a period of three months, unless the right has been noted on the record within that period or the amount of the claim has been agreed upon or judicial action on the right has been commenced.

Attachment and sale in execution

Article VI

The Convention includes a number of regulations for settlement of the questions which arise in case of attachment or sale of an aircraft in execution.

According to Article VI, in the event of attachment or sale in execution of an aircraft, or of any right therein, the contract-

[1] Riese, "Luftrecht", pp. 295 and 296.

ing States shall not be obliged to recognize, as against the attaching or executing creditor or against the purchaser any right mentioned in Article I (par. 1), or the transfer of any such right, if constituted or effected with knowledge of the sale or execution proceedings by the person against whom the proceedings are directed.

This non-recognition of the rights mentioned in Article I of the Convention is based on bad faith on the part of the debtor whose aircraft is attached. No allowance is made for good or bad faith on the part of the person who has acquired the right.

Article VII

Article VII states that the proceedings of a sale of an aircraft in execution shall be determined by the law of the contracting State where the sale takes place, subject to the following provisions:

"(*a*) The date and place of the sale shall be fixed at least six weeks in advance.

(*b*) The executing creditor shall supply to the Court or other competent authority a certified extract of the recordings concerning the aircraft. He shall give public notice of the sale at the place where the aircraft is registered as to nationality, in accordance with the law there applicable, at least one month before the day fixed, and shall concurrently notify by registered letter, if possible by air mail, the recorded owner and the holders of recorded rights in the aircraft and of rights noted on the record under Article IV, paragraph 3, according to their addresses as shown on the record."

These provisions are intended to supply possible deficiencies in the national laws,[1] while the third paragraph of this article stipulates that:

"The consequences of failure to observe the requirements of paragraph 2 shall be as provided by the law of the contracting State where the sale takes place. However, any sale taking place in contravention of the requirements of that paragraph may be annulled upon demand made within six months from the date

---

[1] These provisions are in accordance with Article 29 of the Convention de Genève concernant l'immatriculation des bateaux de navigation intérieure, les droits réels sur ces bateaux et autres matières connexes, du 9 décembre 1930.

of the sale by any person suffering damage as the result of such contravention." The fourth paragraph of Article VII reads as follows:

"No sale in execution can be effected unless all rights having priority over the claim of the executing creditor in accordance with this Convention which are established before the competent authority, are covered by the proceeds of sale or assumed by the purchaser."

Here we have two alternatives: the claims which take precedence over that of the executing creditor must either be paid out of the proceeds of sale or the purchaser must accept the liabilities attaching to these claims.

This is a point which gave rise to objections from the United States,[1] but the latter finally acquiesced in a situation whereby countries whose legislation provides for cancellation in the case of sale in execution must recognize the validity of such a sale without cancellation, conversely, countries whose legislation does not provide for cancellation on execution must recognize the validity of a cancellation.

In Paragraph 5 a privilege is given to third parties who have suffered injury or damage on the ground by an aircraft in transit, viz.:

"When injury or damage is caused to persons or property on the surface of the contracting State where the execution takes place, by any aircraft subject to any right referred to in Article I held as security for an indebtedness, unless adequate and effective insurance by a State or an insurance undertaking in any State has been provided by or on behalf of the operator to cover such injury or damage, the national law of such contracting State may provide in case of the seizure of such aircraft or any other aircraft owned by the same person and encumbered with any similar right held by the same creditor:

(*a*) that the provisions of paragraph (4) above shall have no effect with regard to the person suffering such injury or damage or his representative if he is an executing creditor;

(*b*) that any right referred to in Article I held as security for an indebtedness encumbering the aircraft may not be set up

[1] ICAO Doc. 4635, p. 110.
ICAO Doc. 5722, p. 136.

against any person suffering such injury or damage or his representative in excess of an amount equal to 80% of the sale price.

In absence of other limit established by the law of the contracting State where the execution sale takes place, the insurance shall be considered adequate within the meaning of the present paragraph if the amount of the insurance corresponds to the value when new of the aircraft seized in execution."

The benefits attaching to the above privilege will not amount to much. If an aircraft causes damage on the surface of the earth, this will often be the result of a catastrophe after which the value of the aircraft is usually nil.

Regulations have already been laid down for the protection of third parties on the ground,[1] though they have not yet come into force.

Consequences of sale in execution

Article VIII

This Article deals with the consequence of a sale in execution:

"Sale of an aircraft in execution in conformity with the provisions of Article VII shall effect the transfer of the property in such aircraft free from all rights which are not assumed by the purchaser."

The above is a logical consequence of Article VII(4).

Execution releases the aircraft from all rights encumbering it, with the exception of those assumed by the purchaser.

Transfer to another nationality register

Article IX

Article IX relates to the transfer of registration of an aircraft to a foreign register. Alienation of the aircraft to another country is one of the chief risks run by the mortgagee. Most of the national legislations prohibit the sale of an aircraft to a foreign country without the consent of the mortgagees. The great difficulty is that it is practically impossible to enforce such a prohibition by means of sanctions.[2] An international convention on this subject is therefore imperative.

---

[1] Convention on damage caused by foreign aircraft to third parties on the surface (Rome, October 1952).

[2] Hofstetter, "L'hypothèque aérienne", p. 253.

There are two possibilities:

1. automatic transfer of all security rights;
2. transfer of registration subject to the approval of the mortgagees.

The second solution is chosen in the Convention. This is regrettable from the standpoint of unification of law, but it is inevitable in view of the system followed in the Convention.

The text of the article in question reads:

"Except in the case of a sale in execution in conformity with the provisions of Article VII, no transfer of an aircraft from the nationality register or the record of a contiacting State to that of another contracting State shall be made, unless all holders of recorded rights have been satisfied or consent to the transfer."

Spare parts of the aircraft

Article X

Regulations concerning rights in the spare parts of the aircraft are given in this article, which also contains a rule on conflict of laws. In order to be eligible for recognition, the rights in the spare parts must be constituted in conformity with the law of the State in which the aircraft is registered. In addition, however, the Article contains unification rules.

The rights must be an extension of a similar right in an aircraft. The conditions of recognition are the same as for rights in aircraft. Further conditions are that the spare parts must be stored in a specified place and that the rights in question must be described in a public notice exhibited at that place.

The consequences of the recognition are the same as those of the recognition of rights in the aircraft itself. The importance of these provisions is evident when one considers that the spare parts represent about 25% of the value of the aircraft.

The spare parts can be replaced by similar parts without affecting the right of the creditor.

The third paragraph of this Article gives an important special rule in favour of the seizor of a spare part:

"The provisions of Article VII, paragraphs (1) and (4) and of Article VIII shall apply to a sale of spare parts in execution. However, where the executing creditor is an unsecured creditor, paragraph (4) of Article VII in its application to such a sale be construed so as to permit the sale to take place if a bid is received in an amount not less than two-thirds of the value of the spare parts as determined by experts appointed by the authority responsible for the sale. Further, in the distribution of the proceeds of sale, the competent authority may, in order to provide for the claim of the executing creditor, limit the amount payable to holders of prior rights to two-thirds of such proceeds of sale after payment of the costs referred to in Article VII, paragraph (6)."

This rule has been severely criticized by various writers.[1] What the criticism amounts to is that once security rights in spare parts of aircraft have been recognized, no further restrictions must be imposed. That is correct. The above rule resembles the privilege of third parties who have suffered injury or damage, as laid down in Article VII(5), but it is more comprehensive because it covers both voluntary and involuntary creditors. In addition, fully 13% more is reserved for such creditors than under the terms of Article VII(5). The question that arises is why the unsecured creditor must be protected in this manner. It is illogical and it is unjustifiably detrimental to creditors who have a mortgage on the spare parts concerned.

Scope of the Convention

Article XI

With a few exceptions the Convention is only applicable to international relationships. It has this in common with the existing conventions relating to mortgages in the field of maritime law.[2]

The first paragraph of Article XI reads:

"The provisions of this Convention shall in each contracting State apply to all aircraft registered as to nationality in another State."

However, certain provisions of the Convention must also be

---

[1] Riese, "Luftrecht", p. 304.
Hofstetter, "L'hypothèque aérienne", p. 262.
Rijks, "Het Verdrag van Genève", p. 178.

[2] Convention de Bruxelles pour l'unification de certaines règles relatives aux privilèges et hypothèques maritimes, du 10 avril 1926.
Convention de Genève concernant l'immatriculation des bateaux de navigation intérieure, les droits réels sur ces bateaux et autres matières connexes, du 9 décembre 1930.

applied to aircraft entered on the national register. The provisions in question are those of Articles II, III and IX, and also the provisions of Article IV unless the salvage or preservation operations have been terminated within the national territory.

Article XII

The applicability of the Convention is limited in Article XII, which reads as follows:

"Nothing in this Convention shall prejudice the right of any contracting State to enforce against an aircraft its national laws relating to immigration, customs or air navigation."

Article XIII

According to this article the Convention does not apply to aircraft used in military, customs or police services.

Final provisions

Article XIV

Under the terms of this article, the competent judicial and administrative authorities of the contracting States can correspond directly with each other.

Article XV

This article obliges the contracting States to take such measures as are necessary for the fulfilment of the provisions of the Convention and to inform the Secretary General of ICAO of these measures.

National law

1. France

According to Article 14 of the "Loi du 31 mai 1924 relative à la navigation aérienne," aircraft are capable of being mortgaged. The provisions of the Law of July 5, 1917, relating to "l'hypothèque fluviale" are declared applicable. Thus the privileges with respect to inland shipping also apply to aircraft.[1] An aircraft can only be mortgaged under the terms of an agreement. The mortgage can be established not only by notarial deed but by a

[1] Lemoine, "Traité de Droit Aérien", p. 183.
Le Goff, "Traité théorique et pratique de Droit Aérien", Paris 1934, p. 526.

simple private contract, and it is only valid against third parties after being recorded in the register of aircraft. The mortgage has real effect and right of precedence. In case of destruction of the aircraft this is replaced by a right to the insurance money (Art. 47 of the Law of 1917). The Law of July 1917 "relative à l'hypothèque fluviale" was amended by the Law of July 19, 1934. Four privileges were then included which take priority over mortgages, viz.:

1. the costs of conservation after attachment, harbour dues and pilotage dues;
2. claims in respect of the wages of the crew and premiums for the social insurances of the crew;
3. remuneration for assistance;
4. compensation for damage resulting from a collision or any other accident, provided that it occurred before the mortgage was recorded.

These privileges are copied from the "Convention de Genève concernant l'immatriculation des bateaux de navigation intérieure, les droits réels sur ces bateaux et autres matières connexes du 9 décembre 1930." Consequently they are typically maritime privileges which are not really appropriate in air legislation.

Aircraft are rarely mortgaged in France, perhaps partly because of the reference to maritime law. It may also be due to the fact that the aircraft is not regarded as a suitable object for a mortgage.[1]

The whole question will undoubtedly be reconsidered in France as a result of the signing of an international convention on this subject.

2. Italy

Mortgages on aircraft have been recognized under Italian law since 1923. The Italian air legislation was completely revised in 1942, when the "Codice della navigazione" [2] was drawn up. This includes regulations concerning mortgages on aircraft. The mortgage can only be established by agreement (Art. 1027). The

[1] Coquoz, "L'hypothèque aérienne", Rev. Gen. de l'Air, 1938, p. 570.
Riese, "Luftrecht", p. 267.
Guldiman, "Dingliche Rechte, besonders Pfandrechte, an Flugzeugen", Schweizerische Juristen Zeitung ,1948, p. 372.

[2] See French translation in R.F.D.A. 1949, Nos. 1–4.

right of the mortgagee extends not only to the aircraft and its appurtenances but also to unpaid freight charges (Art. 1037). Otherwise the mortgage has no special features.

3. Anglo-Saxon countries

United Kingdom. As far as rights in rem are concerned, aircraft are not subject to any special regulations in the United Kingdom. As we have already seen, they are looked upon as ordinary movable property.

According to the Bills of Sale Acts of 1878 and 1882, aircraft can be the object of a chattel mortgage, but in actual practice this is very seldom applied to aircraft.[1]

United States. Movable property is capable of being mortgaged in all the states of the U.S.A. Hence this also applies to aircraft. Chattel mortgages are quite common. There are two types, viz. the chattel mortgage of the title type, whereby title to the chattel is transferred as security for the debt, and the chattel mortgage of the lien type, whereby the debtor grants the creditor priority in the recovery of his claim on the chattel in question. The latter form is particularly suitable for transactions relating to aircraft.

If the aircraft concerned are also used outside the United States, however, the value of the right is often illusory. It is not surprising therefore that the United States – as the principal creditor in the field of aviation – was the first country to ratify the convention signed at Geneva in 1948 on the international recognition of rights in aircraft.

4. The Netherlands

Hitherto the mortgage on aircraft has been unknown in the Netherlands. As the question of ratifying the Geneva mortgage convention of 1948 (which was also signed by the Netherlands) is now under consideration, however, the desirability of introducing this legal device into the national legislation had to be examined. It has been definitely established that in the event of ratification of the Geneva Convention of 1948 by the Netherlands, Dutch legislation will have to be brought into line with

[1] Hofstetter, "L'hypothèque aérienne", p. 124.
Rijks, "Het Verdrag van Genève", p. 54.

the Convention, as may be seen from the following arguments:

1. If the Netherlands does not introduce a record for purposes of private law, the contracting States are not obliged to recognize Dutch rights of property, etc.
2. A Dutch airline cannot buy any aircraft abroad under real security unless a mortgage can be established in the Netherlands.
3. It is also questionable whether the Netherlands recognizes the rights specified in Article I of the Convention if Dutch law is not adapted.
4. The Convention assumes that each contracting State maintains a record for purposes of private law. Such a record must therefore be instituted.
5. According to Article IV, if Dutch law is not adapted the Netherlands will be placed in a situation whereby it is obliged to recognize the high priority of foreign claims in respect of remuneration for assistance outside the Netherlands, while the Netherlands cannot enforce this preferential treatment for assistance rendered in the Netherlands to a Dutch aircraft or to a foreign aircraft.
6. Articles VII and VIII of the Convention are directly enforceable. The provisions of these articles would apply alongside those of the existing law. The only solution is to amend the existing regulations.
7. Article IX of the Convention states that transfer of an aircraft from the record of a contracting State is only feasible after all holders of recorded rights have been satisfied or consent to the transfer. If no satisfaction can be given, and if aircraft cannot be mortgaged in the Netherlands, the mortgagee will not grant permission for the transfer of a foreign aircraft to a Dutch national.
8. Difficulties may also arise in connection with mortgages on spare parts.
9. Lastly, Article XV of the Convention presupposes that the contracting States will adapt their legislation.

Since ratification of the Geneva Convention of 1948 was considered desirable in order to facilitate obtaining credit on the purchase of aircraft outside the Netherlands and granting credit on the sale of aircraft to other countries, preparations were made

– for the reasons summarized above – to adapt the Dutch legislation before proceeding to ratification of the Convention.

An Ad Hoc Committee consisting of Professor J. H. Beekhuis (of Groningen University) and Mr. H. Schadee (average adjuster, Rotterdam) was therefore appointed to draft an Aircraft Recordation Bill. They completed their work in 1953. The draft prepared by this committee adheres as closely as possible to the Geneva Convention, but it differs in two important points. In contrast to the Convention, the draft Bill does not provide for mortgages on spare parts of aircraft. Nor does the draft make any provision for the priority of claims originating from damage caused by aircraft on the surface of the earth. The committee considered that a mortgage on the constantly changing spare parts of an aircraft was incompatible with Dutch law. The question of damage caused by aircraft to third parties on the surface is regulated on an international basis in a convention signed at Rome on October 6, 1952. So far this convention has only been ratified by two [1] of the signatory States (the Netherlands was among the signatories). The committee was of the opinion that it was inadvisable at this stage to lay down a national regulation for one small item, namely the priority of the relevant claim on the aircraft itself.

The draft provides for the establishment of a public register for the recordation of aircraft, in which statutory rights in rem over aircraft can be recorded. The use of the term "statutory rights in rem" implies that foreign rights in rem recorded in the Netherlands can only be real securities in the Netherlands if such rights may be regarded as rights in rem according to Dutch law.

Recordation is no more obligatory for aircraft than it is for ships. The aircraft must be a Dutch aircraft within the meaning of the Dutch Aviation Act in order to be eligible for recordation. To ensure that an aircraft is not entered on more than one record, the recordation can only take place if the aircraft is not recorded elsewhere.

As the statutory regulations concerning the right of repurchase (Articles 1555 et seq., Dutch Civil Code) of purchase and sale on deferred payment terms (Articles 1576 et seq., Dutch Civil

[1] Egypt, Canada.

Code) and of recovery (Articles 230 et seq., Dutch Commercial Code) would affect the right of the owner whose title to the aircraft is regularly recorded, these are declared to be inapplicable.

The draft allows for the creation in Dutch law of the Anglo-Saxon legal construction referred to in Article I(1)b of the Geneva Convention of 1948, in addition to the possibility of making the lease of a recorded aircraft a full right in rem.

Aircraft are declared capable of being mortgaged *in virtue of an agreement*. A claim covered by a mortgage takes precedence over other right in the aircraft – except claims for remuneration for assistance – and also above a possible priority of the fiscal authorities.

Insofar as the nature of the security permits and there is no stipulation to the contrary in the provisions of the draft, the statutory regulations concerning mortgages on immovable property are similarly applicable to mortgages on recorded aircraft.

Like Article 318c of the Commercial Code, the draft Bill gives highest preference to claims for remuneration for assistance.

Execution of an aircraft is only feasible if all claims with priority over that of the seizor are satisfied out of the proceeds of the sale or if these rights are assumed by the buyer. This is in accordance with Article VII(4) of the Geneva Convention of 1948. Options to acquire aircraft by purchase and rights to possession under leases, which take precedence over the right of the executing creditor, are therefore maintained but such rights are only cancelled by the execution insofar as they rank after the claim of the seizor. This is possible because Article 1612 of the Civil Code is declared inapplicable. Pursuant to Article VIII of the Geneva Convention, the sale of an aircraft in execution in conformity with the provisions of Article VII effects the transfer of the property in such aircraft free from all rights which are not assumed by the purchaser. The draft goes even further by not prescribing any formalities whose non-fulfilment makes the sale in execution null and void, as is done in the Convention, but stipulating that transfer of title is only effected when attachment and execution take place in accordance with the provisions of the draft.

In case of bankruptcy of the owner of a recorded aircraft, the holders of rights in the aircraft are placed in the position of separatists. Even when they do not exercise their rights as separatists, however, they are no worse off in case of bankruptcy than they would be in the event of a normal sale in execution. This is because the draft stipulates that the selling trustee shall be regarded as the seizor in virtue of a right which does not hold any priority, i.e. as a rival creditor. The regulations given in the draft for execution and cancellation are then applicable to the sale to be effected by the trustee. It should be noted that if a separatist or the selling trustee wish to exercise their right of execution, they must attach the aircraft after and during the bankruptcy attachment.

The Aircraft Recordation Bill outlined above has been put before the Dutch Parliament and it will probably be enacted without any major amendments.

CHAPTER IV

CIVIL JURISDICTION OVER AIRCRAFT

PRINCIPLES OF THE APPLICATION OF CIVIL LAW

In the previous chapters we have seen that the air space above the territory of a particular State is subject to the sovereignty of that State, that the aircraft possesses a nationality and that it must be regarded as movable property sui generis.

We now come to the question of which law is applicable to acts committed on board aircraft when such acts lie outside the scope of criminal law and jurisdiction. In this connection one must consider such things as the conclusion of agreements, making wills, drawing up birth certificates, marriage certificates and death certificates and, last but not least, the performance of acts which may give rise to an action for tort.

In view of the fact that the aircraft – like a ship – possesses a nationality, it might be assumed that the same principles are applicable with regard to the above points as apply in the case of shipping.[1] This would mean that if the occurrences mentioned above take place on board aircraft which are not within the jurisdiction of a particular State, then the law of the flag (i.e. the law of the country where the aircraft is registered as to nationality) is applicable. On a ship outside territorial waters, the people and goods on board are considered to be within the jurisdiction of the State whose nationality the ship possesses.

No matter how logical it may seem, it is impossible to draw an analogy between air law and maritime law on this point, since aircraft have by no means reached the position accorded to ships in international law.[2] The main reason is that in many cases the transportation of passengers and goods by sea creates

[1] De Bustamante, "Droit International Public," III, p. 158.
[2] McNair, "The Law of the Air," p. 109.

a prolonged connection with a certain ship. Such a ship will often spend a considerable time on the high seas, which are not subject to the sovereignty of any State. It is only natural that *in such a situation* the ship should be identified with the State whose nationality it possesses. It must be borne in mind, however, that this is not just an example of applying the maxim that "a ship is territory."[1] After all, whenever a ship enters the territorial waters of a State other than that whose flag it carries, the nationality of the ship ceases to have any significance from the viewpoint of international law.[2] The nationality of the ship in that event is merely of importance for determining the legal status of the ship itself.[3] So far as our subject is concerned, this importance only exists as long as the ship is on the high seas, in which case the law of the flag of the ship applies with respect to the persons and goods on board.

With regard to aircraft, however, the position is entirely different. The aircraft travels much faster than the ship, and the travelling time is thus a great deal shorter than for sea transportation, so that in air transportation we do not have the aforesaid prolonged connection of persons and goods with the means of transport. [4]

But there is another obstacle to uniformity of air law and maritime law in this respect. Although a ship will often be within territorial waters, in most cases the time spent on the high seas comprises the greater part of the voyage. In contrast to the ship, the aircraft frequently enters the jurisdiction of other States in the course of its flights, since the aircraft spends much of its time above the territory of other States, i.e. in air space which – as already explained – is subject to the sovereignty of the subjacent States.

The application of the law of the flag to persons and goods on board aircraft is therefore not so automatic as in the case of shipping.[5] Where ships are concerned, the law of the flag is only applicable insofar as the occurrences in question have taken place outside territorial waters.

---

[1] Bourquin, "Règles générales du droit de la paix," Rec. 35 (1931, I), p. 128.
[2] Cleveringa, "Het Nieuwe Zeerecht."
[3] See p. 56.
[4] Spaight, "Aircraft in Peace and the Law," p. 17.
[5] Lemoine, "Traité de Droit Aérien," pp. 201–207.

In the case of aircraft, however, adequate regulations on this subject will have to go much further. By reason of the facts noted above, the law of the flag must also apply to acts done while the aircraft is flying over the territory of foreign States. But such a consistent application of the law of the flag represents an encroachment on the diverse territorial systems of law. Needless to say, this will have a very unfavourable influence on the willingness of the various States to accept such regulations. It will therefore be necessary to determine which system is preferable with respect to aircraft, quite apart from maritime law. In this connection we have the choice of the following five systems:

1. The law of the territory flown over (territorial law);
2. the law of the flag;
3. the law of the place of departure;
4. the law of the place of arrival;
5. a combination of the above.

We shall now review each of these system separately.

Territorial law

When occurrences have taken place on board aircraft within the territorial air space, the territorial law is applicable in conformity with the principle of sovereignty. This is due to the fact that the sovereignty of each State over the air space above its territory is fully recognized. As a rule the boundaries of a State are at the same time the boundaries of its jurisdiction. In maritime law, however, a State does not have to confine its judicial authority to its own territory, and consequently this should also be unnecessary in air law. But the system of applying the territorial law to occurrences on board aircraft restricts the jurisdiction of the State to the territorial air space. It is at once apparent that the application of this system in air law will encounter strong objections.

In the first place, the mere application of the territorial system does not provide a solution for application of the law and jurisdiction with respect to periods when the aircraft is flying over the high seas or over territory which is not subject to the sovereignty of any State. International regulations on this subject must certainly not allow such a gap to exist. At any rate, supplementary regulations ought to be drawn up for aircraft flying over "no man's land."

But there is also an objection of a more practical nature. In the course of an international flight the aircraft generally passes through the jurisdiction of several States. On such a flight it is therefore subject to several systems of law. The drawbacks of this are immediately obvious.[1]

What they amount to is that it will often be rather difficult to determine where the aircraft was at the time of a certain occurrence. After all, aircraft travel at high speeds and naturally the various frontiers are not visible from the air. In many cases it will therefore be no easy matter to decide whether a certain event took place in the territorial air space of one particular State, and hence it will be almost impossible to determine which territorial law must be applied.

Apart from the above-mentioned objections to the territorial system, it may be argued that often the State above whose territory the aircraft is flying has not the slightest interest in what happens on board the aircraft and will therefore be unconcerned with questions of the applicable law and jurisdiction.

On the basis of the foregoing we must conclude that it is both unsatisfactory and impracticable to apply to a certain act the territorial law of the State within whose territorial air space the aircraft was located at the time when that act was committed. On the other hand, it will not be possible to discard the territorial law completely in cases where the States flown over are interested in the said act or in its consequences. This is because the States will be reluctant to accept a system which provides for the application of foreign law and foreign jurisdiction in such cases.

Law of the flag

The application of the law of the flag (i.e. the law of the country in which the aircraft is registered as to nationality) to acts committed on board the aircraft during its flight, is based on the relationship between the aircraft and that country. As explained

[1] Karrer, "Die Einflusz der Souveränität im Luftraum auf die Abgrenzung des Privaatrechts," Aarau, 1938, p. 92.

in Chapter II, it must be assumed that the aircraft has a nationality. In this respect the aircraft resembles the ship. However, we have seen that there is no question of a prolonged connection between the passengers and cargo and the aircraft, as is the case with ships. Nevertheless a certain connection does exist, and at all events it has been found sufficient to form a basis for a system of application of the law. This is partly due to practical considerations, as it is obvious that the objections put forward against the system of applying the territorial law can largely be met by adopting the system to be discussed below.

In the first place there must be some law applicable to aircraft flying over the high seas or over territory which is not subject to the sovereignty of any State whatsoever. As the territory flown over does not have any system of law, it is logical that the law of the State of registry of the aircraft should be applied.

Furthermore, if we also apply the law of the flag to acts committed on board the aircraft while it is flying in the territorial air space of a foreign State, we eliminate the objection against application of the law of the State flown over to such acts, viz. the objection that the aircraft is subject to different systems of law in the course of a single flight. The practical difficulties which this would entail, culminating in the frequent impossibility of determining which State's territory the aircraft was over at a time when a certain legal transaction took place, are solved by the application of the law of the flag. But objections have likewise been raised against the application of the law of the flag.[1] We shall deal with De Visscher's comments on this subject in more detail. In his opinion, application of the law of the country whose nationality the aircraft possesses is "un monstrueux simplisme." According to him, the nationality of the aircraft is a circumstance which may be taken into account, but it is certainly not the only one for which allowance must be made. De Visscher goes into the problem at considerable length. In the case of a birth on board an aircraft he would like the child to be regarded as having been born in the country where the mother is domiciled. He does not favour an analogy with maritime law on this point. He

[1] Lortsch, Revue de Droit Aérien, Vol. 13, 1929, p. 7.
De Visscher, "Les Conflicts de Lois en Matière de Droit Aérien," Recueil des Cours de l'Académie de Droit International à la Haye, 1934, II, p. 352.
Coquoz, "Le droit privé international aérien," p. 291.

takes the view that the birth is "un fait nécessairement accidentel qui ne détermine aucune attache spéciale avec le pays de la nationalité de l'aéronef." The law of the country where the air transport company has its principal place of business would have to be applicable to accidents, while in the case of a marriage on board an aircraft the national law of the parties would have to apply.

De Visscher also proposes a widely differentiated system with respect to contracts concluded on board aircraft. As far as the applicable law is concerned, he suggests two classes of legislative provisions, viz.:

"dispositions supplétives ou interprétatives"

(these do not affect the freedom of the parties to declare which law shall be applicable to the contract) and

"dispositions impératives ou prohibitives"

(these are mandatory).

I. Dispositions supplétives ou interprétatives.

In principle the parties can freely determine which law is to be applicable, but if nothing is mentioned on this subject then the following circumstances must be taken into account:

1. Nature of contract;
2. Common domicile;
3. Common nationality;
4. Place where contract is entered into.

A modest place is thus set aside for the aircraft, as being the place where the contract is concluded. In such cases De Visscher would prefer application of the "loi du lieu d'exécution du contract."

II. Dispositions impératives ou prohibitives.

Here the contract relates to interests which are protected by mandatory provisions of the various national legislations. De Visscher logically considers that the "loi du lieu d'exécution du contract" should likewise be applicable in this case.

When public instruments are involved and these have to be drawn up by an official, De Visscher would like to apply the law of the country whose nationality the official possesses.

De Visscher's observations are extremely interesting, but in our opinion his system is too complicated. The objections of the other writers may briefly be summarized as follows: it seems illogical that an accidental choice of aircraft should determine the law which must be applied to a certain legal transaction. To my mind, this objection does not amount to much. There must be an applicable law, and why not the law of the State whose nationality the aircraft possesses? The nationality of the aircraft appears to be a reasonable starting-point. Any other choice of law would be much more arbitrary. In addition to this comparatively unimportant practical objection, however, an argument of fundamental importance against application of the national law is that it violates the principle of sovereignty. This is undoubtedly correct. Acceptance of the system discussed here represents an encroachment on the sovereignty of the State flown over. In general, the States flown over will not attach any significance to the acts referred to in this chapter. After all, the majority of these acts do not affect the interests of the State within whose territorial air space they occurred. The States in question will have no interest in the application of their national legislation and the exercise of their national jurisdiction with respect to such acts. But the States flown over may well have an interest in certain other occurrences on board aircraft, and then the States concerned will be more reluctant to acquiesce in the aforesaid encroachment upon their sovereignty. Consistent application of the law of the flag will therefore be impracticable in any international regulations on this subject. There is no doubt, however, that application of the above principles is an improvement on the mere application of the territorial law. Acceptable regulations on this subject will have to provide for application of the law of the flag in as wide a field as possible.

Law of the place of departure and law of the place of arrival

The objection to the application to either of these two systems is that as a general rule the State where the aircraft arrives or departs has not the slightest interest in acts committed on board the aircraft during the flight. Its interest in the relevant application of the law and jurisdiction will therefore be negligible. Furthermore, it seems very arbitrary to let a random place of departure or arrival determine which law is applicable to an occurrence that took place during the flight. For this reason the mere adoption of one of these systems appears to be impracticable and undesirable.

Combined system

As is clearly apparent from the foregoing, the application of a single principle can never lead to an acceptable solution. A search has therefore been made for a system which represents a compromise in regard to the application of various principles.[1] The most acceptable of the combined systems is that in which the law of the flag finds general application, except in those cases where the States flown over have an interest in the acts concerned – in which cases the territorial law is applied.

Provision is thus made for national sovereignty in the air space above the territory of the States flown over. The objection put forward against unrestricted application of the law of the flag, viz. that such unrestricted application implied an infringement of the sovereignty principle, does not arise in this case. Attempts to regulate this matter on an international level have therefore been directed along the above line.

Ever since the subject under discussion began to occupy the attention of legal experts, there has been a tendency to dissociate the aircraft from the territorial law of the States over whose territory it flies, as far as acts committed on board the aircraft are concerned. That would mean excluding the influence of sovereignty over the air space in regard to such acts. Most States will only tolerate an encroachment of this nature so long as they have no interest whatsoever in the acts concerned. Hence the application of the territorial law and the competence of the territorial court in cases where the interests of the State flown over are at issue. In the majority of cases these interests will be of minor importance, but allowance must also be made for cases where a wrongful act does concern the State flown over. A combination of the application of the law of the flag and the territorial law as indicated above therefore seems to be the most correct system.

In the following pages we shall discuss the steps taken to regulate this matter on an international basis.

---

[1] Hamel, "Nationalité et conflicts de lois du droit aérien," Revue de droit international privé, 20 (1925), p. 211.

International Law

Institute of International Law

Fauchille, who devoted attention to practically all the problems which still exist in air law, likewise went into this subject. In the report that he submitted to the Institute of International Law in preparation for the sessions at Paris and Madrid in 1910 and 1911 respectively,[1] there was a draft code of regulations for civil aviation.[2] Article 13 of this draft deals with the question now under consideration. The text of that article reads as follows:

"Aıticle 13

1. Les actes passés à bord des aérostats publics et privés en quelque partie que ce soit de l'espace tombent sous la compétence des tribunaux de l'Etat auquel appartiennent les aérostats et sont jugés selon les lois de cet Etat.

2. Toutefois, les actes portant atteinte au droit de conservation de l'Etat sous-jacent, ou qui causent un dommage à son territoire ainsi qu'aux personnes de ses habitants, doivent être jugés par les tribunaux et selon les lois de l'Etat territoire."

Obviously Fauchille was already convinced that unrestricted application of a single principle could not lead to a solution. He at once introduces the application of a combined system. In principle he prefers the law of the flag, which must only be overridden by territorial law if the acts in question affect the interests of the State flown over. Fauchille has thus abandoned the principle of complete freedom of the air (with the exception of a small territorial zone), which he originally advocated. The combined system is to be found in practically all subsequent drafts of regulations on this subject.

The proposal which Von Bar submitted to the Institute of International Law in 1910 [3] formed a counterpart to Fauchille's proposal.

Von Bar went much further than Fauchille in the direction of unrestricted application of a single principle, as may be seen from the following text:

---

[1] See note p. 11.
[2] Institut de Droit International, Annuaire 1911, pp. 105–122.
[3] Ibid., Annuaire 1910, p. 318.

"1. Les aérostats *sont réputés faire partie du territoire de l'Etat* dans les registres duquel ils sont inscrits, aussi longtemps qu'ils se trouvent dans les airs, sans contact avec le sol et à quelque proximité qu'ils soient de celui-ci.

2. Toutefois, en ce qui concerne les dommages et lésions, causés soit par un aérostat même, soit par les personnes à bord, à des objets ou à des personnes qui ne se trouvent à son bord ni à bord d'un aérostat de la même nationalité, la loi territoriale sera appliquée tant pour la responsabilité pénale que pour les actions en dommages intérêts.

3. Lorsqu'il est impossible de constater avec une certitude suffisante si, lors de l'événement donnant naissance à une action pénale ou à une action civile, l'aérostat se trouvait dans la zone enveloppant le territoire d'un autre Etat, on appliquera la loi nationale de l'aérostat."

Von Bar thus assumes that aircraft must be looked upon as airborne parts of territory of the State on whose nationality register they are entered. If he had left it at that, the implication would be that the aircraft must be regarded as exterritorial. Naturally there are a lot of drawbacks to this; such an arrangement was not even adopted for ships. We shall have to start from the assumption that the law of the flag can only be applied if this is permitted by the territorial system of law. That is the only system which may be considered internationally acceptable. To regard the aircraft as part of the territory of the State in which it is registered, is a legal fiction which cannot possibly secure international acceptance.

Although both Fauchille and those who later followed in his footsteps attach primary importance to the application of the law of the flag, they take good care to respect the sovereignty of the States flown over. Von Bar likewise makes concessions in this connection, though to a much smaller extent. In his proposal he declares the national law to be applicable to all acts performed on board the aircraft; the territorial law only applies when the aircraft itself or persons on board the aircraft cause damage to persons or goods outside the aircraft. Von Bar thus recognizes the fact that the interests of the State flown over must be protected, but his proposal definitely does not go far enough to make this internationally acceptable. The fiction of regarding the aircraft as airborne territory is an infringement of the legal system of the States flown over. It is correct to make the law of the flag of the aircraft apply to occurrences on board the aircraft which do not affect the interests of the States flown over. But if one accepts Von Bar's fiction that an aircraft is airborne territory, the inference is that the States flown over have nothing to do with what happens on board the aircraft within their territorial air space. Despite the fact that Von Bar makes provision for the interests of the States flown over, the latter will certainly not approve of a proposal which so encroaches on their sovereignty. Of course Fauchille's proposal also encroaches on the sovereignty of the States flown over, but in addition to the fact that Fauchille allows more scope for the territorial system of law, he does not base the application of the national law on an unacceptable legal fiction. The proposal of Fauchille is therefore preferable in every respect to that of Von Bar.

Paris Convention of 1919

Like the Chicago Convention of 1944, the Paris Convention of 1919 did not contain any regulations concerning application of the law and jurisdiction with respect to occurences which take place on board aircraft in flight. But this does not mean that the problem was completely ignored at the time when the Convention was drawn up.

On the contrary, Article 23 of the draft prepared by the "Sous-Commission Juridique de la Commission de l'Aéronautique de la Conférence de la Paix" contained the following provisions on this subject: [1]

"1. Toute personne à bord d'un aéronef doit se conformer aux lois et règlements de l'Etat où elle se trouve.

2. En cas de survol sans escale, de frontière à frontière, toute personne à bord doit se conformer aux lois et règlements édictés par le pays survolé, en vue de rendre inoffensif le passage.

3. Les rapports de droit qui se forment entre personnes à bord d'un aéronef en vol sont régis par la loi du pays dont l'aéronef porte nationalité."

The draft thus adopts the system which we referred to above

[1] Roper, "La Convention Internationale du 13 octobre portant réglémentation de la navigation aérienne" (Paris, 1930), pp. 155–157.

as the combined system. The territorial system of law is to apply, but legal relations between persons on board the aircraft are to be governed by the law of the flag.

However, some delegates expressed the view that this article was both unnecessary and superfluous. It was remarked that the provisions of paragraphs 1 and 2 already ensue from the fact that each State has sovereignty over the air space above its territory, while the provisions of paragraph 3 relate to a point of international private law which should not be settled in the Paris Convention but in a subsequent agreement. On account of these objections, the contents of the above-mentioned article were omitted from the Paris Convention.

That is rather unsatisfactory, especially because the draft also contained provisions with respect to criminal law which – as we shall see later – were likewise discarded. The situation of the aircraft outside the territorial air space could not be imagined. In the year 1919 such a thing was quite understandable, although it showed a certain lack of foresight.

Comité Juridique International de l'Aviation

The Comité Juridique International de l'Aviation (CJIA) also devoted attention to the subject under review.

Provisions relating to the choice of law and jurisdiction with respect to happenings on board aircraft in flight were included in the draft international air code drawn up by CJIA.[1]

During the VIth Congress of CJIA at Rome in 1924 the final text of the following articles for the proposed international air code was adopted, after having been discussed at Geneva in 1912, at Monaco in 1921 and at Prague in 1922.

Chapitre VI

Article 23. L'aéronef qui se trouve au-dessus de la pleine mer ou d'un territoire qui ne dépend pas de la souveraineté d'aucun Etat est soumis à la législation et la jurisdiction de pays dont il a la nationalité.

Article 24. Lorsqu'un aéronef se trouve au-dessus du territoire

[1] Projet de Code International de l'Air du Comité Juridique International de l'Aviation (VI Congrès, Rome 1924), Chapitre VI, De la législation applicable et de la juridiction compétente en matière de locomotion aérienne.

d'un Etat étranger, les actes accomplis et les faits survenus à bord et qui seraient de nature à compromettre la sécurité ou l'ordre public de l'Etat sous-jacent sont régis par la législation de cet Etat et jugés par ses tribunaux.

Article 25. La réparation des dommages causés aux personnes et aux biens sur le territoire de l'Etat sous-jacent est régie par la législation de cet Etat.

Article 30. Les actes accomplis et les faits survenus dans l'espace à bord de l'aeronef et qui n'intéresseraient pas la sécurité ou l'ordre public de l'Etat sous-jacent, restent soumis à la législation et à la jurisdiction du pays dont l'aéronef a la nationalité.

Article 31 deals with the recording of births and deaths on the logbook of the aircraft.

In this draft the principles which ought to govern the application of law and jurisdiction with respect to acts committed on board aircraft are laid down in acceptable form for the first time. An aircraft flying above "no man's land" or above the open sea is subject to the laws and jurisdiction of the State whose nationality it possesses. As soon as the aircraft is over the territory of a certain State, it is subject to the jurisdiction of that State insofar as acts committed on board the aircraft affect the safety and public order in the State flown over. Claims in respect of damage sustained by persons and goods on the territory of the State flown over are likewise subject to the laws and jurisdiction of that State. (In the meantime this subject has been dealt with in an international convention.[1] As we shall see later, however, the solution to the jurisdiction problem in that convention is not entirely satisfactory.)

Acts which do not affect either the safety or the public order of the State flown over are subject to the laws and jurisdiction of the State whose nationality the aircraft possesses.

The above draft thus gives expression to the principle enunciated by Coüannier [2] as early as 1910, viz. that the nationality of the aircraft forms the foundation of the international system of law in aviation. But the jurists who drew up the above regulations rightly realized that there must not be any encroach-

[1] Convention on damage caused by foreign aircraft to third parties on the surface, Rome, 1952, ICAO Doc. 7364.

[2] Couännier, "De la nationalité et du domicile des aéronefs", Revue Juridique Internationale de la Locomotion Aérienne, 1910, p. 165.

ment on the sovereignty of the surface States over the air space above their territory. An arrangement whereby the sovereignty of the States flown over was insufficiently respected would never have any chance of finding widespread acceptance. If international regulations on this subject are to be succesful, they must be drawn up in accordance with the perfectly correct principles indicated in the CJIA draft.

It is therefore extremely regrettable that the CJIA draft, like the other subjects which this organization endeavoured to regulate in a "Code de l'Air," has not received more international attention. It was mainly the French legislators who got in touch with CJIA when framing their national law on this question. Now that it is once again the subject of international interest – the Legal Committee of ICAO has put the legal status of aircraft on its agenda – the relevant regulations which the International Law Association drew up and embodied in a draft convention are being taken as a basis.

International Law Association

The International Law Association also realized the importance of regulations on this subject. The Aviation Law Committee of the International Law Association compiled a report which included a draft for a set of regulations concerning jurisdiction in civil and criminal matters over all persons carried in aircraft. This draft was discussed during the 31st conference of the International Law Association at Buenos Aires in 1922,[1] and it received further consideration during the 33rd conference at Stockholm in 1924.[2] The following rules were recommended for inclusion in an international convention:

"(*a*) Civil Jurisdiction:

Art. 1.

The airship which is above the open sea or such territory as is not under the sovereignty of any State is subject to the laws and civil jurisdiction of the country of which it has the nationality.

[1] International Law Association, Report of the Thirty-First Conference, Buenos Aires, 1922, p. 211.

[2] Ibid., Report of the Thirty-third Conference, Stockholm, 1924, pp. 113 et. seq.

Art. 2.
A public airship which is above territory of a foreign State remains under the exclusive jurisdiction of the State of which it has the nationality.

A private airship which is above the territory of a foreign State is subject to the laws and jurisdiction of such State only in the following cases:

1. With regard to every breach of its laws for the public safety and its military and fiscal laws.
2. In case of a breach of its regulations concerning air navigation
3. For all acts committed on board the airship and having effect on the territory of the said State.

In all other respects a private airship follows the laws and jurisdiction of the State of the flag."

The next section of the rules is concerned with criminal jurisdiction, which will be dealt with in the following chapter.

The above rules are roughly the same as those laid down in Chapter VI of the "Code de l'Air" drafted by the Comité Juridique International de l'Aviation, which was discussed earlier in the present chapter.[1] There was a certain amount of liaison between the two organizations on this subject.[2] In view of the fact that the Paris Convention of 1919 did not contain any regulations governing the application of law and jurisdiction with respect to acts committed on board aircraft,[3] the International Law Association considered it desirable that this subject should be regulated by international agreement. However, it was felt that the time was not yet ripe. The subject was then left in abeyance until the conferences at Copenhagen in 1950[4] and Lucerne in 1952.[5] During the Copenhagen conference in 1950 it was decided to ask the Air Law Committee to prepare a revised draft of the rules drawn up in 1924 (see above). In 1951 the Air Law Committee appointed Professor John C. Cooper as rapporteur for this revision. The latter submitted to the Air Law

[1] See p. 109.
[2] International Law Association, Report of the Thirty-first Conference, Buenos Aires, 1922, p. 212.
[3] See p. 108.
[4] International Law Association, Report of the Forty-fourth Conference, Copenhagen, 1950, pp. 226 et seq.
[5] International Law Association, Report of the Forty-fifth Conference, Lucerne, 1952, pp. 113–138.

Committee a number of questions which might form a basis of discussion.[1]

Among the questions raised by Cooper were the following:

Question A: Should the Chicago Convention as now in effect be accepted both in principle and terminology as the background for the proposed new convention on the respective conflicts and jurisdiction of the State of the flag of the aircraft and other States?

That is a rhetorical question. Naturally the answer will have to be in the affirmative, but nevertheless we shall examine the arguments summed up by Cooper.

The Chicago Convention is now in force between practically all the States engaged in international aviation on this side of the Iron Curtain. As Cooper rightly points out, it will involve a great deal of trouble to amend the Chicago Convention and consequently no efforts in this direction may be anticipated in the near future. Since the Chicago Convention in its present form will serve as a constitution for international aviation for a long time to come, it would show very little sense of reality if the principles and the terminology of the Chicago Convention were not taken into account in preparing a draft convention on the subject of acts committed on board aircraft. The draft convention will have to be worded in such a way that the States which ratified the Chicago Convention can accept it without discussion. The terminology of the socalled Stockholm draft of 1924 must therefore be revised in any case. This Stockholm draft, for example, refers to "airships," whereas the Chicago Convention speaks of "aircraft." In the Stockholm draft a distinction is made between public and private airships, while the Chicago draft makes a distinction between civil and state aircraft. In the next chapter we shall also see that Article 12 of the Chicago Convention, which deals with breaches of air traffic regulations, contains rules of jurisdiction which do not fit in with the system of the Stockholm draft.

Question B: Should the new convention seek to deal with all problems of criminal and civil jurisdiction within the same limited document as did the Stockholm draft, or should the International Law Association seek to divide the problem and

[1] Ibid., p. 114.

deal first with the question which is most urgent, namely criminal jurisdiction?

According to Cooper there are three problems: [1]

a) competence and jurisdiction for the punishment of crimes committed on board aircraft;

b) the same as to births, deaths and marriages occurring on board;

c) the same as to other occurrences giving rise to questions of civil jurisdiction such as torts committed on board aircraft or contracts there entered into.

Regulations covering these three fields are essential, and Cooper advises the International Law Association to concentrate its attention on the first problem, i.e. regulations with respect to crimes and offences committed on board aircraft.

Question C: Assuming that an effort is made to amend the Stockholm draft so as to cover in a satisfactory manner the question of crimes committed on board aircraft, should such convention cover both state and civil aircraft as defined in the Chicago Convention?

Since this question relates to criminal jurisdiction, we shall discuss it in the next chapter.

Question D: Should the jurisdiction or jurisdictions provided in the draft convention be exclusive of all existing state legislation?

Cooper recommends that the proposed regulations should not override the national laws.[2] He asserts that a convention which overrides the national legislation will be internationally unacceptable. However, this objection can hardly be raised against the Stockholm draft, because the latter does full justice to the national law. Anyway Cooper's standpoint is fundamentally wrong. The future international regulations will derive much of their value from the fact that the national legislation has to give way on certain points.

Question E: What general rules of jurisdiction should be provided as to civil aircraft in the draft convention in addition to existing national legislation as to crimes committed on board?

Like Question C, this question is entirely concerned with crimi-

[1] Ibid., p. 116.
[2] Ibid., p. 117.

nal law and it will therefore be discussed in the next chapter.

At its 45th conference in Lucerne in September 1952 the International Law Association decided to give priority to the problem of criminal jurisdiction,[1] as recommended by Cooper, and consequently its further activities relate to criminal law.

We shall now consider the rules of jurisdiction under the Conventions of Warsaw and Rome.

Warsaw Convention of October 12, 1929

The convention for the unification of certain rules relating to international carriage by air, which was signed at Warsaw on October 12, 1929,[2] has met with a very wide acceptance.[3] This is really not surprising, as one of the points regulated in the Warsaw Convention is extremely important for international air transport, namely the liability of the air carrier. Under the terms of this Convention, the carrier is liable for damage sustained in the event of the death or wounding of a passenger or any other bodily injury suffered by a passenger, if the accident which caused the damage took place on board the aircraft or in the course of any of the operations of embarking or disembarking.[4] The carrier is likewise liable for damage sustained in the event of the destruction or loss of, or of damage to, any registered baggage or any goods, if the occurrence which caused the damage so sustained took place during the carriage by air.[5] In addition, the carrier is liable for damage occasioned by delay in the carriage by air of passengers, baggage or goods.[6] He is not liable if he proves that he and his agents have taken all necessary measures to avoid the damage or that it was impossible for him or them to take such measures.[7] The passenger or the shipper must therefore prove the existence of the contract of carriage, but it is sufficient if he states the damage. The carrier can exculpate himself.

An extremely important point for the carrier, however, is

[1] Ibid., p. 109.

[2] Ratified by the Netherlands on April 6, 1933 (Statute Book 149) and published by Royal Decree of July 7, 1933 (Statute Book No. 365).

[3] The Convention has been ratified by forty six States.

[4] Article 17 of the Warsaw Convention of 1929.

[5] Article 18 of the Warsaw Convention of 1929.

[6] Article 19 of the Warsaw Convention of 1929.

[7] Article 20 of the Warsaw Convention of 1929.

that in the carriage of passengers his liability for each passenger is limited to the sum of 125,000 gold francs (31,000 Dutch guilders).[1] The passenger can only fix a higher limit for the carrier's liability by means of a special contract with the carrier. In the carriage of registered baggage and of goods, the liability of the carrier is limited to a sum of 250 gold francs per kilogram, unless a special declaration of value was made to him at the time when the goods or baggage were handed over for carriage by air. In that case the carrier will be liable to pay a sum not exceeding the declared value, unless he proves that this is greater than the actual value to the consignor, at delivery. As regards objects of which the passenger takes charge himself, the liability of the carrier is limited to 5,000 gold francs per passenger.[2] The carrier's liability is only unlimited if the damage is caused by his wilful misconduct or by such default on his part as, in accordance with the law of the court seised of the case, is considered to be equivalent to wilful misconduct.[3]

Actions for damage in connection with the liability described above must be brought, at the option of the plaintiff, in the territory of one of the High Contracting Parties, either before the court having jurisdiction where the carrier is ordinarily resident, or has his principal place of business or has an establishment by which the contract has been made, or before the court having jurisdiction at the place of destination.[4] The plaintiff therefore has the choice of a number of courts. The framers of the Convention have not adapted one of the systems discussed earlier in order to determine the competent court. Their objective has been to make it as easy as possible for the plaintiff to institute proceedings by giving him the choice of four courts. They have undoubtedly succeeded in this endeavour, but there is still a difficulty in regard to the enforceability of the judgment when this is passed by a court whose nationality is different from that of the carrier. In actual practice the carrier will always pay the damages awarded against him, because his international

[1] If the Protocol for Revision of the Warsaw Convention (The Hague, September 1955) is ratified, this amount will be increased to 250,000 gold francs (62.000 guilders).
[2] Article 22 of the Warsaw Convention of 1929.
[3] Article 25 of the Warsaw Convention of 1929.
[4] Article 28 of the Warsaw Convention of 1929.

position is usually vulnerable and so he cannot afford to disregard the judgment of a foreign court.

A further drawback of the rules of jurisdiction under the Warsaw Convention is that they do not ensure uniform application of the Convention. This has been realized for some time past and attempts have been made to find a way out of the difficulty. Before discussing these solutions we shall consider the rules of jurisdiction under the Rome Convention, since the solutions also apply to that Convention.

Rome Convention of 1952

On October 7, 1952, a convention on damage caused by foreign aircraft to third parties on the surface [1] was signed at Rome. This Convention supersedes an earlier convention on the same subject, which was signed in 1933 but – unlike the Warsaw Convention – found practical no acceptance. In the almost twenty years of its existence the 1933 Convention has only secured five ratifications,[2] while up till now the 1952 Convention has only been ratified by two countries.[3] This is mainly due to the fact that on the one hand the airlines do not attach very much importance to regulation of the subject covered by the Convention, while on the other hand the liability system of the Rome Convention is based on the principle of absolute liability of the operator of the aircraft. The Convention lays down rules of liability with respect to damage caused to third parties on the surface of the contracting States by aircraft registered in another contracting State, i.e. foreign aircraft. Consequently, the Convention does not give any rules of liability for damage caused on national territory by national aircraft; this is left to the legislature of the country concerned. The object of the Convention is to ensure compensation for persons on the ground who suffer damage from an aircraft and are not engaged in aviation themselves but simply have to tolerate aircraft flying overhead. That is why a system of absolute liability has been introduced. The liability of the aircraft (i.e. of the operator) exists as soon as it

[1] Convention on damage caused by foreign aircraft to third parties on the surface Rome, 1952, ICAO Doc. 7364.

[2] Belgium, Rumania, Guatemala, Brazil, Spain.

[3] Egypt, Canada.

is proved that the damage was caused by an aircraft in flight or by persons or things falling from it.[1] Consequently the injured party does not have to prove fault and the operator of the aircraft cannot even exculpate himself. This was the system already adopted in the Convention of 1933. It was also agreed to for the 1952 Convention by a large majority of votes, although some countries (including such an important aviation country as the United States) were opposed to it. While the Convention imposes an absolute liability on the operator, at the same time it limits the amount of this liability.[2] The limit of liability, however, is so high [3] that normal damage is certainly covered and only the risk of a catastrophe is excluded. Apart from this restricted absolute liability, the operator of the aircraft is liable without limitation if he is proved guilty of wilful misconduct or default considered equivalent to wilful misconduct. Numerous objections to this system have been put forward in the course of the years.[4] The principal argument against the absolute liability is invariably the fact that an aircraft must no longer be looked upon as something which is dangerous in itself but should be treated like other means of transport.

Another objection to the Convention, which brings us back to our subject, concerns the rules of jurisdiction. Under the Rome Convention of 1933, two courts were declared competent, viz. the judicial authorities in the defendant's place of residence and

---

[1] Article 1 of the Rome Convention of 1952.

[2] 500,000 francs for aircraft weighing 1,000 kilogrammes or less;

500,000 francs plus 400 francs per kilogramme over 1,000 kilogrammes for aircraft weighing more than 1,000 but not exceeding 6,000 kilogrammes;

2,500,000 francs plus 250 francs per kilogramme over 6,000 kilogrammes for aircraft weighing more than 6,000 but not exceeding 20,000 kilogrammes;

6,000,000 francs plus 150 francs per kilogramme over 20,000 kilogrammes for aircraft weighing more than 20,000 but not exceeding 50,000 kilogrammes;

10,500,000 francs plus 100 francs per kilogramme over 50,000 kilogrammes for aircraft weighing more than 50,000 kilogrammes.

The francs mentioned here are "gold francs" consisting of 65½ milligrammes of gold of millesimal fineness 900.

Converted into Dutch currency, the present value of one gold franc is approximately 0,25 guilder.

[3] Expressed in Dutch guilders the limit of liability for certain widely used types of aircraft is as follows:

Dakota	1,000,000 guilders
Convair 240	1,500,000 ,,
Constellation	2,600,000 ,,
Super Constellation	3,000,000 ,,

[4] ICAO Doc. 6029–LC/126, p. 32.

those of the place where the damage was caused, whereas the Rome Convention of 1952 only recognizes one court, namely that of the place where the damage occurred. The parties can only deviate from this rule by mutual consent and subject to the provisions of Article 20(1) of the Convention. This restriction to a single forum represents a safeguard for the operator of the aircraft. As far as the injured party is concerned, however, it has the disadvantage that in most cases – since he will usually have to seek regress against an airline which has no assets in the country where the damage occurred – he must try to obtain enforcement of the judgment of the national court in a foreign country. The advantage of the single forum lies in the fact that the limits of liability specified in the Convention will not be exceeded, as would otherwise be possible if actions could be brought before a number of courts. The attraction of the single forum system lies in its simplicity and logic. If it is adopted, however, then rules must also be laid down for enforcement of the judgments. The difficulty in this connection is that no country will accept enforceability of a judgment obtained from the court of the place where the damage occurred. The Convention endeavours to circumvent this difficulty by means of certain provisions[1] which may be summarized as follows.

A final judgment is enforceable in Contracting States other than that in which the judgment was pronounced, viz.:

(*a*) in the Contracting State where the operator has his principal place of business;

(*b*) if the assets available in that State are insufficient to satisfy the judgment, in any other Contracting State where the operator has assets.

Notwithstanding these provisions, execution may be refused on the following grounds;

(*a*) the judgment was given by default and the defendant did not receive adequate notice of the proceedings;

(*b*) the defendant was not given a reasonable opportunity to defend his interests;

(*c*) the judgment relates to a cause of action concerning which an earlier judgment or arbitral award is recognized as final in the place where execution is applied for;

[1] Article 20 of the Rome Convention of 1952.

(*d*) the judgment has been obtained by fraud of one of the parties;

(*e*) the party applying for execution is not the party entitled to enforcement of the judgment.

The above conditions are reasonable and logical. They do not in any way prevent a consistent application of the principle of enforceability in other contracting States of the judgment passed by the forum loci delicti. But they are not the only conditions, as the Convention also provides that execution may be refused if the judgment is contrary to the public policy of the State in which execution is requested. Here we once again encounter the eternal "escape clause" which invariably makes its appearance in the existing bilateral agreements on the execution of judgments. Public policy is such a comprehensive and vague term that the national court will nearly always be able to refuse execution of the judgment in those very countries against whose administration of justice protection ought to be offered. In this way most of what was given with the one hand is taken back with the other hand. The remarkable feature is that although this extremely far-reaching proviso was included in order to make the Convention acceptable, the enforceability of judgments is a point which makes a great many States hesitate to ratify the Convention. Apparently they feel that it means an undesirable encroachment on their sovereignty rights. Apart from the foregoing objections to the rules of execution, the rules of jurisdiction under the Rome Convention give rise to the same objection which we mentioned earlier in connection with the Warsaw Convention, i.e. that it is impossible to secure a uniform application of the Convention.

We shall therefore investigate how the existing objections to the jurisdiction rules of the Warsaw and Rome Conventions might be overcome. After indicating the solutions which have already been suggested in the past, we shall discuss the solution which seems most appropriate for the future. We shall begin with the attempts that have been made to arrive at a more uniform interpretation of the various conventions.

Advisory opinions from CITEJA

Among the topics discussed during the Third International Conference on Air Law at Rome in 1933 (when another air law convention was signed besides the one referred to here) [1] was the desirability of securing a uniform interpretation of the various conventions in the field of air law and the possibility of utilizing the services of CITEJA in this connection. A formal resolution was adopted and CITEJA then made a study of the subject.[2] The rules drafted by the First Commission of CITEJA empowered this body to give advisory opinions on the interpretation of international air law conventions if asked by a State, an international organization, a public authority or an interested party. The foregoing might lead to a uniform interpretation and application of the said conventions, but of course it does not offer an effective solution to the problem of jurisdiction. However, this draft never reached the stage of being discussed at a full session of CITEJA. Nevertheless objections were raised against the principle of CITEJA giving advisory opinions.[3] Since CITEJA no longer exists, there is no point in going into these objections. It may be remarked that one of the chief arguments in favour of the proposal was that the members of CITEJA had been responsible for drafting the various conventions and were thus in a position to give the correct explanation of the meaning of the text. This was not a strong argument, however, as there had been numerous changes in the membership of the committee. CITEJA's successor, the Legal Committee of ICAO, seems even less suitable for this function.[4] as its membership alters even more frequently, while the fact that the members of the Legal

[1] Convention for the unification of certain rules relating to the precautionary arrest of aircraft, Rome, May 29, 1933 (published by Royal Decree of Feb. 7, 1938, Statute Book No. 12).

This Convention came into force for the Netherlands on April 28, 1938, after the Dutch legislation had been adopted to it by the Act of November 4, 1937 (Statute Book No. 207) through addition of the seventh section a) to the IVth Title of Book III of the Dutch Code of Civil Procedure.

Convention on damage caused by foreign aircraft to third parties on the surface, Rome, May 29, 1933. This Convention has never been ratified by the Netherlands.

[2] CITEJA Document 239, 1934.
,, ,, 298, 1936.
,, ,, 334, 1937.
,, ,, 362, 1938.
,, ,, 487, 1946.

[3] CITEJA Document 239, 1934.
,, ,, 293, 1936.

[4] Drion, "Towards a uniform interpretation of the private air law conventions," Journal of Air Law and Commerce, Vol. 19, Autumn 1952, No. 4, pp. 426–427.

Committee hold office as representatives of their States does not guarantee the necessary independence of these members.

Apart from this matter of giving advisory opinions, a more far-reaching solution has been sought in the form of regulations governing the whole question of jurisdiction. This solution lies in the creation of an international court.

International court

The idea of international administration of justice is not a new one. In the course of the years a number of proposals have already been submitted for the establishment of an international court to deal with civil actions.[1] It is an idea which is warmly supported by the Netherlands, but it may be expected that many States will be unwilling to submit to the jurisdiction of an international judicial authority. On the other hand, in view of the international character of civil aviation it is probable that there will be less opposition to the concept of an international court for all questions of air law. Although the resistance in this field must not be underestimated, the goal certainly justifies attempts to find a solution in that direction. In 1948 Professor Cleveringa presented an interesting report to the International Bar Association, which met at The Hague in August of that year.[2] He suggested the establishment of a permanent court of arbitration, to which parties could agree to submit their disputes in the field of maritime law and air law. It is questionable whether there is any sense in this project as far as law is concerned. Drion [3] rightly points out that those who have a choice of several courts

---

[1] Proposal of E. Roguin and A. Darras for the Institute of International Law in 1895 and 1897, Annuaire 1895 and 1897 (XVI), 106, 108.

Proposal of Prof. de la Pradelle for the 38th Conference of the International Law Association in 1934 at Budapest, Report of the 38th Conference, pp. 71–75.

Carabiber, "Les juridictions internationales de droit privé," Neuchatel, 1947, pp. 265–279.

Gidel, Report to the Institute of International Law, "La Clause Juridictionelle dans les Conventions d'Union notamment celles relatives à la Propriété Industrielle et à la Propriété Artistique et Littéraire," 39 Annuaire de l'Institut de Droit International, Brussels, 1936, p. 248.

Charlier in Compte Rendu des Réunions de la lère Commission du CITEJA, Paris, janvier 1946, Doc. No. 487.

[2] Prof. R. P. Cleveringa, proposal to set up an international court of arbitration in the field of maritime and air law, submitted to the 2nd Conference of the International Bar Association at The Hague in 1948.

[3] See p. 121.

under the conventions at present in force would not benefit much by submitting their claim to an international court of arbitration, as that would probably involve more expense than submitting the claim to the court of their choice.

Another report on the same subject was drawn up by Professor P. Chauveau for the conference of the International Law Association at Dubrovnik in 1956.[1] He considers it advisable to set up an international tribunal for the sake of obtaining a uniform interpretation and application of international private law. He proposes the creation of a court of first instance and a court of appeal. The court of first instance will have to be designated in each of the States adhering to the relevant convention. Chauveau suggests that the appeal court should sit in Strasbourg. Its members must be appointed by the President of ICAO on the nomination of the States represented on the Council of ICAO.

Although Dutch opinion is more in favour of making use of the International Court of Justice in The Hague, Chauveau's proposal is regarded as an extremely important one and a welcome contribution towards the development of the concept of international administration of justice.

In addition to setting up an entirely new international court, consideration has also been given to the idea of making use of the existing International Court of Justice, although this body was established to settle disputes between States.

International Court of Justice

An advantage of making use of the International Court of Justice in order to secure a uniform interpretation of international private law is that this Court has great authority and experience. The idea was already adopted to some extent in 1931 when a number of States signed a Protocol whereby they agreed to submit to arbitration by the Permanent Court of International Justice at The Hague (the forerunner of the International Court of Justice) in the event of a dispute as to the interpretation of the treaties drawn up at The Hague Conference on International Private Law of 1928.[2] In 1948 a new article (27b) of the same

[1] Proposal of Prof. P. Chauveau for the conference of the International Law Association at Dubrovnik in 1956.

[2] Dutch Statute Book 1935, No. 444.

The Protocol was ratified by Belgium, the Netherlands, Esthonia, Portugal, Norway, Denmark, Sweden and Finland.

tenor was added to the Berne Convention governing international copyright.

In any case it is always possible to appeal to the International Court of Justice in disputes concerning the interpretation of a treaty (under the terms of Article 36, Par. 2, of the Statute of this Court), since the States which have accepted this Statute can declare that they recognize the jurisdiction of the Court as compulsory – in relation to every State which does the same – in all disputes concerning the interpretation of a treaty. Consequently this is also feasible with regard to treaties in the field of air law, such as the Conventions of Warsaw, Rome and Geneva.

So far as the present writer is aware, that possibility has never been utilized. Holland has always advocated making use of an international authority to settle disputes arising out of the international conventions on the subject of air law.[1] As an argument in support of this, it was repeatedly pointed out that such a procedure is the only way of guaranteeing uniform application of the said conventions. Up till now, however, the response has not been favourable. That is why proposals involving a less far-reaching solution have also received attention. Following the 1933 proposal that advisory opinions relating to the various air law conventions should be given by CITEJA, it is now suggested that the International Court of Justice should be called upon to give advisory opinions in this connections.

Advisory opinions from the International Court of Justice

In the paper which we have already referred to above,[2] Drion suggests making use of the authority and experience of the International Court of Justice in order to realize "the possibility of promoting uniform interpretation by way of advisory opinions." In his paper Drion indicates a way of finding a satisfactory procedure for this. The method which he proposes is certainly worthy of consideration. His proposal is as follows. The Legal Committee of ICAO will first find out which questions of interpretation have arisen with respect to the conventions in the field of air law. The Legal Committee will then submit the questions to the Council of ICAO with comments and advice regarding

[1] ICAO Doc. 7379–LC/34, p. 56.
[2] See p. 121.

the desirability of obtaining a decision from the International Court of Justice. Since ICAO is recognized as a specialized agency of the United Nations (Article X of the Agreement between the United Nations and ICAO), the Council of ICAO can ask the International Court for an advisory opinion on these questions. Under the terms of the second paragraph of Article 96 of the United Nations Charter, "specialized agencies (of the United Nations), which may at any time be so authorized by the General Assembly, may request advisory opinions of the (International) Court (of Justice) on legal questions arising within the scope of their activities." There are undoubtedly a number of advantages attaching to the above arrangement. On account of the authority which the International Court of Justice enjoys, these opinions are not likely to be disregarded in actual practice. Another extremely important point is that a new convention is unnecessary, as the possibility already exists.

At the moment, however, it appears that the need for a more far-reaching arrangement has become increasingly urgent, due to the following reasons.

The rules of jurisdiction given in the Rome Convention are regarded as unsatisfactory by numerous States. The objections to these rules could largely be met by creating an international court for the settlement of disputes relating to the execution of the various air law conventions. If the Rome Convention of 1952 is to secure wide ratification, satisfactory rules of jurisdiction must be found, and for this purpose the possibilities of arriving at an international judicial procedure ought to be thoroughly investigated.

Furthermore, in the course of the preparatory discussions on a convention to regulate liability in the case of aerial collisions, it has become apparent that a proper solution to the jurisdiction problem can only be found along the lines of an international system of judicature.

Dutch proposal for an International Tribunal [1]

Even before the importance of an international court was so evident as it is now, viz. while the draft which ultimately led to the Rome Convention of 1952 was being dealt with by the Legal

[1] ICAO Doc. 7379-LC/24, p. 56.

Committee of ICAO, the Netherlands put forward a proposal for such a court. The Dutch suggestion for solving the problems of jurisdiction under the Rome Convention took the following form.

Actions for damage can only be brought before the competent court of the place where the damage occurred. Within a period of three months from the date of the accident, however, the operator of the aircraft concerned can request this court to fix the total amount of this liability, for which amount he deposits a security. If the operator fails to do so, the injured party can bring an action at all places where the court declares itself to be competent pursuant to its national law. Naturally the injured party can bring an action before the court in the country where the accident occurred. In that event all other contracting States will have to give their exequator to the judgment ,and if they refuse to do this then the case will be brought before an international arbitral tribunal to be appointed for this purpose. The members of this tribunal will be a judge designated by the country where enforcement of the judgment was sought, a judge designated by the country where the judgment was passed, and a third to be appointed jointly by the other two, or if no agreement can be reached, by the President of the International Court of Justice. The verdict of this tribunal shall be enforceable in all contracting States.

The above proposal found little support, partly because of its complexity and partly because it was felt that the time was not yet ripe for the establishment of an international tribunal.

This Dutch proposal is certainly rather complicated, but that is due to the very fact that it goes so far to meet possible objections from States which are jealous of their sovereign rights. If the States were willing to place more confidence in the objectivity of an international tribunal, a simpler procedure could be followed.

Now that the Legal Committee of ICAO has put the study of the possibility of international jurisdiction on its agenda as a priority item, apparently the idea is beginning to gain ground that a satisfactory solution for the adjudication of aviation disputes can only be found in the direction of an international court.

Up till now we have considered the problem insofar as private air law conventions are concerned, but perhaps public law – as embodied in the Chicago Convention of 1944 – should also be included in the settlement of the jurisdiction problem.

Chicago Convention of 1944

The Chicago Convention likewise contains provisions with respect to the settlement of disputes relating to the interpretation or application of the Convention. In Article 84 [1] it is stated that if any of the contracting States disagree upon the correct application of the provisions of the Convention, the dispute shall be decided by the Council of ICAO. Any contracting State may appeal from the decision of the Council to the International Court of Justice or to an ad hoc arbitral tribunal. It is very doubtful, however, whether the Council of ICAO is an appropriate authority to give decisions. After all, the Council is composed of representatives of the different States, who act in accordance with instructions given by their governments. There is no guarantee of impartiality. The Council is a political organ.[2] It is essential to have confidence in the impartiality of every authority that administers justice. Since they are bound to adhere to their instructions, the members of the Council of ICAO cannot be expected to be impartial.

It therefore seems definitely advisable that when the possibility of creating an international court is being studied, provision should also be made for the disagreements which may arise in regard to the application of the Chicago Convention, for which the existing rules of jurisdiction are inadequate.

Some national legislation on this subject, which again raises the question of the application of civil law, will now be reviewed.

---

[1] Article 84 of the Chicago Convention of 1944, reading as follows:

"If any disagreement between two or more contracting States relating to the interpretation or application of this Convention and its Annexes cannot be settled by negotiation, it shall, on the application of any State concerned in the disagreement, be decided by the Council. No member of the Council shall vote in the consideration by the Council of any dispute to which it is a party. Any contracting State may, subject to Article 85, appeal from the decision of the Council to an ad hoc arbitral tribunal agreed upon with the other parties to the dispute or to the Permanent Court of International Justice. Any such appeal shall be notified to the Council within sixty days of receipt of notification of the decision of the Council."

[2] Goedhuis, Pacta sunt servanda," 1952, p. 20.

National law

1. France.

In Article 10 of the "Loi relative à la navigation aérienne (du 31 mai 1924)" we find that the law of the flag is declared applicable to acts which have taken place on board foreign aircraft above French territory. The article in question reads as follows;

"Les rapports juridiques entre les personnes qui se trouvent à bord d'un aéronef étranger en circulation sont régis par la loi du pavillon de cet aéronef, toutes les fois que la loi territoriale serait normalement compétente."

Here we are concerned with rules of maritime law transplanted to air law. This was done at the instance of Ripert, who was one of the jurists responsible for drafting the above Law.[1] They ventured to lay down a single principle in the Law, namely that of application of the law of the flag of the aircraft involved. It is worth noting that in this case the proposal which Von Bar submitted to the Institute of International Law in 1910 with regard to an international regulation [2] is almost entirely put into effect in a national law. Von Bar's motivation, however, was quite different from that of Ripert, since the former started from the theory that "les aérostats *sont réputés faire partie du territoire de l'Etat.*" This fiction, which we have already rejected as incorrect,[3] was by no means the starting-point for Ripert when he introduced into French legislation the principle of application of the law of the flag of the aircraft to acts committed on board aircraft. His motives for regarding this principle as the correct one are identical to those which led to application of the law of the flag in maritime law, viz. the fact that during the flight of the aircraft a small community is formed, which must be subject to rules of law. It is logical that in choosing a system of law one should take the law of the State whose flag the aircraft carries. Lemoine [4] gives the following definition of this community:

"société organisée d'hommes ayant une certaine nationalité, dont l'équipage s'est formé sous le contrôle de l'Etat dont le

---

[1] Lemoine, "Traité de Droit Aérien," p. 206.
[2] Institut de Droit International, Annuaire 1910, p. 318.
[3] See page 107.
[4] Lemoine, "Traité de Droit Aérien," p. 201.

navire bat pavillon, et qu'il est logique dès lors de soumettre aux lois de cet Etat."

In France we thus have a territorial system of law which, insofar as relations between persons on board aircraft are concerned (as we shall see in the next chapter, French law does not go the same length with respect to crimes and offences committed on board aircraft), is overridden by the law of the State whose nationality the aircraft possesses.

The framers of the "Loi relative à la navigation aérienne" maintained close contact with the Comité Juridique International de l'Aviation (CJIA) regarding the principle embodied in Article 10. CJIA likewise adopted the principle of the law of the flag in its draft for a "Code de l'Air". In view of the fact that the rules laid down by CJIA were intended to have an international sphere of operation, however, it was considered necessary to respect certain sovereign rights. The CJIA rules therefore stipulated that the law of the flag of the aircraft should apply when the safety or the public order of the State flown over were not affected.[1]

The above Law of May 31, 1924, only applies locally and so Article 10 merely refers to foreign aircraft. It was unnecessary to make any provision with respect to French aircraft because they are naturally subject to the territorial system of law.

French law on this subject is undoubtedly correct, and it is in this direction that a solution will have to be sought on an international level.

2. Belgium.

In the "Loi de juin 1937 portant révision de la loi du 16 novembre 1919 relative à la réglementation de la navigation aérienne," which came into force on March 31, 1954, we find the following provisions relating to the application of law and jurisdiction with respect to acts committed on board aircraft.

"Art. 10. Les rapports de droit qui se forment entre personnes se trouvant à bord d'un aéronef en vol sont réputés s'être formés sur le territoire du pays dont l'aéronef possède la nationalité,

---

[1] Projet de Code International de l'Air du Comité Juridique International de l'Aviation, Art. 30.

à moins que les intéressés ne soient convenus de l'application d'une loi déterminée.

"Lorsque les tribunaux belges sont compétents, le tribunal du lieu de l'atterrisage pourra être valablement saisi."

The Law also contains provisions in the field of criminal law, which will be discussed in the next chapter. In this connection, however, it may be remarked that a sort of "Code de l'Air" has been established in Belgium [1] whereby the application of law and jurisdiction with respect to occurrences on board aircraft is satisfactorily regulated.

3. United Kingdom.

As far as our present subject is concerned, we must distinguish between

(*a*) torts, i.e. acts whereby damage is caused to another party,
(*b*) contracts, and
(*c*) births, deaths and marriages.

a. Torts

The position is quite clear as regards competence to take cognizance of claims in respect of damage resulting from a tort committed on board an aircraft.[2] The action in question can be brought before a British court in the following cases:

(i) in all cases in which the defendant is amenable to the process of the court by being present within the jurisdiction at the time when the writ is served on him, or
(ii) where he voluntarily submits to the jurisdiction, or
(iii) where leave for service of process out of the jurisdiction has been given on the grounds laid down in Order 11 of the Rules of the Supreme Court, 1883.

As to the law which must be applied, we can make a distinction between the following three cases.[3]

I. Acts committed in or over the United Kingdom

The act is assimilated with one which has taken place on the

[1] Goldstein, "La nouvelle législation aérienne belge," Revue Française de Droit Aérien, avril-juin 1954, p. 115.
Litvine, "Précis Elémentaire de Droit Aérien," Bruxelles, 1953.
[2] McNair, "The Law of the Air," 1953, p. 122.
[3] Shawcross and Beaumont on Air Law, 1951, p. 80.

land or territorial waters flown over. In other words, the territorial principle is simply applied in this case. The law of the flag is not recognized as far as foreign aircraft are concerned.

II. Acts committed over non-British territory
According to Dicey: [1]

"An act done in a foreign country is a tort and actionable as such in England, only if it is both

(1) actionable as a tort, according to English Law, or in other words, is an act which, if done in England, would be a tort; and

(2) not justifiable, according to the law of the foreign country where it was done."

It must be assumed that in this case too the British court assimilates such acts committed on board an aircraft over non-British territory which acts committed in that territory itself, irrespective of the nationality of the aircraft. The court will only take cognizance of the act if it was not justifiable according to the law of the foreign country. The territorial system of law of the foreign country is thus recognized.

III. Acts committed over the high seas
a) Torts. McNair [2] comes to the conclusion that such an act "is cognisable by the jurisdiction of any country which can render the tortfeasor amenable to its jurisdiction by the service of a writ or notice of a writ." He also concludes that "the law governing such a tort is, in the case of the United Kingdom, either the common law of the part of the United Kingdom in which the action is properly brought, or, in the case of a tort falling within the scope of the maritime law, such as a collision between ships, or between a ship and another object, the maritime law."

b. Contracts. Here we can distinguish between two groups of cases.

I. Contracts entered into over land or territorial waters. The

---

[1] Dicey, "Conflict of Laws" (6th ed., 1949, under the general editorship of J. H. C. Morris).

[2] McNair, "The Law of the Air," 1953, p. 127.

standpoint adopted in the United Kingdom [1] is that such contracts are made in the country flown over. Thus the territorial principle is again recognized in such cases.

II. Agreements entered into over the high seas. Should a dispute arise with respects to the contract, it may be assumed that – on the analogy of what was explained above in regard to torts – the British court will deem itself competent to take cognizance of the case, though this does not necessarily mean that the law of the United Kingdom will also be applicable. It can be taken for granted, however, that the common law of the United Kingdom will be declared applicable by the British court if such action is necessary to obviate a legal vacuum.[2]

c. Births, deaths and marriages. Under Section 32(5) of the British Nationality Act, 1948, "a person born aboard a registered ship or aircraft, or aboard an unregistered ship or aircraft of the government of any country, shall be deemed to have been born in the place in which the ship or aircraft was registered or, as the case may be, in that country."

According to Section 55 of the Civil Aviation Act, 1949, births and deaths must be recorded in the log book of the aircraft concerned.

Recapitulation. On the basis of the foregoing it may be stated that as far as acts committed on board an aircraft are concerned, under the laws of the United Kingdom the applicable law and jurisdiction depend on the place where the aircraft was at the time when the act in question was committed.

In contrast to the French and Belgian legislation on this point, the law of the flag of the aircraft is very rarely applied. In British legal writings,[3] however, it is stressed that an international agreement on these matters is essential, and at the same time it is pointed out that application of the law of the flag of the aircraft is preferable.

---

[1] Ibid., p. 136.

[2] In Godfrey's Case, 1625 (Latch 11; 82 English Reports 249), the Court of Kings' Bench confirmed that the Admiralty Court has jurisdiction over contracts made at sea.

[3] McNair, "The Law of the Air", 1953, p. 145.

Conclusion

In the preceding pages we have discussed the question of which law must be applicable to acts committed on board aircraft, insofar as such acts do not come within the scope of criminal law and there are no international conventions on the subject. We have also examined the rules of jurisdiction, with particular reference to the rules concerning jurisdiction under the various air law conventions. With regard to the application of civil law, it may be observed that consistent application of a single principle – whether it is the principle of nationality or the territorial principle or any other principle – cannot lead to a practicable international solution. Accordingly, if international regulations on this subject are to have any chance of acceptance, these regulations must be in the form of a compromise between the existing systems. That brings us to a combined system. In principle, the law of the flag of the aircraft will have to be applicable, subject to the proviso that the interests of the States flown over must not be prejudiced. If the act in question affects the State flown over, then the latter's law must be applicable, but in all other cases the law of the flag of the aircraft will apply. This is the only feasible solution in view of the ever-increasing speed of air traffic. In many cases it will be impossible to determine which country the aircraft was over at the time of a certain occurrence, and in those cases the law of the flag of the aircraft must apply. Should the interests of the State flown over be harmed by a tort committed on board the aircraft, it will certainly be possible to determine the territorial jurisdiction within which the occurrence took place.

The position with respect to jurisdiction is the same as outlined above in connection with the application of civil law. No State will feel inclined to exercise its jurisdiction with respect to acts committed on board an aircraft in transit if the State itself is in no way interested in such occurrences. A State will only do so when it has an interest in the acts committed on board the aircraft. Thus the system which we indicated above for the application of civil law must also be adopted with regard to jurisdiction. In principle the State of the flag of the aircraft has jurisdiction. As soon as the State flown over has an interest in the act committed, however, it will come under the jurisdiction of that State. This seems to be the best solution.

Admittedly there is still another solution, one which is dear to the hearts of Dutch jurists, namely to bring all aviation matters under the jurisdiction of an international court. It is to be expected that a great many States will be unwilling to submit to the jurisdiction of such an international court. A start might therefore be made by establishing a court of arbitration which will merely be entrusted with the settlement of disputes relating to the application of the various air law conventions. This restriction of the activities of the international court is purely for practical reasons. From a legal viewpoint it is quite unnecessary for an international court to confine itself to giving decisions on disputes relating to the application of international conventions.[1]

The following procedure has also been suggested in the Netherlands with a view to promoting uniform interpretation of air law conventions: ICAO, as a specialized agency of the United Nations, should request the International Court of Justice to give advisory opinions on the interpretation of the international air law conventions. This could be done after the Legal Committee had first examined all the questions raised by the various States in regard to the interpretation of the conventions in the field of air law. The great advantage of this method is that use can be made of existing legal institutions, while the authority of the International Court of Justice will ensure that the opinions given are not lightly disregarded. Moreover, the acceptance of such a proposal would represent an important first step towards an international system of law.

In the field of public air law, we already have an international authority for the settlement of disputes relating to the execution of the Chicago Convention. According to this Convention, States which disagree on the application or interpretation of it can submit their dispute to the judgment of the Council of ICAO. Since the members of the Council hold office as mandatories of their respective governments, however, there is no real

---

[1] Cleveringa, Int. Bar. Ass., 2nd Conference of the legal profession at The Hague, Aug. 16–21, 1948, p. 5.

guarantee for the impartiality of the Council in giving its decisions.

Furthermore, the members of the Council are not appointed by their governments with a view to performing a function of this nature, so that the majority of the members lack the necessary legal training.

From the foregoing it is obvious that the situation as regards the application of civil law and jurisdiction with respect to acts committed on board aircraft is anything but satisfactory.

Apart from a few national legislations, which incorporate the system recommended by us, and the rules of jurisdiction laid down in some conventions, there exists a legal vacuum in this field.

While admitting that regulations with respect to crimes and offences committed on board aircraft are more urgently required, attention must also be devoted to the civil sector. The draft of the International Law Association, which has been discussed in this chapter, is certainly a step in the right direction and should undoubtedly be taken as a starting-point for further study. Amongst other things, as already remarked, it will have to be brought into line with the standard aviation terminology of the present day. Perhaps the question of jurisdiction could be regulated in the draft in such a way that an international court is entrusted with the administration of justice. The composition and rules of procedure of this international tribunal would likewise have to be regulated in the draft. This is all the more imperative because the rules of jurisdiction laid down in the Rome Convention of 1952 (for the settlement of damage caused by aircraft to third parties on the surface) are regarded by many States as being very unsatisfactory and will form an obstacle to general satisfaction of this Convention. The creation of an international court may provide a solution for cases where international law has to be applied, as well as for cases where national law is applicable.

At the meeting of the Legal Committee of ICAO at Montreal in September 1954, it also became apparent that the jurisdiction problems which arise in connection with the settlement of liability in the event of a collision between aircraft can only be properly solved by introducing an international jurisdiction.

We therefore come to the final conclusion that as far as the application of law to occurrences on board aircraft is concerned, in principle the law of the flag of the aircraft must apply, while the territorial system of law must only be applied when the interests of the States flown over are affected.

As to the question of jurisdiction, a solution will have to be sought along the lines of an international procedure.

CHAPTER V

CRIMINAL JURISDICTION OVER AIRCRAFT

PRINCIPLES OF THE APPLICATION OF CRIMINAL LAW

A State has jurisdiction to prosecute and punish crimes and offences committed on board aircraft within the area of its sovereignty, which also includes the air space above its territory (according to Article 1 of the Chicago Convention of 1944). However, it is questionable whether a State will wish to exercise this jurisdiction under all circumstances, particularly when its interests are not harmed in any way whatsoever. In the case of a crime committed on board an aircraft over French territory during a flight from the United Kingdom to Italy, for example, there will be very little inclination to commence legal proceedings in France in connection with such a crime, unless French interests are affected.

Moreover, this raises the important question of which criminal law is applicable to crimes and offences committed on board aircraft flying over the high seas or above territory that is not subject tot the sovereignty of any State. The well-known case of the United States v. Cordova [1] may serve to illustrate this. In that particular case an American airliner was flying from Puerto Rico to New York; while the aircraft was over the high seas a fight started on board, and when the pilot intervened he was attacked by the passenger Cordova. Criminal proceedings were instituted but the U.S. court declared that it did not have jurisdiction to punish the offence, since American criminal law only covers United States territory. This meant that the criminal law of the United States was not applicable to offences committed on board U.S. aircraft above the high seas. Commenting on the court's decision, Arnold W. Knauth observed that "it was ap-

[1] United States Aviation Reports, 1950, R.1.

parently, at the date of this writing in June 1950 legally safe to commit almost any crime in the calendar, while travelling in an American airplane over the ocean." [1]

As we shall see later, this deficiency in the legislation of the United States has meanwhile been remedied.

It is natural that attempts should have been made to find a solution to the above-mentioned problem by reference to maritime law. As a general rule the seafaring powers declare their criminal law applicable to persons who commit a crime or offence on board vessels carrying their national flag. It is only a short step to extend this rule to aircraft. A number of States, including the Netherlands, [2] even go so far as to apply their criminal law without any restriction in regard to the place where the aircraft is situated. Thus their criminal law is also applicable when an aircraft carrying their flag is located in or over the territory of another State.

Here we come to an extremely complex legal problem, viz. the extent to which a State is entitled to declare its own criminal law applicable to a person who commits an offence in a foreign country, irrespective of the existing criminal legislation in the foreign country concerned. In the first place there are the standards of the Law of Nations, which restrict the power of a State in that respect. According to the rules of international criminal law, a State only has jurisdiction over offences committed by aliens abroad when such an offence is also punishable in the country where it is committed.

Another question that arises is whether a State renounces the right to try offences committed on board foreign aircraft within its territory, if it has incorporated the above-mentioned rule of law into its criminal legislation. As already remarked, an aircraft which is located within the territory of a foreign State certainly does not form an enclave of national territory there. [3] Consequently the national criminal law cannot be applied to offences committed on board that aircraft to the exclusion of a foreign

---

[1] Knauth, "Crime in the High Air, A Footnote to History," 25 Tulane L. Rev. (1950/51), pp. 447, 460; Hilbert, "Jurisdiction in High Seas Criminal Cases," J.A.L. 1951, p. 427; 1952, p. 25.

[2] Article 3 of the Dutch Criminal Code.

[3] See p. 107.

criminal law. Nor is the foreign State obliged to waive its own criminal jurisdiction.

The result is a conflict of criminal laws, which is usually solved in such a way that the criminal of the State where the offence was committed is declared applicable. As explained in the previous chapter, aircraft present special difficulties in regard to the operation of criminal law. When an aircraft is flying across Europe, for instance, it is no easy matter to determine which State it was over while a certain offence was committed. The following four principles are generally employed to determine the standard by which the applicability of the national criminal law is limited:

(1) the territorial principle,
(2) the active personality principle,
(3) the passive personality principle, and
(4) the universality principle.

But these principles cannot be strictly applied in regard to offences committed on board aircraft. Owing to the exceptional character of air traffic, other doctrines will apply. The doctrines in question will be the same as those outlined in the previous chapter [1] concerning acts which lie outside the scope of criminal law, viz.:

1. the territorial principle;
2. the nationality principle;
3. application of the law of the place of departure of the aircraft;
4. application of the law of the place of arrival of the aircraft;
5. a combination of the above systems. [2]

Territorial law

According to the territorial principle, every offence committed within the territory of a certain State can be prosecuted under the criminal law of that State. As we have seen, a number of States regard their ships and aircraft as national territory for the purposes of the administration of law. This, however, is not an application of the maxim that "a ship is territory." In international law such a rule only applies to naval vessels. We shall

[1] See p. 100.
[2] Meyer, Revue Générale de l'Air IX (nouv. série) pp. 545, 615.

therefore have to speak of application of the national law of the aircraft to acts committed on board the aircraft, but in that case, we are applying the nationality principle.

The remarks in the previous chapter regarding the application of territorial law to occurrences outside the scope of criminal law are also relevant here. In the present case, however, the objections against exclusive application of this system are even stronger. What these objections amount to is that the territorial system does not offer a solution for acts committed on board an aircraft while flying over the high seas or above a region which is not subject to the sovereignty of any State, and also that the State flown over may not be interested in prosecuting the offence. Although exclusive application of this system is undesirable, it cannot be completely abandoned, since the Chicago Convention is governed by the territorial principle. Article 1, in conjunction with Article 12 of the same Convention, does not leave any doubt on the subject. Furthermore, the forum delicti is the place where the sense of justice will be most outraged and where the judiciary in general can most easily perform its task. [1] Here too the principle cannot simply be disregarded even though it is not entirely applicable to acts committed on board aircraft. No matter which system is followed, provision will have to be made for application of the territorial principle. It will therefore be necessary to seek a combination of principles.

The law of the flag

The system of applying the law of the flag is the antithesis of the territorial principle. As stated in the previous chapter in connection with non-criminal acts, it lacks some of the disadvantages of the application of the territorial principle. It provides a solution to the difficulty of not being able to determine which State the aircraft was over at the time when the offence was committed, besides solving the problem of offences committed above the high seas.

On the other hand, the application of the law of the flag conflicts with the rule that the States have complete sovereignty

---

[1] François, "Handboek van het Volkenrecht", Vol. II, p. 13.

over the air space above their territory. Nevertheless it is desirable that application of the law of the flag should be given precedence in a system based on a combination of principles.

Law of the place of departure and law of the place of arrival

Supporters of these two theories argue that they offer the best conditions for prosecution of the offender, [1] but it is not clear why such prosecution cannot be guaranteed in the event of application of the nationality principle. So far as offences committed on board aircraft over the high seas are concerned, the State whose nationality the aircraft possesses will probably be the only one to take any interest in the matter.

There is not the slightest connection between the offence and the criminal law of the place where the aircraft happens to land after the offence has been committed or where it took off prior to the offence. The theories mentioned here are certainly peculiar to air law but they are unsatisfactory, mainly because the State where the aircraft landed or took off will show very little interest in prosecuting the offence in question.

Combined system

As is evident from the foregoing, it is advisable to draw a demarcation line between the jurisdiction of the ground State and the jurisdiction of the State whose nationality the aircraft possesses.

This was already realized in the early years of aviation. A Dutch jurist, Miss Lijcklama à Nijeholt, advocated a combined system for the application of criminal law as far back as 1910. [2] She proposed that the territorial law should be applied in the first instance and that the law of the flag of the aircraft should only be applicable so long as the public order and safety of the State flown over are not affected, as well as in cases where it is

---

[1] Morpurgo, "Quelques considérations sur les conflits internationaux de juridiction en matière pénale aéronautique à propos de la mort du banquier Loewenstein," 2 Rev. Jur. Int. de Locomotion Aérienne, pp. 397, 408, 414 (1928).

Pholien, "Des Crimes et Délits à bord d'aéronefs en vol," R.D.A. 1929, p. 289.

Lortsch, "Le Statut Juridique du Passager d'aéronef," R.D.A. Vol. 13, 1929, pp. 7 et seq.

[2] Lijcklama à Nijeholt, "Luchtvaart in het Volkenrecht," Leyden, 1910.

impossible to determine the country above which the offence took place. [1]

In the following account of the efforts to reach international agreement on this subject, we shall see that a solution has always been sought along the lines of a combined system.

INTERNATIONAL LAW

Institute of International Law. Even when aviation was still in its infancy, attempts were made to draw up a convention which would provide a solution for the special problems involved in the application of criminal law and jurisdiction with respect to aircraft. Again it was Fauchille who submitted one of the earliest proposals. The draft code of air law that he prepared for the Institute of International Law in 1910 contained two articles relating to the application of law and jurisdiction with respect to offences committed on board aircraft. [2]

"Article 15.
Les crimes et délits, commis à bord des aérostats en quelque part que ce soit de l'espace, par les gens de l'équipage ou par toutes autres personnes se trouvant à bord, tombent sous la compétence des tribunaux de la nation à laquelle appartient l'aérostat et sont jugés selon les lois de cette nation quelle que soit la nationalité des auteurs."

Here Fauchille starts from the nationality principle, but he supplements it with the protection principle, as may be seen from the next paragraph of Article 15:

"Toutes les infractions qui portent atteinte à la sûreté ou la fortune d'un Etat, telles que conspiration, trahison, fausse monnaie, etc. doivent, en quelque endroit qu'elles aient été commises, être jugées par les tribunaux et selon les lois de l'Etat lésé."

---

[1] See also:

Steidle, "Das Luftfahrzeug als Begehungsort strafbarer Handlungen" Cologne, 1934.

Hazeltine, "The Law of the Air" (Three lectures delivered in the University of London at the request of the Faculty of Laws. Second lecture: "The Principles and Problems of National Law"). Spaight, "Aircraft in Peace and the Law," 1919.

Volkman, "Crimes et dèlits à bord des aeronefs en droit international," Droit Aérien, 1931, p. 26.

[2] Institut de Droit International, Annuaire 1910, p. 297.

In this case too, just as in the case of non-criminal acts, [1] Fauchille did not wish to base his system on a single principle. He makes provision for the jurisdiction of the State whose public order and safety are threatened by the offences committed. Von Bar is the only one who – as mentioned in the previous chapter [2] – tries to enforce a single principle, namely the principle of nationality. But in the proposal which he submitted to the Institute of International Law in 1910, [3] even Von Bar makes some concessions to the territorial system of law. We have already explained the objections to his basic assumption that "les aérostats sont réputés faire partie du territoire de l'Etat." [4] If Von Bar's proposal were to be put into effect, one consequence would be that every foreign aircraft on or over our territory must be regarded as foreign territory. Offences committed on board such an aircraft within Dutch territory could therefore go unpunished in the Netherlands. Few States will feel inclined to renounce their sovereign rights in this manner.

In 1937 a report entitled „Le Règlement des compétences pénales en Droit Aérien" [5] was presented to the Institute of International Law by M. F. de Visscher. The regulations which he proposed read as follows:

"Article 1.
Indépendamment de tous autres chefs de compétence reconnus par la législation des Etats contractants, la compétence des infractions de droit commun commises à bord d'un aéronef privé en cours de vol appartient

1. à l'Etat dans le territoire duquel l'aéronef se trouvait au moment où les actes constitutifs de l'infraction ont été accomplis;
2. à l'Etat de la nationalité de l'aéronef;
3. à l'Etat dans le territoire duquel l'infraction a produit son effet;
4. à l'Etat sur le territoire duquel l'aéronef vient atterrir;

---

[1] See p. 106.
[2] See p. 107.
[3] Institut de Droit International, Annuaire 1910, p. 318.
[4] See p. 107.
[5] De Visscher, "Le Règlement des Compétences en Droit Aérien," R.G.D.A. 1937, p. 329 et seq.

Néanmoins la compétence de cet Etat ne s'exercera vis-à-vis ces deux Etats précédents qu'à titre subsidiaire, pour le cas où aucun d'eux n'exerce sa propre compétence."

Thus the territorial principle is put first, although it does not take precedence over the second and third bases of jurisdiction mentioned. Only the fourth basis, that of the jurisdiction of the State where the aircraft lands after its flight, is assigned a subsidiary place. The other three rank equally. The question of which criminal law is applicable will therefore have to be settled on the basis of a general rule of conflicts of law.

"Article 2.
La violation, à bord d'un aéronef en cours de vol, des lois et règlements édictés par un Etat pour le survol de son territoire, relève de la compétence pénale de celui-ci."

"Article 3.
La violation, à bord d'un aéronef en cours de vol, des lois et règlements édictés par l'Etat dont l'aéronef a la nationalité, en vue de la navigation aérienne en dehors de son territoire, relève de la compétence pénale de cet Etat.

Cette règle ne porte aucun préjudice à la compétence reconnue à l'Etat sous-jacent par l'article précédent."

These two articles deal with breaches of the rules of the air, The State whose air traffic rules are violated during a flight over its territory has jurisdiction, irrespective of the nationality of the aircraft involved. The State of registry of an aircraft also has jurisdiction with respect to every contravention of its rules of the air by this aircraft outside its territory. If the violation of the rules of the air of the State of registry of the aircraft is at the same time a violation of the air traffic rules of the State flown over, the latter has jurisdiction.

"Article 4.
Toute infraction commise en cours de vol par des passagers contre les règlements de bord, comme tout acte de désobéissance commis par eux contre l'autorité du commandant de l'aéronef, relève de la compétence de l'Etat de la nationalité de l'aéronef."

Such a provision is necessary so long as the position of the aircraft commander is not regulated in international law. [1]

"Article 5.
Toute infraction commise (en cours de voyage) par des gens de l'équipage contre les règlements ou la discipline de bord relève de la compétence de l'Etat de la nationalité de l'aéronef. (L'Etat du lieu d'atterrisage demeure compétent pour toute infraction commise contre ses propres règlements par des membres d'un équipage pendant la durée de l'escale. Sa juridiction à cet égard s'exerce par priorité vis-à-vis de l'Etat de la nationalité de l'aéronef, aussi longtemps que l'inculpé se trouve sur son sol.)"

This article deals with breaches of discipline by the crew of the aircraft. Quite logically, the State whose nationality the aircraft possesses is declared competent. However, the State where the aircraft lands after its flight still has jurisdiction with respect to violations of its own regulations during this flight. While the offender is in the latter's territory, the jurisdiction of that State takes precedence over that of the State whose flag the aircraft carries.

"Article 6.
Moyennant avis officiel donné par les autorités compétentes soit de l'Etat où l'infraction a été commise, soit de l'Etat de la nationalité de l'aéronef, chaque Etat s'engage, sous conditions de réciprocité, a poursuivre conformément à ses propres lois les infractions visées aux articles 2 et 3 et qui auraient été commises à bord d'aéronefs venant à atterrir sur son territoire. (Au cas d'infractions prévues par les articles 4 et 5, alinea ler, chaque Etat s'engage à prêter main-forte au consul ou autres autorités compétentes de l'Etat de la nationalité de l'aéronef pour l'arrestation et la mise en détention éventuelles des inculpés.)"

It is apparent from the foregoing that the draft devotes considerable attention to measures for the safety of air traffic. Air safety is considered so important that offences in this field

[1] Kamminga, "The Aircraft Commander in Commercial Air Transportation," Leyden, 1953.

(see Arts. 2 and 3 of the draft) shall be prosecuted by the State where the aircraft lands after its flight, on receipt of an official notification from the State above whose territory the offence was committed or from the State whose flag the aircraft carries; this is to be done on a basis of reciprocity.

The system proposed by De Visscher, which we have explained above, has many advantages. Several courts are declared competent, so that there is very little risk of an offence not being prosecuted because the State having jurisdiction is not interested in prosecuting the offence. Nor is there any encroachment on the sovereignty of the States over the air space above their territory. De Visscher's draft was therefore adopted by the Institute of International Law.

Paris Convention of 1919. In the previous chapter [1] we discussed the clauses which were drafted for – but not included in – the Paris Convention of 1919, concerning the application of civil law and jurisdiction with respect to acts committed on board aircraft. The second part of the regulations in question, originally drafted as Article 23 of the Paris Convention, related to crimes and misdemeanours. The text reads as follows:

"En cas de crime ou de délit entre personnes à bord d'un aéronef en vol, la loi de l'Etat survolé n'a compétence que si, commis contre l'un des ressortissants de cet Etat, le crime ou délit est suivi d'un atterrisage sur le territoire de ce même Etat.

L'Etat survolé a compétence:

1. A l'égard de toute infraction aux lois de protection, militaire ou fiscale;
2. En cas d'infraction à ses prescriptions relatives à la navigation aérienne." [2]

This was similar to what Fauchille had proposed to the Institute of International Law in 1910. In the previous chapter we have already explained why the above clauses were omitted from the final text of the Paris Convention of 1919. [3]

Comité Juridique International de l'Aviation. As mentioned earlier,

---

[1] See p. 108.
[2] Roper, "La Convention Internationale du 13 octobre 1919," p. 156.
[3] See p. 109.

the code of international air law drafted by CJIA [1] also contained provisions on the choice of law and jurisdiction with respect to offences. [2] This draft likewise gave effect to the two principles embodied in Fauchille's draft for the Institute of International Law, viz.: applicability of the criminal law of the country whose flag the aircraft carries and, in a few cases, applicability of the criminal law of the country whose interests are harmed as a result of the offence. [3]

However, the various sections of the Comité Juridique International de l'Aviation also submitted a number of proposals, some of which were based on other principles. At a meeting of the German section of CJIA in April 1929 [4] Dr. V. Niemeyer presented a report on the application of law and jurisdiction with respect to offences committed on board aircraft. The three principles underlying this report are as follows:

"1. Les délits commis à bord d'un aéronef en cours de vol sont réputés commis sur le territoire de l'Etat survolé, à moins qu'ils affectent ni l'intérêt de l'Etat survolé ni celui de ses habitants, quant à leurs personnes ou quant à leurs biens, auquel cas ils sont réputés l'être dans le pays duquel l'appareil est ressortissant. Ils seront également réputés commis dans ce dernier pays s'ils ont été commis au-dessus de la haute mer, d'un territoire sans maître, ou d'un territoire indéterminé.

2. Quand, dans l'un des cas visés au paragraphe précédent, l'aéronef ne porte aucune marque de nationalité ou qu'il porte une fausse marque de nationalité, le délit est réputé commis dans le pays de la juridiction duquel relève son auteur.

3. Ne sont pas modifiées les dispositions concernant les délits commis à bord d'aéronefs dont les vols sont limités à un même territoire national."

Niemeyer begins by giving precedence to the jurisdiction of the State over whose territory the aircraft was flying when the

---

[1] Projet de Code International de l'Air du Comité Juridique International de l'Aviation (VI Congrès, Rome 1924, Chapitre VI, "De la législation applicable et de juridiction compétente en matière de locomotion aérienne").

[2] See p. 109.

[3] See p. 110.

[4] Niemeyer, Revue de Droit Aérien, Vol. 13, 1929, p. 285.

offence was committed, but at the same time he restricts this jurisdiction to cases in which the interests of the State flown over are harmed. In his report he also asserts that only the State flown over can decide whether its interests have been harmed. If these interests have not been harmed, then the State of the flag of the aircraft has jurisdiction. If the aircraft does not carry any nationality markings then the State whose nationality the offender possesses has jurisdiction. No rules are given in regard to crimes committed on flights wholly performed above the territory of one State, nor is this necessary, since application of the territorial principle offers an adequate solution in such cases.

When the Belgian section of CJIA met in June 1929, Pholien submitted a report [1] which introduced a new theory – or at least one which had not yet been discussed by CJIA. Pholien proposed that the State where the aircraft lands on completion of a flight should be designated to prosecute and punish the offence committed during the flight. This idea had previously been suggested by Morpurgo and Lortsch. [2] The following articles were contained in Pholien's proposal:

"Article 1.
En cas de crime ou de délit commis à bord d'un aéronef, quelle qu'en soit la nationalité et quel que soit le lieu de l'infraction, les tribunaux du pays d'atterrisage sont compétents."

Here Pholien gives precedence to the jurisdiction of the State where the aircraft lands after completing a flight. He wishes to exclude from his system the fact that the aircraft possesses a nationality. He also severs every connection with maritime law, as he wants a system to suit the specific needs of air law.

"Article 2.
La personne revêtue de l'autorité à bord prendra toutes mesures pour la constation du fait, la conservation des pièces à conviction et la mise à la disposition de l'autorité judiciaire de l'inculpé."

---

[1] Pholien, Revue de Droit Aérien, Vol. 13, 1929, p. 289.
[2] Supra.

A clause of this nature is certainly appropriate pending an international agreement on the legal position of the commander of an aircraft. [1]

"Article 3.
Elle avertira par T.S.F., ou par les voies les plus rapides, l'autorité judiciaire compétente de la plus prochaine escale, et, au moment de l'atterrisage lui remettra, avec l'inculpé, les pièces à conviction et les éléments. Elle veillera à ce que les témoins ne s'éloignent pas."

This clause would also have to be studied in relation to an international convention on the legal status of the aircraft commander. What is lacking in air law is an equivalent of the legislative provisions concerning order and discipline on merchant vessels, mainly because these provisions also prescribe the action to be taken by the captain when a crime is committed on board. [2] Until the position of the aircraft commander is regulated on an international basis, however, provisions such as those mentioned above cannot be omitted from a draft like the one under consideration.

"Article 4.
L'autorité judiciaire du lieu d'atterrisage fera dans l'avion toutes constatations utiles sans retarder le départ de celui-ci."

Such a clause is indispensable in a system based on the principle of the jurisdiction of the State where the aircraft lands after its flight. In many cases the State where the aircraft lands will not take any measures unless such action is called for under the terms of an international convention.

"Article 5.
Dans le case où l'autorité judiciaire du lieu d'atterrisage estimerait ne pas devoir exercer de poursuites, elle libérera l'inculpé et portera sa décision à la connaissance du Gouvernement sur le

---

[1] Kamminga, "The Aircraft Commander in Commercial Air Transportation," Leyden, 1953.
[2] Honig, "De Positie van de Gezagvoerder van een Luchtvaartuig," N.J.B. 21-4-51, p. 317.

territoire duquel le crime ou le délit aura été commis et lui transmettra, en même temps, les pièces de la procédure. Ce dernier Gouvernement reste libre de poursuivre."

The circumstances outlined in this article will occur rather frequently. Such an arrangement is necessary and provides a flexible solution.

"Article 6.
En cas de crime ou délit politique, l'Etat survolé peut donner à l'aéronef l'injonction d'atterrir immédiatement sur son territoire. En cas de désobéissance après avertissement l'aéronef peut être abattu."

This last clause is a logical consequence of the principle that the States have sovereignty over the air space above their territory.

We have already drawn attention [1] to the fact that a system on the lines suggested by Pholien has a serious drawback, due to the fact there is no connection between the crime committed and the criminal law of the country where the aircraft lands on completion of its flight. The provisions of Article 5 of the draft would have to be applied on numerous occasions.

Two Hungarian jurists, de Danivolics and de Szondy, likewise prepared a draft which they submitted to CJIA for discussion at the Budapest congress of this organization in 1930. [2]

The draft consisted of two parts. Part I dealt with "Des crimes et des délits commis à bord d'un aéronef se trouvant au-dessus de la mer," while Part II was concerned with "Des crimes et des délits commis à bord d'un aéronef se trouvant dans le domaine aérien d'un Etat étranger."

The crimes and misdemeanours referred to in Part I are subject to the law of the State where the aircraft is registered as to nationality. On the other hand, the crimes and misdemeanours dealt with in the second part are governed by the law of the State flown over or by the law of the flag of the aircraft concerned. The draft contained the following provisions:

[1] See p. 141.
[2] De Danilovics and de Szondy, "Des crimes et des délits commis à bord d'un aéronef," Revue de Droit Aérien, Vol. 14, 1930, p. 412.

"Article 1.
Les aéronefs se trouvant au-dessus de la pleine mer ou d'un territoire qui ne dépend de la souveraineté d'aucun Etat, sont réputés faire partie du territoire de l'Etat auquel ils appartiennent et les crimes et délits commis à bord de ces aéronefs tombent sous les lois pénales de l'Etat qui les a revêtus de sa nationalité.

La loi pénale du lieu de l'infraction est celle de l'Etat auquel appartient l'aéronef à bord duquel se trouve, au moment de l'action criminelle, l'auteur du fait délictueux."

This is in conformity with the proposal submitted by Von Bar to the Institute of International Law in 1910. [1] The objections raised against the rule that "an aircraft is territory" [2] do not apply to Part I of the draft prepared by de Danilovics and de Szondy, since in this case the dictum only refers to aircraft above the high seas. As we shall see in a moment, however, these objections do apply to Part II of the draft.

"Article 2.
Si dans les cases prévus à l'article 1, l'action criminelle est dirigée contres des personnes et des biens qui ne se trouvent pas à bord de l'aéronef et lorsque les effets de cette action se réalisent dans une partie de l'espace soumise à la souveraineté d'un autre Etat, la justice pénale de ce pays pourrait également juger et punir l'action en question d'après les règles qui régissent la matière des crimes et délits commis sur les territoires de différents Etats."

This article too is obviously based on Von Bar's proposal. But in his proposal Von Bar also speaks of actions for damages, and purely from a viewpoint of criminal law there does not seem to be much sense in such an article. After all, the consequences of a crime committed on board an aircraft against persons and property outside that aircraft will always occur outside the aircraft. Even without the above article, the place where the crime takes effect can be regarded as the place of the crime.

---

[1] Institut de Droit International, Annuaire 1910, p. 318.
[2] See pp. 107 and 128.

"Article 3.
Si les effects d'une action criminelle prévue à l'article 1 se réalisent ou, d'après l'intention de l'auteur, devaient se réaliser sur un autre aéronef ou hydravion qui appartient à un Etat étranger, il y aura une compétence pénale double dont l'une dûment exercée par prévention, exclura l'autre."

Here the place of the crime is construed in a broad sense and two courts are declared competent, with due provision to obviate a conflict of jurisdiction.

"Article 4.
Si les effets d'une action criminelle prévue à l'article 1 se réalisent ou, d'après l'intention de l'auteur, devaient se réaliser sur un navire ou hydravion étranger navigant sur la mer sous-jacente, le principe non bis in idem doit également être appliqué."

As in the previous article, care is taken to ensure that the guilty party shall not be punished twice if the consequences of the crime do not take effect in the place where the crime was committed.

Part II of the draft, which we shall now discuss, deals with "Des crimes et des délits commis à bord d'un aéronef se trouvant dans le domaine aérien d'un Etat étranger."

"Article 5.
La compétence territoriale concernant les crimes et les délits commis à bord d'un aéronef qui se trouve au-dessus du territoire terrestre, fluvial ou maritime d'un Etat étranger, appartient à l'Etat sous-jacent.

Cet Etat peut punir, sans aucun égard à la loi pénale de l'Etat auquel appartient l'aéronef et sans tenir compte de la nationalité du criminal, tous les crimes et délits commis à bord des aéronefs qui se trouvent dans son domaine aérien, à tous les actes de juridiction ou de police (l'arrestation des malfaiteurs etc.)."

In contrast to the first part, the second part of the draft is quite simply based on the territorial principle. The State flown over has jurisdiction not only with respect to crimes which harm its interests, but also with respect to all crimes committed in its territory. In this case we are therefore concerned with a departure – in fact one might say a step backward – from the drafts so far discussed.[1] The framers of the draft do not make any allowance for the special difficulties presented in this respect by air traffic. They completely ignore a problem which we have already referred to, namely the fact that it will often be impossible to determine which State the aircraft was over at the time when the crime was committed.[2] From the following article it appears that the drafters realized what difficulties may ensue from application of Article 5.

"Article 6.
Cependant l'Etat auquel l'aéronef appartient est autorisé à assimiler les délits et les crimes commis à bord de cet aéronef aux actes délictueux accomplis sur son propre territoire terrestre et à juger les auteurs des crimes en question sans tenir compte de la loi pénale de l'Etat sous-jacent et de même sans aucun égard à la nationalité du coupable."

In this article the drafters take back practically all that they first laid down in Article 5. Here they adopt Von Bar's principle that "an aircraft is territory." [3] The provisions of Article 5, however, seem to be incompatible with those of Article 6. There ought to be some indication of when the system prescribed in Article 5 is to be followed and when the system of Article 6 is to apply, but no ruling is given on this point.

"Article 7.
Si la loi d'un Etat tiers prescrit au juge d'appliquer les dispositions du Code Pénal en vigueur sur le territoire où le crime ou le délit a été commis, et lorsque en l'espèce, il s'agit de crimes et de délits qui se sont produits à bord d'un aéronef se trouvant dans le domaine aérien d'un Etat étranger, l'Etat tiers susmentionné pourrait considérer la loi du pavillon comme loi du lieu dans tous les cas où le survol a eu lieu sans atterrisage et où le crime ou le

[1] Supra.
[2] See p. 140.
[3] Institut de Droit International, Annuaire 1910, p. 318.

délit commis à bord de l'aéronef n'a porté aucune atteinte à la personne ou aux biens des ressortissants de l'Etat sous-jacent et n'a pas lésé ou menacé ni les personnes et les biens se trouvant sur le territoire de l'Etat sous-jacent, ni l'ordre public et la sécurité de cet Etat."

The provisions of this article relating to an "Etat tiers" are highly acceptable. Without going so far as to adopt the fiction that an aircraft is territory, as is done in Article 6, the possibility is left open for application of the law of the flag of the aircraft.

"Article 8.
Aucune poursuite ne peut être dirigée pour crime ou délit commis à bord d'un aéronef contre un ressortissant ou un étranger qui justifie avoir subi ou prescrit sa peine soit dans l'Etat sous-jacent, soit dans l'Etat auquel l'aéronef appartient.

"Article 9.
Chaque Etat doit exercer le pouvoir de police aérienne dans la zône de l'espace atmosphérique soumise à sa souveraineté et il est obligé d'organiser les services de sa police aérienne en mettant à la disposition de cette dernière, en nombre nécessaire, des aéronefs armés."

CJIA did not adhere to the above draft but decided upon the following text at its 9th session in Budapest. [1]

"Article 1.
Au point de vue pénal les actes commis à bord d'un aéronef sont soumis à une compétence spéciale: la compétence pénale de droit aérien.

"Article 2.
La compétence pénale de droit aérien appartient d'une part à l'Etat du pavillon et d'autre part à l'Etat survolé.

---

[1] Les Editions Internationales, Paris 1931.

"Article 3.
Les effets de la compétence pénale de droit aérien sont les mêmes que ceux de la compétence territoriale.

"Article 4.
La compétence pénale de droit aérien n'exclut pas l'exercice de la répression sur d'autres bases que celles de la territorialité.

"Article 5.
Quand l'aéronef n'a pas la nationalité de l'Etat survolé celui des deux Etats compétents qui tient en son pouvoir le prévenu, a priorité de compétence.

"Article 6.
Au regard des autres Etats le règlement des compétences s'opère par priorité des compétences speciales de droit aérien et le règlement des compétences spéciales de droit pénal aérien s'opère par priorité de la loi du pavillon sauf:

1. si l'acte est de nature de compromettre la sécurité et l'ordre public de l'Etat sous-jacent;
2. si l'acte lèse les ressortissants de l'Etat sous-jacent.

"Article 7.
L'Etat qui n'admet pas l'extradition de ses nationaux est obligé de les punir quand ils reviennent sur son territoire après d'être rendus coupables à bord d'un aéronef étranger d'une infraction prévue par sa législation pénale.

Cette disposition ne sera pas applicable si dans un tel cas l'extradition d'un étranger ne pouvait être accordée."

CJIA thus abandoned the system proposed by de Danivolics and de Szondy. Admittedly this text is based on two principles, the principle of nationality and the principle of territoriality (i.e. a combined system), but in contrast to the system of the two Hungarian jurists, the sphere of applicability of both principles is logically defined. Furthermore, it is not based on the incorrect principle that an aircraft is territory. Both the law of the flag and the law of the State flown over are declared applicable to crimes committed on board aircraft, but a sort of order of precedence in jurisdiction is indicated. In the first place, the State in whose power the offender is held as the right to prosecute and punish. If the offender is in a State other than the state flown over or the State whose flag the aircraft carries, then the law of the State of the flag is applicable, unless the crimes in question harm the interests of the State flown over.

However, such an order of precedence only makes sense if it ensures that in the event of acquittal by the State having primary jurisdiction, for example, criminal proceedings can still be brought in the State having secondary jurisdiction. De Danivolics and de Szondy turn their attention to this subject in Article 8 of their draft.

The lines along which CJIA attempted to find a solution do not seem very appropriate. After all, the most logical system is to apply the law of the flag of the aircraft and only to make exceptions to this rule if the interests of the State flown over are harmed. It would therefore have been better if CJIA had adopted Niemeyer's proposal. [1]

At approximately the same time as Niemeyer, Schrieber submitted a report based on identical principles to the Air Transport Committee of the International Chamber of Commerce. [2] As remarked earlier, [3] the work of CJIA did not receive the attention that it deserved – especially after the formation of CITEJA in 1925.

International Law Association. The International Law Association has also gone into the question of crimes committed on board aircraft. The draft convention on "Jurisdiction in Civil and Criminal Matters over all Persons carried in Aircraft," [4] which we referred to in the previous chapter, contained the following provisions with respect to crimes and offences:

"Article 2.
A public airship which is above territory of a foreign State remains under the exclusive jurisdiction of the State of which it has the nationality.

[1] Niemeyer, R.D.A. 13, 1929, p. 285; see p. 146.
[2] Schrieber, "Principles of a draft convention on nationality of aircraft" (prepared for the Air Transport Committee of the International Chamber of Commerce, 1929).
[3] See p. 111.
[4] Supra.

A private airship which is above the territory of a foreign State is subject to the laws and jurisdiction of such State only in the following cases:

1. With regard to every breach of its laws for the public safety and its military and fiscal laws.
2. In cases of a breach of its regulations concerning air navigation.
3. For all acts committed on board the airship and having effect on the territory of the said State.

In all other respects a private airship follows the laws and jurisdiction of the State of the flag."

"Article 3.
If at the commencement or during the progress of any flight of any aircraft passing over any State or States or their territorial waters or over the high seas without landing, any person on board such aircraft commits any crime or misdemeanour, the person charged shall forthwith be arrested if necessary. Such felony or misdemeanour may be inquired into and the accused tried and punished in accordance with the Rules given under Art. 2. The State of the place where such aircraft lands shall be bound to arrest the accused if necessary and to extradite him to the State which has jurisdiction over him."

"Article 4.
Acts committed on board a private aircraft not in flight in a foreign State shall be subject to the jurisdiction of such State, and any person or persons charged with the commission of such acts shall be tried and, if found guilty, punished according to the laws of such State."

The general rule laid down in this draft is that the law of the flag of the aircraft is applicable to crimes and offences committed on board an aircraft in all cases where the interests of the State flown over are not harmed. On the other hand, if the interests of the state flown over are harmed, then this State is entitled to prosecute and punish the wrongdoer.

In Article 3 of the draft it is assumed that the aircraft commander or somebody else on board the aircraft has the power to arrest the person guilty of the crime. As we have already seen, [1] however, there is still no international agreement on this point.

Article 3 also speaks of extradition of the accused to the State which has jurisdiction over him, but such extradition may be incompatible with the existing extradition treaties. These treaties are practically all the same in one respect, namely that extradition can only be applied for in cases where the crime of which a person is accused is also regarded as a crime in the State where extradition is requested. The draft prepared by the International Law Association was put aside till 1950, [2] when Prof. John C. Cooper was asked to draw up a report on the subject. [3] Cooper submitted a number of questions, some of which were mentioned in the previous chapter, [4] to the Air Law Committee of the International Law Association. Amongst other things, Cooper asserts that the draft cannot be reconciled with Article 12 of the Chicago Convention of 1944. The text of this article, whose origin has already been discussed, [5] reads as follows:

"Each contracting State undertakes to adopt measures to insure that every aircraft carrying its nationality mark, wherever such aircraft may be, shall comply with the rules and regulations relating to the flight and maneuver of aircraft there in force.

Each contracting State undertakes to keep its own regulations in these respects uniform, to the greatest possible extent, with those established from time to time under this Convention.

Over the high seas, the rules in force shall be those established under this Convention. Each contracting State undertakes to insure the prosecution of all persons violating the regulations applicable."

Under the terms of this article, each State is entitled to prosecute a breach of its air traffic rules by any aircraft over its territory, besides being entitled to prosecute a breach of the air traffic rules of another country by an aircraft carrying its flag. The result is that in a number of cases two States have jurisdiction contrary to what is stated in Article 2 of the draft where "in case of a breach of its regulations concerning air navigation" only

---

[1] Honig, op. cit., N.J.B. 21-4-51, p. 317.
[2] Supra.
[3] Supra.
[4] See pp. 113 et seq.
[5] See p. 148.

the State flown over has jurisdiction. Cooper declares that a proposed new convention must be in conformity with the Chicago Convention.

In an article published in the "Zeitschrift für Luftrecht" [1] Meyer opposes Cooper's views on Article 12 of the Chicago Convention. According to Meyer, Article 12 is merely a recommendation to the contracting States and is not intended to lay down new rules with respect to the jurisdiction of a State. He has endeavoured to find a way of avoiding the consequences of Article 12, which are often undesirable. But what Meyer says is incorrect. Article 12 is not a recommendation. It does indeed contain the fundamental principle on which the States must base their regulations. As Cooper rightly points out, the system of the draft – whereby the jurisdiction of the various States is clearly defined and concurrent jurisdiction of more than one State is excluded – cannot be maintained once it has been agreed that the proposed new draft must not conflict with the Chicago Convention. Meyer likewise insists that the terminology and the principles of the Chicago Convention should be adhered to when preparing a draft convention. However, he is unwilling to accept the consequences of Article 12, hence his erroneous interpretation. On the other hand, Cooper accepts the consequences of Article 12 and so he is forced to adopt a system which differs from the one laid down in Article 2 of the draft. He proposes that the following principles should be embodied in a draft convention.

"Article 1.
The jurisdiction of a contracting State extends
(a) to all aircraft which bear its nationality mark wherever such aircraft may be;
(b) to all aircraft within its territory, including its air space.

"Article 2.
For the purposes of conferring jurisdiction in case of a crime committed in the air space, such crime may be deemed to have been committed in the air space of any contracting State through which the aircraft has passed, beginning with the last departure of the aircraft preceding the crime until the first landing thereafter.

[1] Meyer, Zeitschrift für Luftrecht, Vol. I, 1953, p. 58.

"Article 3.
When the accused is apprehended in a contracting State which does not assume jurisdiction, the accused will be delivered, if at all, to the first contracting State, formally requesting extradition which has jurisdiction hereunder.

"Article 4.
Any person tried under the provisions of this convention may not be tried again for the same offence by the courts of another contracting State.

"Article 5.
This convention does not alter or set aside other bases for criminal jurisdiction which a State may have incorporated into its national laws."

The above principles are based on what Cooper refers to as "concurrent jurisdiction." This is necessary because Article 12 of the Chicago Convention of 1944 is based on these principles, and Cooper regards that article as the background for the proposed new convention. According to these principles, the State of the flag of the aircraft, the State of departure, the State of arrival and the State over whose territory the aircraft has flown all have jurisdiction. In most cases the criminal proceedings will be instituted in the State where the aircraft lands. Cooper also deals with the problem of extradition. He is fully aware that the extradition rule given by him in Article 3 may be incompatible with the existing international agreements on that subject, and so he has added the words "if at all."

Meyer strongly disapproves of Cooper's proposal to confer jurisdiction on every contracting State over which the aircraft has flown in the case of a crime committed in the air space above a contracting State. [1] He agrees with Cooper that the principles and the terminology of the Chicago Convention must be adhered to in drafting regulations on the application of criminal law and jurisdiction with respect to crimes and offences committed on board aircraft, but since he considers that Article 12 of the Chicago Convention is nothing more than a recommended procedure

[1] Ibid.

for the contracting States, he does not think it necessary to follow Cooper's lead in regard to concurrent jurisdiction. Meyer therefore proposes that:

a. the State above whose territory the crime or offence has been committed should have jurisdiction in the first instance;

b. the State of the flag of the aircraft should have jurisdiction in the second instance

(1) if it is impossible to determine the exact position of the aircraft at the time when the crime or offence was committed.

(2) if the State flown over decides not to prosecute.

Application of these principles certainly has some advantage over the system developed by Cooper. Conflicts of jurisdiction are obviated in this case, because the jurisdiction is accurately defined, whereas Cooper's system leaves the door wide open for such conflicts. In conclusion Meyer formulates his principles as follows: [1]

"1. Crimes committed on board of aircraft in flight above the territory of a State are subject to the laws and the jurisdiction of this State, excepting the cases mentioned in paragraph 2.

2. Crimes committed on board of aircraft in flight above the territory of a State follow the laws and jurisdiction of the State of the flag

(*a*) if it was practically impossible to determine where the crime has been committed,

(*b*) if the State in the air space of which the crime has been committed decides in a proper space of time not to assume the jurisdiction."

The above text is different from the text which Meyer outlined in an article in the "Revue Générale de l'Air" in 1946. [2] In that article Meyer argued that the State flown over ought to have jurisdiction insofar as its interests were harmed. In his latest proposal quoted above, Meyer says that the State flown over has jurisdiction unless it decides not to assume jurisdiction. Commenting on this change, Meyer remarks that it is merely a question of

[1] International Law Association, Report of the Forty-fifth Conference, Lucerne, 1952, p. 130.

[2] Meyer, R.G.A. IX, pp. 545, 615.

a different wording. That is rather an understatement, for Meyer's last proposal represents a much broader application of the territorial principle than his first proposal. According to the first proposal, the State flown over can only prosecute if its interests have been harmed, whereas the second proposal does not involve any such restriction. Obviously Meyer is now more inclined to favour a stricter limitation of the sphere of operation of the law of the flag than in 1946. This is also evident from his otherwise unmotivated remark that it is inadvisable to enforce the nationality principle to the extent that Cooper does in Article la of his proposal. Another opponent of Cooper's proposal is Chauveau. [1] Like Meyer, he considers that Article 12 of the Chicago Convention does not conflict with the draft adopted at the 24th conference of the International Law Association in Stockholm in 1924. Furthermore, he points out that Cooper gives practically no explanation of why a convention on the subject of crimes and offences committed on board aircraft should be given priority over a convention relating to contracts, births, etc. According to Chauveau, the rules proposed by Cooper for the application of criminal law and jurisdiction lead to:

"(*a*) Conflits éventuels entre les diverses juridictions compétentes;
(*b*) Incertitude quant à la loi compétente pour qualifier l'infraction, déterminer la peine, etc. ...
avec possibilité pour le même fait d'être considéré comme licite ou illicite suivant la juridiction saisie."

In contrast to Meyer, Chauveau advocates application of the law of the flag of the aircraft. He argues that the law of the flag can easily be determined, while in addition it has "une valeur permanente pendant toute la durée du vol." The State whose flag the aircraft carries will always have an interest in the maintenance of order on board. However, Chauveau realizes that the territorial system of law cannot be entirely eliminated. In the connection he refers to Meyer's draft of 1946, [2] in which Meyer gives the following rule:

"Tombent sous le coup du droit pénal et de la compétence pénale de l'Etat du lieu des crimes et délits commis à bord d'un

[1] Chauveau, International Law Association, Report of the Forty-fifth Conference, Lucerne, 1952, p. 132.
[2] Meyer, R.G.A. IX, pp. 545, 615.

aéronef lors de la traversée d'un espace aérien étranger *dans la mesure seulement ou ils touchent les intérêts de l'Etat survolé, de ses habitants ou de leurs biens.* S'il n'en est pas ainsi, ces actes relèvent du droit pénal et la juridiction pénale de l'Etat national de l'aéronef. Il en sera encore ainsi lorsqu'on ne pourra établir avec certitude dans le domaine aérien de quel Etat a été commis le crime ou délit."

This means that what Chauveau wants is a combined system of jurisdiction whereby the law of the flag of the aircraft takes precedence except when the interests of the State flown over are affected. Once again we wish to emphasize that in our opinion this is the only correct system.

De la Pradelle likewise raised objections to Cooper's proposal [1] saying:

"Est-il utile, dans ces conditions, de faire un traité qui ne poserait aucune règle obligatoire pour les contractants, soit sous la forme d'une règle obligatoire pour les contractants, soit sous la forme d'une règle de fond uniforme ou sous la forme d'une règle de solution des conflits de lois?" He thinks that both De Visscher's draft (presented to the Institute of International Law in 1937) [2] and Meyer's draft are better formulated. In these drafts, in contrast to Article 5 of the draft which Cooper prepared, it is specifically stated when the territorial system of law must be applied.

Another point in Cooper's draft which De la Pradelle objects to is the concurrent jurisdiction. He feels that an order of precedence ought to be introduced.

Lastly, Professor Arnold W. Knauth has submitted a draft convention on aviation crimes [3] to the Air Law Committee of the International Law Association. Article 1 contains a number of definitions, while Article 2 deals with jurisdiction, which Knauth expressly differentiates from the application of law. The text of Article 2 deals with jurisdiction, which Knauth expressly differentiates from the application of law. The text of Article 2 reads as follows:

---

[1] De la Pradelle, International Law Association, Report of the Forty-fifth Conference, Lucerne, 1952, p. 104.

[2] See p. 143.

[3] Draft of a Convention on Aviation Crimes by Prof. Arnold W. Knauth, International Law Association, Report of the Forty-fifth Conference, Lucerne, 1952, p. 135.

"Article 2.

Jurisdiction of crimes in, on and about Aircraft. Every crime committed in, on or about any aircraft when in flight or on the ground or on or in water outside the territory and airspace of the State of its Flag *shall be deemed to have been* committed in: –

(*a*) the first place within the State of its Flag where it lands after the commission of the crime with the accused person on board, and also

(*b*) if the aircraft first lands at a place outside the State of its Flag, then at the first place outside the State of its Flag where it lands after the commission of the crime with the accused person on board;

(*c*) if the person accused leaves the aircraft while it is in flight, jurisdiction of such person and of the offence shall exist at (a) and at (b) and at the place where such person first touches the earth."

Here Knauth starts from the same principle as Pholien,[1] namely the principle of jurisdiction of the State where the aircraft lands after its flight, but he elaborates it with greater care. His wording would therefore be preferable to that of Pholien. The drawback of this principle has already been mentioned,[2] viz. in many cases the State where the aircraft lands will show little inclination to institute legal proceedings. If one goes so far as to lay down mandatory rules with regard to jurisdiction, why not give jurisdiction in the first instance to the State whose flag the aircraft carries, with certain concessions to the territorial system of law?

Knauth devotes a separate article to the application of law:

"Article 3.

What Law applies?

The criminal law to be applied to the case shall, in the discretion of the court acquiring jurisdiction according to Article 2, be selected from the following laws, in order of preference stated:

First preference: the law of the State of the Flag of the aircraft, if such State has an appropriate criminal law. Second preference:

[1] Pholien, R.D.A. 13, 1929, p. 289.

[2] See p. 150.

the law of the place where the aircraft first lands after the commission of the crime (with the accused person on board).

Third preference: the law of the State and of the place where the aircraft first lands after the commission of the crime. (This may be an emergency landing place, or a scheduled landing place).

Fourth preference: the law of the State and of the place where the aircraft was first scheduled to land, or where a first landing had been planned when the flight commenced, as the normal end of the flight during which the crime was committed. (This will not be an emergency landing place.) Fifth preference: the law of the place where the aircraft last ascended into flight prior to the commission of the crime.

Any of these laws may be shown to the court by any person and in any evidenting manner."

Unlike Pholien, Knauth makes a distinction between the rules for the application of law and the rules of jurisdiction. Admittedly his proposal generally means that the State having jurisdiction will apply its own law, but of course it is possible that this State may not have any "appropriate criminal law." It is therefore correct to do as Knauth does in Article 3 and indicate an order of preference for the application of different criminal laws. As far as the procedure is concerned, still another rule is given.

"Article 4.
What law of Procedure applies?

The procedure shall be governed by the law of the court acquiring jurisdiction according to Article 2."

The above rule is perfectly logical. It would be extremely impractical for a court to have to apply a foreign law of procedure. The next article lays down the principle of non bis in idem:

"Article 5. Double Jeopardy
If any person is either convicted or acquitted by any court having jurisdiction of an offence committed in, on or about an aircraft, such person shall not be again put in jeopardy for the same offence by the courts of any of the High Contracting Parties, nor by the courts of any other State."

A provision such as the foregoing is indispensable in a convention dealing with criminal jurisdiction.

In the following article Knauth introduces an optional clause. Apparently he also sees the drawback of the State where the aircraft lands having very little interest in prosecuting an offence committed during the flight.

"Article 6. (*Optional Clause*). When Jurisdiction shall not be taken No High Contracting Party will exercise criminal jurisdiction of act or of omissions to act in or on aircraft when the following conditions concur:

(*a*) The aircraft does not possess the nationality of such State, and

(*b*) The act or omission to act did not occur in the airspace or upon the territory of such State, and

(*c*) The aircraft does not first land in such State after the commission of the crime."

If this optional clause is adopted, as is desirable because the above-mentioned drawback will thus be eliminated, then an extradition rule must be included. Knauth does so in Article 7:

"Article 7. Extradition
The principles of extradition of persons accused of criminal offences shall be applied by the High Contracting Parties to the cases of persons accused of crimes committed in, on or about aircraft in flight or on the ground, in any and every place, upon the request of the State where the aircraft first lands after the commission of the crime, in the same manner as when a crime of similar character is alleged to have been committed within the State making the request."

This draft of Knauth is very well thought out and carefully formulated. The objection to it, however, is that it does not make adequate provision for the territorial system of law. A convention which does not take the territorial law into account is very unlikely to secure international acceptance. Up till now the draft established during the 33rd conference of the International Law Association at Stockholm in 1924 seems to offer the best prospects in this respect, provided that the terminology is adapted to that of the Chicago Convention of 1944. This brings us to the end of our review of the efforts to reach international agreement on the application of law and jurisdiction with respect to crimes committed on board aircraft. There are hardly any tangible results. That in itself is not surprising, since the development of international criminal law has not yet made much progress. It was only after the First World War that this subject attracted more interest and was subjected to a closer study. At present the punishment of piracy is really all that has been internationalized. This is based on custom and not on treaties. It is an established international custom that a pirate can be tried and punished by the courts of all nations, but it will be difficult to secure acceptance for a similar custom with respect to aviation crimes. In view of the international character of aviation, it is only natural to suggest that aviation crimes should be brought before an international court. In 1937 a convention was even drawn up for the formation of an International Criminal Court. [1] However, the convention was never ratified by any State and so this Court has not been set up. Besides, such a Court would only have been competent to try individuals accused of violating the convention on suppression of terrorism. We also have international trials of war criminals, but otherwise there is no international criminal jurisdiction. All we can say is that the idea of international criminal law has found slightly more acceptance. Before giving our final conclusions we shall examine a number of national legislations.

NATIONAL LAW

France

The Law of May 1924 only contains one article dealing with crimes and offences committed on board aircraft. This article, the first part of which was discussed in the previous chapter, [2] reads as follows:

"Article 10.

Les rapports juridiques entre les personnes qui se trouvent à bord d'un aéronef étranger en circulation sont régis par la loi du pavillon de cet aéronef, toutes les fois que la loi territoriale serait

---

[1] Journal Officiel de la Société des Nations, 1938, p. 36.

[2] See p. 128.

normalement compétente. Toutefois, au cas de crime ou délit commis à bord d'un aéronef étranger, les tribunaux français sont compétents si l'auteur ou la victime est de nationalité française ou si l'appareil atterrit en France après le crime ou délit."

Although the first paragraph is based entirely on the principle of application of the law of the flag of the aircraft, in the second paragraph an exception is made with respect to crimes and offences. In this connection Lemoine remarks that: [1] "En attribuant comme une dérogation au principe posé dans le premier alinéa (cf. le mot 'toutefois') compétence aux tribunaux français si l'auteur ou la victime est de nationalité française, le législateur paraît avoir perdu de vue ces règles habituelles de conflits de lois pénales." According to these rules of the conflict of laws, Lemoine continues, the States whose nationality the offender or the victim possesses can always exercise jurisdiction. But what the law does not expressly stipulate is that the French State must have jurisdiction when a crime committed on board a foreign aircraft has consequences within French territory. The wording of Article 10 is rather unsatisfactory in this respect.

Article 10 also makes the French court competent if the aircraft lands on French territory after the crime has been committed. The question that arises is whether this refers to the first landing after the crime. Le Goff [2] advocates a wide interpretation of Article 10. Lemoine concurs in this view, so it must be assumed that the French court has jurisdiction if the offender is still on board and in freedom when the aircraft lands within French territory, irrespective of whether a landing has already been made outside French territory.

Belgium

In the "Loi du juin 1937 portant révision de la loi du 16 novembre 1919 relative à la règlementation de la navigation aérienne," which came into force on March 31, 1954, we find the following article devoted to offences committed on board aircraft.

"Article 36.

Les infractions commis à bord d'un aéronef belge en vol sont

[1] Lemoine, "Traité de Droit Aérien," p. 799.

[2] Le Goff, "Traité Théorique et Pratique de Droit Aérien," Paris 1934.

réputés commises en Belgique et peuvent y être poursuivies même si l'inculpé n'est pas trouvé sur le territoire du Royaume.

Sont compétents pour la poursuite de ces infractions et de celles prévues par la présente loi et par les arrêtes pris pour son exécution, le procureur du Roi ou l'officier du ministère public près le tribunal de police du lieu de l'infraction, celui de la résidence de l'inculpé, celui du lieu où il pourra être trouvé et, à leur défaut, celui de Bruxelles.

Les articles 6 à 13 de la loi du 17 avril 1878 formant le titre préliminaire du Code de procédure pénale s'appliquent aux infractions commises à bord d'un aéronef étranger en vol, comme si le fait s'était accompli hors du territoire du Royaume. En outre, le coupable d'un crime ou d'un délit commis à bord d'un aéronef étranger en vol pourra être poursuivi en Belgique, si lui-même ou la victime est de nationalité belge ou si l'appareil atterrit en Belgique après l'infraction.

Sont compétents pour la poursuite des infractions visées à l'alinéa précédent, le procureur du Roi du lieu de la résidence de l'inculpé, celui du lieu oû l'inculpé aura été trouvé, celui du lieu de l'atterrisage, et, à leur défaut, le procureur du Roi de Bruxelles."

According to the article quoted above, offences committed on board a Belgian aircraft are deemed to have taken place within Belgian territory.

On the other hand, offences committed on board a foreign aircraft are considered to have taken place outside Belgian territory even in the case of a flight over Belgium.

However, a person who is guilty of an offence committed on board a foreign aircraft can only be prosecuted in Belgium if either he or the victim are Belgian nationals or if the aircraft lands in Belgium after the offence.

Switzerland

The "Loi fédérale sur la navigation aérienne du 21 décembre 1948" includes provisions of criminal law. These are merely intended to supplement the Swiss Criminal Code, since Article 95 states that: "Les dispositions du Code pénal sont en outre applicables." In view of the unique character of aviation, special provisions are necessary. [1] These are to be found in Articles 96–98 of the same Act, and they are based on the territorial principle. For a continental State like Switzerland this is only to be expected, but a few concessions are made to application of the law of the flag of the aircraft. The following exceptions are made by Article 96, which states that the provisions of criminal law are only applicable to a person who commits an offence in Switzerland:

"Art. 89.4.
Est aussi punissable celui qui a piloté ou fait piloter un aéronef en dehors de la Suisse portant sans droit des marques suisses.

"Art. 97.1.
Les prescriptions du droit pénal suisse sont applicables aux actes commis en dehors de la Suisse à bord d'un aéronef suisse employé dans le traffic commercial, quand l'auteur se trouve en Suisse et qu'il n'est pas extradé ou lorsqu'il a été extradé à la Confédération en raison de cet acte.

"Art. 97.3.
Les membres de l'équipage d'un aéronef suisse employé dans le traffic commercial sont toujours soumis au droit pénal suisse, s'ils ont commis l'acte à bord de l'aéronef ou dans l'accomplissement de leurs fonctions professionnelles.

Dans des cas particuliers, l'auteur d'un crime ou d'un délit commis à l'étranger contra la Suisse, contra un Suisse ou par un Suisse, selon les articles 4 à 6 du Code pénal."

The above act also contains a number of provisions with respect to violations of the rules of the air (Arts. 88, 89 and 90).

Spain
The following is an English translation of part of Article 9 of the "Codigo de Justicia Militar":

"Art. 9.
On the basis of locality, the military courts shall have jurisdiction

---

[1] Guldimann, "Le nouveau droit aérien suisse," Revue Française de Droit Aérien, No. 1 Janvier-Mars 1949, p. 25.

in proceedings against any person for delicts (delitos) and contraventions (faltas) which, while not covered by Article 16 of this Code, are committed: (c) In the air space subject to the national sovereignty or in the air space of the protectorate; on board aircraft whether stationed in airfields or Spanish waters or in flight through the above-mentioned air space, including foreign commercial aircraft which land in Spanish territory before crossing the frontier, or cause damage to Spanish nationals, property or interests, or on board other national aircraft, without prejudice to the exceptions which may be established by special acts or international treaties for the purpose of dealing with delicts or contraventions committed in aircraft, missions or places used for civil air navigation or in specified cases, and without prejudice to the provision whereby alien members of foreign crews who, on board the aircraft to which they are assigned, commit offences amongst themselves, may be handed over to the diplomatic or consular representatives of the countries concerned."

In this case the Spanish legislation confers jurisdiction on military courts with respect to aviation crimes committed in the air space under Spanish sovereignty. These military courts also have jurisdiction with respect to crimes committed on board foreign aircraft within the Spanish air space, in the event of such aircraft landing in Spain before crossing the frontier. Furthermore, these courts have jurisdiction if the crimes committed on board the aircraft cause damage to Spanish interests.

When a crime has taken place on board a Spanish aircraft outside Spanish territory, jurisdiction may be exercised by the Spanish court to which the diplomatic or consular officials can most easily send the offender (Art. 37). All this is based on the Spanish Criminal Code, Article 19 of which states that:

"There shall also be considered as Spanish territory, by extension for these purposes: Spanish vessels and aircraft on the high seas, or in the free zone of the air, or anchored in a foreign port, or in a foreign aerodrome."

The nationality of the aircraft is thus taken by the Spanish legislators as a basis for determining the jurisdiction over crimes committed on board the aircraft concerned. With regard to foreign aircraft, as we saw above, a Spanish criminal is only applicable under certain circumstances.

Mexico

The "Codigo Penale" of August 13, 1931, contains the following provisions:

"Art. 5.

The following offences shall be deemed to have been committed in the territory of the Republic:

I. Offences committed by Mexicans or aliens on the high seas on board Mexican vessels.

II. Offences committed on board Mexican warships in foreign ports or foreign territorial waters. This provision shall apply also to Mexican merchant vessels, if the offender has not been judged in the country to which the port belongs.

III. Offences committed on board foreign vessels in Mexican ports or in territorial waters of the Republic, if the offence causes a breach of the peace or if the offender or the aggrieved person is not a member of the crew. The converse case shall be governed by the law of reciprocity.

IV. Offences committed on board Mexican or foreign aircraft in Mexican or foreign territory, air space or territorial waters in circumstances similar to those specified in the foregoing paragraphs with respect to vessels."

Just as in the Spanish legislation referred to above, the nationality of the aircraft serves as a basis to determine the jurisdiction with respect to offences committed on board aircraft.

Uruguay

The air legislation in the "Registro Nacional de Leyes y Decretos" (Vol. 65, 1942, p. 1466) includes a clause reading as follows:

"Article 3.

The laws of Uruguay govern all acts occurring on board an aircraft, whether in flight or not, and all aircraft activities affecting third persons or property not on board, in so far as they occur in the territory, territorial waters or air space of Uruguay.

The law of Uruguay shall also apply to any act which occurs on board any Uruguayan aircraft, if the act takes place outside the territorial waters or the air space of Uruguay."

As may be seen from the above English translation, the Uruguayan legislature is more "territorial-minded" than the Spanish and Mexican legislators. An offence committed on board a foreign aircraft within the sovereign jurisdiction of Uruguay is always governed by the laws of Uruguay. This is a straight forward application of the territorial principle. Offences committed on board Uruguayan aircraft, however, will always be governed by Uruguayan law, even if the aircraft was in foreign territory at the time. Apparently the idea of reciprocity has not been considered at all.

Italy

Article 4 of the "Codice della Navigazione" of March 30, 1942, states that Italian aircraft over the high seas or in a part of the air space which is not subject to the sovereignty of any State, are looked upon as Italian territory.

With regard to the applicability of the provisions of criminal law of the Codice, however, the Italian legislator goes a step further. In Article 1080 of the "Codice della Navigazione" it is stipulated that an Italian citizen or alien belonging to the passengers or crew of an aircraft shall be punished in accordance with the rules laid down in the Codice if he commits a crime within the meaning of the Codice while outside Italian territory. Even when the guilty party is sentenced abroad, he will be tried again in Italy, but only at the request of the Minister of Justice. The provisions of criminal law in the Codice are not applicable to the passengers and crew of foreign aircraft, unless otherwise stipulated.

Thus Italy also takes the nationality of the aircraft as a basis for the application of criminal law and jurisdiction. This implies that the criminal provisions of the Codice in general are declared inapplicable to foreign aircraft.

United Kingdom

The following provisions are contained in the Civil Aviation Act of November 24, 1949:

"Section 60.
Any offence under any enactment to which this Part of this Act applies or under an Order in Council or regulation made under either any such enactment or this Part of this Act shall, for the purpose of conferring jurisdiction, be deemed to have been committed in any place where the offender may for the time being be.

"Section 62.
(1) Any offence whatever committed on a British aircraft shall, for the purpose of conferring jurisdiction, be deemed to have been committed in any place where the offender may for the time being be."

According to this, anybody who has committed an offence on board a British aircraft anywhere in the world or has contravened the statutory provisions relating to civil aviation, can be punished by a British court if he is subsequently found in the United Kingdom. In contrast to the legislation of the other countries which we have discussed above, there are no provisions relating to offences committed on board foreign aircraft. If an offence is committed on board a non-British aircraft while flying within the British jurisdictional domain, this offence is deemed to have taken place within British territory. The State whose flag the foreign aircraft carries is not granted any jurisdiction whatsoever. The United Kingdom thus adheres unilaterally to the principle of application of the law of the country whose flag the aircraft carries.

United States of America
The undernoted paragraph was added to § 7 Title 18 of the United States Code (Crimes and Criminal Procedure) after the notorious case of the United States v. Cordova, [1] which we mentioned earlier:

"(5) Any aircraft belonging in whole or in part to the United States or any citizen thereof, or to any corporation created by or under the laws of the United States, or any State, Territory, district, or possession thereof, while such aircraft is in flight over the high seas, or over any other waters within the admiralty and

[1] U.S.Av.R.1.

maritime jurisdiction of the United States and out of the jurisdiction of any particular State."

As a result of the above addition to the title dealing with the applicability of U.S. criminal law, the latter is declared applicable to crimes committed on board American aircraft so long as they are over United States territory or over the high seas or "no man's land." As may be seen from the foregoing, the U.S.A. does not go so far as to declare its criminal law applicable to American aircraft wherever they may be. The American legislature is certainly not a supporter of the nationality principle. The territorial principle is adopted as a starting-point, with a single necessary concession to the principle of nationality.

The Netherlands
Since August 5, 1952, according to Article 3 of the Dutch Criminal Code, Dutch criminal law is applicable to any person who commits an offence on board a Dutch vessel or aircraft outside the Kingdom of the Netherlands in Europe. The criminal law of the Netherlands thus applies also to Dutch aircraft situated within the territory of another State. No exception is made in favour of foreign aircraft within Dutch territory; the latter are therefore subject to Dutch criminal law. In this case too we have a unilateral application of the law of the flag of the aircraft.

CONCLUSION

From the foregoing analysis of the various drafts for international conventions on the application of criminal law and jurisdiction with respect to crimes committed on board aircraft, as well as a number of national legislations on this subject, one must inevitably conclude that it is extremely difficult to arrive at an internationally acceptable system.

It must be borne in mind that two principles have become firmly established in international law, viz. the principle *of nationality* of the aircraft and the principle of the *sovereignty of each State in the column of air above its territory*. This in itself is a source of conflict. If both principles are enforced, an aircraft will be subject to two systems of criminal law when it enters the air space above the territory of a State other than that whose nationality it possesses. Needless to say, this will lead to conflicts of jurisdiction. Any convention which is intended to regulate the punishability of crimes committed on board aircraft must guard against this if the regulations are to be satisfactory. The territorial system of law in the different countries will have to be respected as much as possible, but nevertheless it is obvious that the nationality of the aircraft should be taken as a basis for the application of criminal law in order to avoid having a period in which no criminal law whatsoever would apply, namely when the aircraft is over the high seas or above territory that is not subject to the sovereignty of any State. As we have already seen, [1] a number of States have declared their criminal law applicable wherever the aircraft may be, i.e. even when it is in or over the territory of another State. This means that we are confronted with the conflict of laws mentioned above, since there is bound to be a clash with the territorial system of law. In order to obviate this, it would be necessary to differentiate between national and foreign aircraft within the territorial air space, in such a way that the territorial law will only apply to foreign aircraft in certain cases. Some States already do so. [2] If all States were to enact in their national legislations that the nationality of the aircraft must be the basis for the application of criminal law to crimes committed on board an aircraft and that the territorial system of law should merely apply in cases where the interests of the State flown over were affected, then a convention on the subject would be superfluous. For the sake of unification of law, however, preference must be given to a convention. It is very tempting to toy with the idea of internationalizing aviation crimes, but such a project would be very difficult to put into effect. It would be necessary to start from the universality principle. Aviation crimes might be included in an international criminal law. The logical corollary of this idea is that the crimes should be brought under the jurisdiction of an international court, or at least that an international court of appeal should be set up. The development of international criminal law does not hold out much prospect of a solution in that direction, as there are too many delicate matters

[1] Including Belgium, Spain, Mexico, Uruguay and the Netherlands.
[2] Including Belgium, Spain and Mexico.

of sovereignty involved. All that has been accomplished in this field up till now amounts to the trial of war criminals. Although aviation crimes are certainly eligible for internationalization from a theoretical viewpoint, a practicable solution will have to be sought elsewhere.

The draft convention prepared by the International Law Association more than thirty years ago [1] undoubtedly offers better possibilities. The almost unfeasible task of compiling an international Criminal Code can be dispensed with. After all, it must be taken for granted that the aircraft is subject to the laws and the jurisdiction of the State whose nationality it possesses. The territorial principle is rightly applied in three particular cases, the sphere of application of the national and territorial principles being correctly defined. It must be admitted that the system is not altogether ideal, as jurisdictional problems are bound to arise from the fact that in many cases the offender will have to be extradited if the court of the State of the flag of the aircraft has jurisdiction. The draft makes provision for this, but difficulties may occur if the offender has to be extradited from Europe to America (or vice versa) on account of a minor offence. Concurrent jurisdiction, as envisaged by Cooper, [2] might provide a solution, but the risk of conflicts ensuing from such a solution is so great that it must be rejected.

Another objection to the principle of nationality is that the passenger's choice of aircraft is or may be very accidental, so that it would be incorrect to let this determine the application of law and jurisdiction. It is hard to see why this should be regarded as a drawback. A passenger boarding a Dutch aircraft knows that during the flight he will be subject to Dutch law. If he does not like this, he is free to take a non-Dutch aircraft.

On the other hand, the advantages of the system laid down in the draft of the International Law Association are immediately apparent.

The passengers and crew are governed by a single system of law during the flight of the aircraft, and the territorial system of law will only apply in certain cases in accord with the general legal conviction.

---

[1] Supra.

[2] See p. 159.

The problem of determining which State the aircraft was over at the time when an offence was committed will not arise, since the State of the flag of the aircraft has jurisdiction, while in the three categories of cases where the aircraft is subject to the laws and jurisdiction of the State flown over it will always be clear which State is concerned.

A state of "lawlessness," in the case of flights over the high seas or over territory which is not subject to the sovereignty of any State, such as existed until a few years ago as far as American aircraft were concerned, is obviated. Moreover, the States flown over will seldom feel inclined to prosecute offences committed above their territory unless their own interests are affected, whereas the State of the flag of the aircraft will always have an interest in the maintenance of law and order on board the aircraft.

Absolute enforcement of the nationality principle would be impracticable in view of the existing territorial sensitivities, although it would undoubtedly be theoretically correct. An acceptable compromise has been found in the draft.

Of course there are still a few difficulties to be dealt with. The terminology of the draft will have to be brought into line with that of the Chicago Convention of 1944. Furthermore, the draft presupposes that the commander of an aircraft has the power to arrest a delinquent, but such a power of the aircraft commander is not laid down in any international agreement nor in the majority of national legislations. Attention will certainly have to be devoted to this point.

As was the case in the previous chapter with regard to civil proceedings, we again come to the conclusion that the nationality of the aircraft must be taken as a basis for the application of law and jurisdiction with respect to crimes and offences – subject to concessions to the territorial system of law under certain circumstances. In the field of civil law we saw that there was still a possibility of an international court, but such a possibility must be rejected as unrealistic in the field of criminal law.

CHAPTER VI

CONSEQUENCES OF THE SPECIAL LEGAL STATUS OF AIRCRAFT

Having elucidated the various aspects of the special legal status of aircraft, we shall now determine the consequences of this special status.

A. CONSEQUENCES FOR THE STATE IN WHICH THE AIRCRAFT IS REGISTERED

Registration

As the aircraft possesses a nationality, the State concerned must see to it that the aircraft carries evidence of that nationality.

According to Article 6 of the Paris Convention of 1919 and Article 17 of the Chicago Convention of 1944,[1] aircraft have the nationality of the State in which they are registered. Article 20 of the Chicago Convention also provides that aircraft must bear nationality and registration marks in order to be able to take part in international air transport operations.[2]

If it is to serve the purpose for which it was constructed, namely to engage in air navigation, the aircraft must therefore be entered on a register. This is a register intended solely for purposes of public law. The register referred to in Article 17 does not play any role whatsoever in connection with the transfer of title to aircraft, though Article 21 of the Chicago Convention makes it obligatory for the States to supply each other with information concerning the registration and ownership of aircraft.[3]

---

[1] Article 17
Aircraft have the nationality of the State in which they are registered.

[2] Article 20
Every aircraft engaged in international air navigation shall bear its appropriate nationality and registration marks.

[3] Article 21
Each contracting State undertakes to supply to any other contracting State or to

It appears that the Chicago Convention is exclusively concerned with aircraft which possess a nationality, since – for example – there are no clauses relating to the status of aircraft operated by international organizations or aircraft that are not entered on any national register. The Convention does, however, contain a rule to prevent double registration.[1]

The International Civil Aviation Organization has published an annex to the Chicago Convention (Annex 7) on the subject of aircraft nationality and registration marks. Chapter 6 of this Annex requires the contracting States to maintain a register, but there is no obligation to enter aircraft on this register. As mentioned above, an aircraft cannot engage in international air navigation without being entered on the register of aircraft, and according to most national legislations it cannot take part in domestic air navigation either, so that in case of non-registration the aircraft is practically worthless to its owner.

It must be emphasized that registration does not create the nationality of the aircraft: the entry on the register is merely a proof of nationality. Each State is free to stipulate the conditions under which an aircraft may be entered on its nationality register.

Airworthiness

Before it can be allowed to fly, however, the aircraft must fulfil other requirements besides that of registration. A certificate of airworthiness is also necessary. Under the terms of Article 31 of the Chicago Convention, an aircraft to be used for international air transport must be provided with a certificate of airworthiness.[2]

---

the International Civil Aviation Organization, on demand, information concerning the registration and ownership of any particular aircraft registered in that State. In addition, each contracting State shall furnish reports to the International Civil Aviation Organization, under such regulations as the latter may prescribe, giving such pertinent data as can be made available concerning the ownership and control of aircraft registered in that State and habitually engaged in international air navigation. The data thus obtained by the International Civil Aviation Organization shall be made available by it on request to the other contracting States.

[1] Article 18

An aircraft cannot be validly registered in more than one State, but its registration may be changed from one State to another.

[2] Article 31

Every aircraft engaged in international navigation shall be provided with a certificate of airworthiness issued or rendered valid by the State in which it is registered.

As was the case with the registration of aircraft, international agreement has been reached on this purely technical subject. ICAO has likewise published an annex to the Chicago Convention dealing with airworthiness requirements.[1] The purpose of this annex (Annex 8) is described as follows:

"*a*) To ensure that all aircraft engaged in international air navigation are certificated and inspected according to uniform procedures; and

b) To establish airworthiness categories of aircraft, which shall define a minimum level of airworthiness for each such category and shall be exclusive in that no Contracting State will classify an aircraft in an ICAO airworthiness category unless the aircraft meets the airworthiness standards governing that ICAO category."

Article 33 of the Chicago Convention ensures that uniformity will be achieved in actual practice, since the contracting States undertake to recognize certificates of airworthiness which have been issued by other contracting States with due observance of the standards established in the relevant Annex.[2]

Flight documents

International rules have also been laid down with regard to the flight documents.

Among the documents to be carried by an aircraft engaged in international air navigation, according to Article 29 of the Chicago Convention, is the journey log book. The captain of the aircraft is responsible for keeping this log book (Annex 6, Chapter 4).[3]

The operator of the aircraft has to provide the crew with an

---

[1] See p. 180.

[2] Article 33

Certificates of airworthiness and certificates of competency and licenses issued or rendered valid by the contracting State in which the aircraft is registered, shall be recognized as valid by the other contracting States, provided that the requirements under which such certificates or licenses were issued or rendered valid are equal to or above the minimum standards which may be established from time to time pursuant to this Convention.

[3] Annex 6, 4.5.5.

The pilot-in-command shall be responsible for the maintenance of the Journey Log Book.

operations manual.[1] Chapter 11 of Annex 6 specifies certain minimum requirements which this manual must fulfil.

In addition, the operator has to keep a maintenance release indicating the position with regard to maintenance work on the aircraft.[2]

Lastly, the operator of the aircraft must see to it that records of emergency and survival equipment carried are available at all times, so that this information can be communicated to the organizations for the rescue and salvage of aircraft.[3]

Crew

In spite of all the efforts to draft an acceptable international convention on the legal status of the crew of an aircraft, no success has been achieved as yet.[4]

On the other hand, the *technical requirements* which must be met by the flight crew members of an aircraft have been internationally agreed upon. Article 37 of the Chicago Convention states that, amongst other things, ICAO shall publish an annex to the Convention dealing with the licensing of operating and mechanical personnel.[5] This has been done in the form of Annex 1 (Personnel Licensing).

---

[1] Annex 6, 4.2.1.

An operator shall provide, for the use and guidance of operations personnel, an Operations Manual in accordance with 11.1.

[2] Annex 6, 8.3.1.

An operator shall ensure that there is provided, for the use and guidance of maintenance organizations and personnel, a Maintenance Manual containing the information specified in 11.2.

[3] Annex 6, 11.5.

Operators shall at all times have available for immediate communication to rescue co-ordination centres, lists containing information on the emergency and survival equipment carried on board any of their aircraft engaged in international air navigation.

[4] CITEJA Doc. 17, 37, 434, 493, 496.

International Labour Office, Report V, 24th Session, Geneva, 1938. ICAO Doc. 4006 (Feb. 1947).

Cf. Kamminga, "The Aircraft Commander in Commercial Air Transportation," Leyden, 1953.

Bucher, "Le Statut Juridique de personnel navigant de l'aéronautique civile," Lausanne, 1949.

Bratschi, „Die Rechtstellung des Luftfahrtpersonals," Berne, 1951.

Knauth, "The Aircraft Commander in International Law," Journal of Air Law and Commerce, 1947.

Honig, „De positie van de gezagvoerder van een luchtvaartuig," Nederlands Juristenblad 1951, p. 317.

[5] Article 37

Each contracting State undertakes to collaborate in securing the highest practic-

The annex in question enumerates the various certificates of competency (licences) for flight crew members and specifies the requirements which must be met by the crew members to whom these certificates of competency are issued. Article 33 of the Chicago Convention[1] makes it obligatory for the contracting States to recognize the certificates of competency issued by another contracting State, provided that such certificates were issued in conformity with the standards laid down in the relevant annex.

Owing to the fact that only the technical requirements to be met by flight crew members have been regulated on an international level, the majority of the national legislations likewise confine themselves to this. The result is that in these States the legal relations between the operator and the crew of an aircraft are governed by common law. So far as could be ascertained, the undernoted States have special legislative measures governing the position of the crew of an aircraft.:

France	– Law of April 4, 1953, No. 53–285.
Italy	– Codice della Navigazione (1942), Arts. 883 et seq.
Brazil	– Law of June 8, 1938.
Cuba	– Decree No. 548 of April 21, 1928.
Ecuador	– Law of September 12, 1936.
Mexico	– Law of February 19, 1940.
Norway	– Law of December 7, 1923.
Uruguay	– Law of February 22, 1928.

---

able degree of uniformity in regulations, standards, procedures, and organization in relation to aircraft, personnel, airways and auxiliary services in all matters in which such uniformity will facilitate and improve air navigation. To this end the International Civil Aviation Organization shall adopt and amend from time to time, as may be necessary, international standards and recommended practices and procedures dealing with:

(*a*) Communications systems and air navigation aids, including ground marking;
(*b*) Characteristics of airports and landing areas;
(*c*) Rules of the air and air traffic control practices;
(*d*) Licensing of operating and mechanical personnel;
(*e*) Airworthiness of aircraft;
(*f*) Registration and identification of aircraft;
(*g*) Collection and exchange of meteorological information;
(*h*) Log books;
(*i*) Aeronautical maps and charts;
(*j*) Customs and immigration procedures;
(*k*) Aircraft in distress and investigation of accident; and such other matters concerned with the safety, regularity, and efficiency of air navigation as may from time to time appear appropriate.

[1] Art. Supra, 33, Chicago Convention.

B. CONSEQUENCES FOR THE RELATIONSHIP WITH STATES OTHER THAN THE STATE OF REGISTRY

With regard to the applicability of air regulations at least, the legal relationship between the aircraft and other States which have ratified or adhered to the Chicago Convention of 1944, is governed by this Convention.

Article 11 of the Chicago Convention[1] adopts the territorial principle in connection with the applicability of air regulations: the national laws on this subject are to apply to the aircraft of all contracting States, irrespective of their nationality.

In virtue of Article 12 of the Convention[2] – which was discussed earlier – the contracting States even undertake to insure that every aircraft within their territory and every aircraft carrying their nationality marks, wherever such aircraft may be, shall comply with the local rules and regulations relating to air navigation. Quite logically the States also undertake to keep their own regulations uniform, to the greatest possible extent, with those established under the Chicago Convention. At the same time Article 12 states that the rules of the Convention shall apply over the high seas.

Apart from the fact that an aircraft has *obligations* towards other States which have ratified or adhered to the Chicago Convention, it likewise has certain *rights* which must be recognized by these States.

Under the terms of Article 33 of the Chicago Convention,[3] the contracting States are obliged to recognize as valid the certificates of airworthiness issued by other States, as well as the certificates of competency of the crew of the aircraft, provided that the requirements under which such certificates were issued are equal to or above the minimum standards specified in the relevant annex to the Convention.

In this connection reference must also be made to Articles 5

[1] Article 11
Subject to the provisions of this Convention, the laws and regulations of a contracting State relating to the admission or departure from its territory of aircraft engaged in international air navigation, or to the operation and navigation of such aircraft while within its territory, shall be applied to the aircraft of all contracting States without distinction as to nationality, and shall be complied with by such aircraft upon entering or departing from or while within the territory of that State.

[2] See p. 48

[3] Supra, Art. 33, Chicago Convention.

and 6 of the Chicago Convention,[1] whereby the contracting States agree to allow aircraft registered in another State to fly over or into their territory – though often subject to very restrictive conditions, as we have already seen. As explained in Chapters IV and V, neither the jurisdictional problem nor the application of regulations other than those of air law have been settled on an international basis.

C. CONSEQUENCES FOR HOLDERS OF RIGHTS IN AIRCRAFT

In the Final Act of the International Civil Aviation Conference which was held at Chicago in 1944 and led to the Convention of that name, we find the following recommendation:

"TRANSFER OF TITLE TO AIRCRAFT"

Considering:

That the sale of aircraft to be used in international operations will render it desirable for the various governments to reach a common understanding on the legal questions involved in the transfer of title;

The International Civil Aviation Conference Recommends:

That the various governments represented at this International Civil Aviation Conference give consideration to the early calling of an international conference on private international air law for the purpose of adopting a convention dealing with the transfer of title to aircraft and that such private air law conference include in the bases of discussions:

a) The existing draft convention relating to mortgages, other real securities, and aerial privileges; and

b) The existing draft convention on the ownership of aircraft and the aeronautic register, both of which were adopted by the Comité International Technique d'Experts Juridiques Aériens (CITEJA) in 1931."

As a result of this recommendation, the Convention on the International Recognition of Rights in Aircraft was signed at Geneva on June 18, 1948.[2] It will be recalled that rights of

[1] See pp. 25 and 26
[2] See pp. 78 et seq.

property were given a minor place in this Convention, the main purpose of which was to safeguard security rights. The Convention only gives detailed regulations on the latter subject. In Chapter III we drew attention to the fact that the Convention is mainly concerned with rules of the conflict of laws and consequently it does not contribute much to the unification of law. Naturally this is very disappointing. Another drawback is that the Convention entirely depends on the establishment of a record (for purposes of private law) by the several States, but the Convention does not make the establishment of such records obligatory.

D. CONSEQUENCES WITH RESPECT TO CARRIAGE BY AIR

As far as international carriage is concerned, the transport of goods and passengers by aircraft is regulated in the Convention signed at Warsaw on October 12, 1929, for the unification of certain rules relating to international carriage by air.[1] This Convention contains general rules relating to the liability of the carrier. There is no necessity for the carrier to enter into separate contracts with the shippers and the passengers in regard to the extent and the limits of his liability, since that is settled in the Convention. Any provision intended to relieve the carrier of his liability or to fix a limit lower than that specified in the Convention is null and void. This might appear to have been inspired by the Hague Rules, in which clauses excluding the liability of the shipowner are prohibited, but such a conclusion would be mistaken. In this case the prohibition of clauses excluding liability forms the necessary counterbalance to the rules of the Convention, insofar as the latter deal with the non-liability of the carrier. Provisions exonerating the carrier from liability are useless here because they have been incorporated into general rules. The Convention establishes the non-liability of the carrier for the majority of cases in which the carrier concerned might be able to achieve this by means of special clauses. However, preference has rightly been given to rules embodied in the Convention. After all, a contractual agreement is merely effective through voluntary acceptance by the parties to the agreement, in which

[1] See p. 115

case the carrier can only invoke non-liability clauses if the passenger or the shipper of the goods has consented to those clauses. How is the carrier to obtain the consent of the traveller? He will have to get the traveller to sign the passenger ticket or the luggage ticket, on which the provisions tending to relieve the carrier of liability must be printed. Notwithstanding the existence of a law which recognizes non-liability clauses, the carriers run the risk that a judicial opinion may develop against them, in view of the fact that their clients are not adequately informed of the non-liability clauses. The rules of the Convention bar legal proceedings on the subject. From the carrier's standpoint, the Convention creates a system of liability based on default with reversal of the burden of proof. The carrier is thus liable for damage sustained during the carriage by air, unless he proves that he and his agents took all necessary measures to avoid the damage or that it was impossible to take such measures. The liability of the carrier, however, is limited.[1]

The Warsaw Convention met with world-wide acceptance[2] and has definitely answered to its purpose of unifying certain rules relating to international carriage by air.

E. CONSEQUENCES WITH RESPECT TO DAMAGE CAUSED TO THIRD PARTIES ON THE SURFACE

The question of damage caused to third parties on the ground by aircraft in transit has been internationally regulated in the Convention on Damage Caused by Foreign Aircraft to Third Parties on the Surface, signed at Rome in 1952.[3] Under the terms of this Convention, the liability of the operator of an aircraft is based on the "Théorie du Risque." Although several States had repeatedly objected to this principle of absolute liability, it has nevertheless been retained. We have already mentioned that the main objection against the absolute liability has always been that an aircraft should no longer be regarded as something that is inherently dangerous but ought to be treated like other means of transport.[4] We must confess, however, that owing to the specific

[1] See p. 116
[2] See ICAO L.C. Working Draft 395 15/5/53.
[3] See p. 117
[4] Ibid.

characteristics of air transport, it does indeed involve more risks than arise from surface transport. If the principle of absolute liability is not accepted, in most cases the injured third party will be unable to prove fault on the part of the airline, while the airline will frequently be able to plead force majeure.

An economic argument can also be put forward in favour of application of the principle of absolute liability, namely that people who use aircraft for their personal advantage must also be responsible for the consequences of their activity in this field.[1]

Final review

In the light of the foregoing we must inevitably conclude that in various respects the legal status of aircraft has not yet been fully settled. Recapitulating, the conclusion we arrive at is as follows.

With regard to the technical requirements which the aircraft and its crew must satisfy in order to take part in international air transport, a considerable measure of uniformity has been achieved on an international level, thanks to the standards laid down in the relevant Annexes to the Chicago Convention published by ICAO. On the other hand, there are sometimes differences of opinion concerning the formulation of these requirements in the national legislation of the individual States. The material contents of the Annexes are mostly accepted, in spite of the fact that the Chicago Convention – unlike the Paris Convention – allows the contracting States to depart from the standard text in their national legislation.[2] Nevertheless difficulties still occur

[1] Stanesco, "La Responsabilité dans la Navigation Aérienne," Paris, Les Editions Internationales, 1951.

[2] Article 38

Any State which finds it impracticable to comply in all respects with any such international standard or procedure, or to bring its own regulations or practices into full accord with any international standard or procedure after amendment of the latter, or which deems it necessary to adopt regulations or practices differing in any particular respect from those established by an international standard, shall give immediate notification to the International Civil Aviation Organization of the differences between its own practice and that established by the international standard. In the case of amendments to international standards, any State which does not make the appropriate amendments to its own regulations or practices shall give notice to the Council within sixty days of the adoption of the amendment to the international standard, or indicate the action which it proposes to take. In any such case, the Council shall make immediate notification to all other states of the difference which exists between one or more features of an international standard and the corresponding national practice of that State.

in this purely technical field. As an example of such difficulties we refer to what took place in connection with the approval of the Comet airliner for American carriers. Lord Brabazon, Chairman of the British Air Registration Board, accused the U.S. Civil Aeronautics Administration of technical incompetence in connection with its alleged withholding of a certificate of airworthiness for the Comet.[1]

Replying to this charge, Mr. Frederick Lee, Acting Administrator of the CAA, said that a certificate of airworthiness for the Comet had not been refused and could not have been refused, because the CAA had never received a formal request for the issue of such a certificate. There had only been unofficial contact with the British authorities on this subject. At all events, the situation was that – according to Article 33 of the Chicago Convention – the certificate of airworthiness of a Comet flying under the British flag had to be recognized as valid in the United States, but not issued was a certificate of airworthiness for the same type of aircraft flying under the U.S. flag. This possibility is left open by Article 33 of the Chicago Convention. At present a number of States are endeavouring to arrive at a more satisfactory arrangement by means of bilateral agreements. In this way, however, the unification of the technical regulations envisaged by those who drafted the Chicago Convention, can only be partly realized. The existing situation is such that a purely technical matter like the issue of a certificate of airworthiness can be used as a political weapon against the aircraft industry of another country.

Thus the position with respect to technical regulation still leaves something to be desired, but this applies to a much greater degree in the case of the legal status of aircraft as such. In this connection a brief digression may be permitted on the subject of the situation now prevailing in the field of international air law. We regret to say that the development of international air law is not proceeding satisfactorily. Saporta[2] speaks of a "crise de croissance" of international air law. He observes that seven years after the signing of the Geneva Convention of 1948 only four at the moment six States have so far ratified it without reservations, and that the fate of the Convention concluded at

[1] American Aviation Daily, April 28, 1953.

[2] Saporta, "Crise de Croissance du Droit International Aérien," R.G.A. 1955, No. 2.

Rome in 1952 on the subject of damage caused to third parties seems to be even worse. According to Saporta, the slow progress in the creation of international air law is primarily attributable to the large number of States that take part in the discussions on a footing of complete equality and with equal rights: when it comes to voting, the vote of San Salvador weighs just as much as that of the United States. A second drawback, in his opinion, is the use of several languages at the various conferences on air law. Further reference may be made to a circumstance which Saporta does not mention, namely that in contrast to the situation prior to 1940 a compromise must now be found between two legal systems. In the years before World War II the countries on the Continent (of Europe) were mainly responsible for the growth of international air law. The legal systems of these States were based on similar principles and it was possible to draw up an international convention with due observance of the said principles. In such an international agreement the contracting States did not find anything which conflicted with their national legislation. Now that the United States of America plays such an important role in international aviation – and consequently in international air legislation – it appears to be increasingly difficult to bridge the gap between Continental law and Anglo-American law. All this results in the establishment of international conventions which largely consist of rules of reference, as illustrated by the Geneva Convention of 1948. But the much-desired uniformity of law cannot of course be achieved in this manner. If one attempts to secure unification, as in the case of the Rome Convention of 1952, one of the two parties – in this case the U.S.A. – refuses to sign the convention. The solution envisaged by Saporta for the present impasse is the creation of a supranational organ with legislative authority. In view of the great sensitivity of the different States in regard to questions of sovereignty, a solution in that direction seems to be out of the question, at least for the time being. As an alternative Saporta proposes that conventions be concluded by a limited number of States, with the possibility of other States joining this group at a later date. Saporta's suggestion is of course based primarily on a practical standpoint. From a formal legal aspect of unification of international air law, the proposal is unacceptable.

Our personal opinion is that the "crise de croissance" outlined by Saporta also hinders adoption of the remedies recommended by him. We think the causes of the unsatisfactory state of affairs with respect to international air law lie deeper. Saporta, quite rightly, considers that the method of preparing international conventions is incorrect. He therefore seeks for better methods, but even if these were feasible they still would not provide a solution. The root of the trouble, to our mind, is that the States are reluctant to accept an international agreement purely and simply out of fear that they will be obliged to sacrifice part of their sovereignty. This does not imply that the way in which air law conventions are now prepared is ideal, but an improved procedure will not eliminate the cause of failure. Another consequence of the fact that people do not believe in the possibility of creating international legislation is that the care with which this preparation takes place is by no means perfect.

After this gloomy picture of international law-making, we return to our subject, the legal status of aircraft. The abovementioned fear of the various States that they may be forced to surrender even a small portion of their national sovereignty will also be a serious handicap to those who strive for international agreement in this field. However, in the hope that it will gradually be realized that international agreements are more important than rigid adherence to the concept of sovereignty, we shall now summarize the course of development which we should like to see followed with regard to the legal status of aircraft. The basic premise of both the Paris Convention and the Chicago Convention was that aircraft possess a nationality. We believe that in Chapter II we have conclusively demonstrated the justification for this. Although authoritative writers such as Riese[1] still oppose the theory that aircraft possess a nationality, as embodied in the two conventions mentioned above, the nationality of aircraft is as incontestable as that of ships. Since an aircraft possesses the nationality of a certain State, the State in question is obliged to ensure that the airworthiness of that aircraft, as well as the competency of the crew, meet the standard requirements mentioned earlier in this chapter. No rules are

---

[1] See p. 44

laid down with regard to the conditions under which the States can give their nationality to aircraft. The criterion is the fact of being registered as to nationality in the State concerned. The States are entirely free to determine when they will permit such registration. That is logical, as restrictions imposed on the national legislation on this subject would never be accepted. If States have given their nationality to aircraft, then they bear a certain responsibility for these aircraft. But the stage has not yet been reached of using the nationality of the aircraft to solve problems of international law which may arise when the aircraft is located within the sovereign jurisdiction of a foreign State. Up till now, therefore, no action has been taken to determine the legal status of aircraft abroad on the basis of the law of the State whose nationality the aircraft possesses, i.e. the law of the flag, although this ensues from recognition of the nationality of the aircraft. As far as application of law is concerned, there is not a single international rule on this subject. On the other hand, we do find an international rule relating to jurisdiction: the principle of the law of the flag is applied to some extend in Article 12 of the Chicago Convention,[1] which bears the title of "Rules of the Air". Not only the surface State but also the State whose flag the aircraft carries have jurisdiction to prosecute violations of these rules. The nationality principle is thus recognized in this case, though concurrent with the territorial principle. In Chapter II we already discussed the evolution of this article; the origin of which is to be found in the Paris Convention. The wording of the article in question is anything but satisfactory, because it creates a number of uncertainties. If we construe the text literally, an almost superhuman task is imposed on the States since they have to adopt measures to insure that their national aircraft flying over another country shall comply with the rules and regulations there in force. This is factually impracticable. It would therefore be advisable to replace the words "to insure" by a less stringent term. Moreover, in contrast to the title of the article, the text speaks of "rules and regulations relating to the flight and maneuver of aircraft." The question that arises here, is whether the article applies not only to the rules of the air, as

[1] Drion, "The council of ICAO as international legislator over the high seas." (See also p. 161).

the title indicates, but also to the so-called operational instructions, i.e. instructions concerning such things as the minimum quantity of fuel, the instruments, etc., which must be on board the aircraft. This is another point which calls for clarification. Furthermore, each State is to keep its relevant regulations uniform "to the greatest possible extent." It may perhaps be advisable to substitute in place of this phrase the words used in Article 37 of the Chicago Convention, namely "the highest practicable degree." Article 12 also states that over the high seas the rules in force shall be those established under the Convention. Not the slightest variation is permissible in this case. One consequence is that a State whose Flight Information Region extends over the high seas cannot deviate from the rules of the Chicago Convention as far as the area above the high seas is concerned, although variations are permissible in the area above its own territory. The chief objection to this article lies in the fact that it creates concurrent jurisdictional powers. A legal form of this nature is most undesirable, since it is a source of conflict of laws. Such conflicts can only be avoided if one of the two States is given priority of jurisdiction. Accordingly, the initial application of the nationality principle in international air legislation cannot be described as a very happy one.

From the standpoint of criminal law, the nationality of the aircraft is of no significance except when the aircraft is over the high seas of such territory as is not subject to the sovereignty of any State. During the latter period there must be some rule of law, as otherwise a legal vacuum exists. Owing to the fact that the aircraft possesses a nationality, it operates under the flag of a certain State and it is therefore natural that this State should act as upholder of the law. For that reason a large number of States[1] declare their criminal law applicable to offences committed on board aircraft carrying their flag, irrespective of where these aircraft happen to be. From a practical viewpoint this provision is only of importance so long as the aircraft is over the high seas or "no man's land." Within the territory of a foreign State the criminal law of that State will almost invariable apply, in which case the nationality principle cannot be maintained without

[1] Including Belgium, France, Italy, Mexico, Spain.

international agreement to that effect. There is only one country whose national legislation allows the territorial system of law to be overridden by that of the State whose flag the aircraft carries.[1] As we saw, numerous attempts have been made to arrive at an international agreement, but up till now they have not yielded any result.

We must turn to international private law in order to find an international agreement whereby precedence is granted to the law of the State whose flag the aircraft carries. The Geneva Convention on the International Recognition of Rights in Aircraft (1948)[2] is based on the law of the State whose nationality the aircraft possesses, since that convention refers to the law of the flag of the aircraft with respect to the valid constitution and recordation of certain specified rights. As commended earlier, this is the very field in which unification of legislation ought to be aimed at, instead of rules of the conflict of laws. Due to the present impasse as regards international legislation, however, a convention of this nature offered the only solution, but it gives rise to a remarkable situation in that the maxim advocated by us has been applied in a field where we would prefer an entirely different solution. What we should have liked to see was the creation of an international mortgage.

With regard to jurisdiction, in our search for international rules we again arrive back at international private law. Rules of jurisdiction are given in the Warsaw Convention relating to international carriage by air and in the Rome Convention on damage caused by foreign aircraft to third parties on the surface.[3]

The system adopted in the Rome Convention of 1952 was that of the single forum, whereby jurisdiction rests exclusively with the court of the place where the damage occurred. Viewed from a legal standpoint, this is undoubtedly the purest solution, but it remains to be seen whether the system will also lead to the best results in actual practice. Since the only competent court is the court of the State in which the damage occurred, provision must be made for execution of the judgments. The Rome Convention therefore lays down rules on this subject.[4] A much

[1] Belgium, Law of June 1937 (see p. 169).

[2] See p. 78

[3] See p. 115 et seq.

[4] See pp. 117 and 119

simpler solution would have been to create an international judicial authority. Since there is no possibility of this for the time being, if it is desired to make some contribution towards an international legal system, then the States must agree to enforce each other's judgments on a reciprocal basis, subject to certain conditions. In the course of the years a number of bilateral agreements have been concluded for that purpose.[1] Naturally such agreements do not provide a perfect solution; among those who realized this were the drafters of the "Conventions internationales concernant le transport des voyageurs, des bagages et des marchandises par chemins de fer" (C.I.M. and C.I.V., last revised on October 25, 1952). Judgments passed under these two conventions are enforceable in all the contracting States (Articles 55 of the C.I.M. and the C.I.V.). As already remarked, the Convention of Rome starts from the same principle, but in this case the conditions for enforceability of judgments are such that execution will rarely be granted in actual practice. Here we are thinking particularly of the fact that execution of a judgment can be refused if it is deemed to be contrary to the public policy of the State in which execution is requested. Nevertheless the relevant provisions of the Rome Convention are extremely interesting.

Under the Warsaw Convention, an action for damages can be brought before several fora. Hence there is a possibility that contradictory judgments may be pronounced if actions are brought before different courts by more than one party. In a report presented to the Air Law Committee of the International Law Association on the occasion of the conference at Edinburgh in 1954, Garnault submitted the following proposal.

The Warsaw Convention creates a system of liability for the air carrier based on presumption of fault, but at the same time the carrier's liability is strictly limited. If this fault is disproved by the carrier then he is exonerated from liability, but in case of gross negligence or wilful misconduct his liability is unlimited.

Would it not be possible to find a solution to the effect that judgments for amounts below the convention limits would automatically be granted an exequatur, while the defendant could "freeze" this if he denies liability and succeeds in obtaining

[1] See treaty of March 28, 1925, between the Netherlands and Belgium.

dismissal of a suit in connection with the same accident by the court of the country where execution is applied for?

In the majority of cases, judgments for amounts below the limits prescribed by Article 22 of the Warsaw Convention might thus be quickly put into effect.

This brings us to the end of the special regulations at present applicable to aircraft.

There is every reason to appreciate what has been accomplished with a view to determining the legal status of aircraft in the relatively short course of development of air law, but a great deal remains to be done. The regulations governing the legal status of aircraft still compare unfavourably with those relating to ships. Let us now consider the points on which international agreement would be desirable. The most obvious point is the lack of an international convention with respect to crimes and offences committed on board an aircraft in flight. Admittedly, a number of States make provision for this by declaring their national criminal law applicable to anyone guilty of an offence on board an aircraft carrying their flag outside their own frontiers; but this only furnishes a solution if there is no conflict with the territorial system of law of other States. As already indicated, a solution must be sought along the lines of a convention based on application of the law and jurisdiction of the State whose flag the aircraft carries. It would be too much to hope for unification of legislation in this field. An international code of law for aviation crimes would have to be drawn up and every State would have to be able to prosecute the offenders. Aviation crimes would then be governed by a rule of international law such as is only recognized with respect to piracy at the moment. We do not believe that results are attainable in this manner. It is more realistic to start from the law of the flag of the aircraft. An exception to this principle might have to be made in favour of the State flown over, should the latter have any interest in instituting criminal proceedings. In this connection one must allow for the possibility that a citizen of the State flown over committed the offence or that a landing is made in that State. On account of the prevailing sensitivities in regard to matters of sovereignty it would be impracticable to apply the nationality principle alone. There is no question of simply declaring the territorial system of law applicable in aviation, owing to the difficulties of determining the place of the crime, while it is likewise undesirable that an aircraft should be subject to a number of systems of law in the course of a single flight.

As far as jurisdiction is concerned, offences committed during the flight might perhaps be brought under the jurisdiction of the State of arrival or the State of departure. The drawback of such a system is that in most cases these States will have very little interest in prosecuting the offence. We have already expressed the view that the Stockholm draft of the International Law Association of 1924 presents possibilities for a satisfactory arrangement. It would be preferable to proceed in the lines of this draft rather than to take as a starting-point the system of concurrent jurisdiction embodied in Article 12 of the Chicago Convention. The latter system will inevitably lead to large-scale conflict of laws when it is applied to a wider field than breaches of air traffic regulations.

The convention desired by us might be drafted within the framework outlined below.

The first article ought to include a number of definitions (e.g. "aircraft", "air space," etc.) consonant with the Chicago Convention. All acts punishable under the laws of the contracting States would be treated as crimes and offences.

The nationality principle should be embodied in the second article, which could be formulated as follows:

"Crimes and offences committed on board an aircraft in flight shall be governed by the law of the State whose nationality the aircraft possesses, while the offenders shall be subject to the jurisdiction of that State."

The third article would contain an amendment to this in the form of a necessary concession to the territorial system of law. The following wording might be appropriate. "In the case of crimes and offences which jeopardize the public order and safety of the State flown over, however, the law of this State shall be applicable and the offenders shall be brought under its jurisdiction. The State flown over shall likewise have jurisdiction in case of a breach of its air traffic regulations."

The following rule of procedure could be laid down in the fourth article:

"Criminal proceedings shall be conducted in accordance with the rules of the court which shall try the offence."

The fifth article will have to contain an extradition clause, the wording of which might be as follows:

"The State in which the aircraft lands must detain the person who has committed the offence and place him at the disposal of the State having jurisdiction over him, if so requested by that State."

The sixth article will have to provide for the axiom of non bis in idem. Such a rule ought to be worded as indicated below:

"Any person convicted under the provisions of this Convention shall not be tried again for the same offence."

In a seventh article it might be stipulated that the convention is exclusively applicable to civil aircraft. This convention would still have to be supplemented with instructions concerning the steps to be taken by the commander of the aircraft in the event of a crime being committed on board. In our opinion, however, such instructions ought to be included in a convention on the legal status of the aircraft commander. Our views on this subject will be given later, when we discuss the desirability of regulating the position of the aircraft commander.

We believe that a convention relating to aviation crimes could be evolved along the lines indicated above. Although it is based on two principles, we consider that a logical demarcation line is drawn between the sphere of applicability of each principle. In our opinion, neither concurrency of jurisdiction nor an order of precedence is entailed by the above system. Naturally this is only a rough outline of the possibilities and it is certainly capable of amplification and modification.

Though it is not so urgently needed as a convention on criminal acts, an international convention relating to non-criminal acts committed on board an aircraft in flight is likewise desirable. In view of the speed of modern aircraft and hence the comparatively short duration of the flights, the lack of a convention is not so serious. But a convention of this nature is essential in order to avoid being faced with unsolvable legal puzzles in a number of cases. Here too the application of the law and the jurisdiction of the State whose flag the aircraft carries would have to be taken as a basis in drafting a convention.

A concession would again have to be made to the territorial system of law of the State flown over, though not to the same extent as in the case of criminal acts. This would be particularly advisable in the case of acts which might lead to an action for damages. The law of the State of registry of the aircraft could simply be applied with respect to the conclusion of contracts, and the same might be done concerning births and deaths on board aircraft. Rules to this effect are already incorporated in a number of national legislations. Regulations are likewise necessary on the subject of revocation or execution of wills during the flight. Here again the law of the flag can be applied without any objection. It seems totally incorrect to make the applicable law depend on whether the aircraft was over the high seas or above the territory of another State while the will was made, or on whether the aircraft happened to land in a certain State. On the other hand, it would be necessary to stipulate that neither the law of the State of the flag nor the jurisdiction of that State shall be applicable to acts which take place on board the aircraft after it has landed. When the aircraft is standing on foreign soil there is no need for any regime of law other than that of the foreign State concerned.

We should like to have regulations on this subject formulated in approximately the following terms:

"Legal transactions which have taken place on board an aircraft in flight shall be governed by the law of the State whose nationality the aircraft possesses, unless the parties concerned have agreed that another law shall apply." "Births and deaths occurring on board an aircraft in flight shall be deemed to have taken place within the territory of the State whose nationality the aircraft possesses."

"If torts are committed on board an aircraft in flight and the effects thereof will be felt in the State flown over, the law of that State shall apply to such torts."

These regulations might be further supplemented with provisions concerning the obligations of the aircraft commander in the event of a birth or death on board the aircraft. However, this subject will be discussed below. Another deficiency with regard to aircraft is the lack of a convention on the status of the aircraft commander. As indicated above, in a number of cases somebody on board the aircraft has to act as a police officer or registrar. It is logical that the aircraft commander should do so. Up till now, however, there has been no statutory provision for such action. The powers of the aircraft commander in cases of this nature might be included in the regulations outlined above, or in a separate convention on the powers of the aircraft commander as a whole. If the latter course is to be adopted, it will be necessary to establish not only the duties of the aircraft commander in public law but also his other duties, as has been done in great detail in maritime law with respect to the master of a ship. In discussing Kamminga's thesis, Drion comes to the conclusion that there is no need for such a convention.[1] We shall briefly examine the desirability of a convention governing the further statutory powers of the aircraft commander. While in flight the aircraft forms a temporarily independent community, the head of which must be vested with statutory powers irrespective of the short duration. The commander should have certain rights. During the flight he must be entitled to take drastic measures at his own discretion under certain circumstances which he alone can judge (e.g. the jettisoning of cargo and fuel). When a forced landing has been made in some inhospitable region he must have the right to take such measures as may be necessary. This is advisable in the interests of the safety of all on board the aircraft. The foregoing entails that in certain cases the commander of the aircraft shall have authority to bind his company by legal transactions. Most airlines consider this undesirable and unnecessary. They hold that their local representatives appointed all over the world can do whatever is required. It must be admitted that the position in regard to aircraft is indeed somewhat different from that of ships. Although there is no international convention in the field of maritime law either, all of the seafaring States have embodied rules and regulations on this subject in their national legislations. The reason is self-evident. A ship forms an independent community for such a long time that statutory regulations are essential. The much shorter journeys of aircraft certainly make the need for regulation less urgent, though the necessity still remains. In

---

[1] Drion, Rechtsgeleerd Magazijn Themis, 1954, p. 89.

contrast to maritime law, whereby the position is regulated in practically all national legislations, so that an international convention is not so urgently needed, most of the national legislations in the field of air law fail to deal with this point and for that very reason an international convention is desirable. We should like to see a convention clearly defining the rights and duties of the aircraft commander, in addition to regulating his administrative duties.

In our opinion there is no need for a special contract of employment between the operator and the captain or the crew of the aircraft.

What we have missed in most drafts for a convention on the legal status of the aircraft commander is a clause dealing with his personal liability. This is a question which exercises many minds in aviation circles, as may be seen from the following resolution adopted by the International Federation of Airline Transport Pilots Associations during its fifth meeting at Brussels in April 1950:

"It is resolved that a captain of aircraft shall not, in principle, be held liable for loss or damage to property, cargo and valuables carried in aircraft under his command either by passengers or third parties resulting from accident or otherwise either in the air or on the ground and that in so far as he might be held liable this liability shall not exceed that of the operating company and shall be fully covered by an insurence policy taken out by the operating company."

Some of these wishes are met by the proposed revision of the Warsaw Convention, to the effect that the servants and agents of the operator are covered by the limits of liability specified in the convention. If the Hague Protocol to Amend the Warsaw Convention is ratified by thirty States, this will be the case.

In the event of the legal status of the aircraft commander being regulated by an international convention, we recommend that the convention should include a clause corresponding to Article 342(2) of the Dutch Commercial Code, viz. that the aircraft commander shall only be responsible for damage caused by gross negligence or wilful misconduct on his part, while acting within the scope of his employment.

In the light of the foregoing, we consider that there is every justification for a thorough re-examination of the problem of the legal status of the aircraft commander.It is also advisable to secure a greater degree of international uniformity with respect to the legal status of the aircraft itself. The attempts to attain uniformity of legislation in regard to the acquisition of title to aircraft, which were abandoned by CITEJA in 1930, ought to be resumed. At present the situation is such that there are wide variances in the regulations governing the transfer of title to aircraft in the different States. As we have seen, the legislation of almost every State recognizes the fact that the aircraft is movable property sui generis, but only a few States have acted on the logical consequence of this and established a register of aircraft for purposes of private law. The signing of the Convention on the International Recognition of Rights in Aircraft at Geneva in 1948 is undoubtedly an important step towards that goal, but the number of States which have ratified this convention is increasing very slowly indeed. Although the Convention, strangely enough, does not prescribe the establishment of a register for purposes of private law, it assumes that such a record exists. Every State ratifying the convention must therefore make provision for a record of rights in aircraft. The practically universal existence of register books as those used for ships, still appears to be a dream of the future as far as aircraft are concerned. Like the ship, in fact even more so, the aircraft is preeminently an international means of transport. A convention for the unification of the rules relating to rights of property in aircraft is therefore extremely desirable. A first essential for such a convention is that the various States should proceed to establish a national record of aircraft for purposes of private law.

From the above it is clearly apparent that there are still numerous lacunae in air law. This is a field of law in which great development is feasible. Continuous progress may be observed but up till now there has not been much consolidation. Although the phase of initial development is past, regulations on many different subjects are still being evolved.

In the present study we have endeavoured to throw light on the different aspects of the legal status of aircraft. It was found that the existing legislative measures contain a number of gaps.

Our object was to draw attention to these deficiencies and to indicate possible ways of remedying them.

We hope that by so doing we have contributed in some measure to a further development of air law.

APPENDIX

Draft for an international convention on civil and criminal jurisdiction with respect to acts committed on board aircraft, drawn up as a result of the discussions of the International Law Association at its 31st conference in Buenos Aires in 1922 and its 33rd conference in Stockholm in 1924.

(*a*) *Civil Jurisdiction*:

Art. 1.

The airship which is above the open sea or such territory as is not under the sovereignty of any State is subject to the laws and civil jurisdiction of the country of which it has the nationality.

Art. 2.

A public airship which is above territory of a foreign State remains under the exclusive jurisdiction of the State of which it has the nationality.

A private airship which is above the territory of a foreign State is subject to the laws and jurisdiction of such State only in the following cases:

1. With regard to every breach of its laws for the public safety and its military and fiscal laws.
2. In case of a breach of its regulations concerning air navigation.
3. For all acts committed on board the airship and having effect on the territory of the said State.

In all other respects a private airship follows the laws and jurisdiction of the State of the flag.

(*b*) *Criminal Jurisdiction*

Art. 3.

If at the commencement or during the progress of any flight of any aircraft passing over any State or States or their territorial waters or over the high seas without landing, any person on board such aircraft commits any crime or misdemeanour, the person charged shall forthwith be arrested if necessary. Such felony or misdemeanour may be enquired into and the accused tried and punished in accordance with the Rules given under Art. 2. The State of the place where such aircraft lands shall be bound to arrest the accused if necessary and to extradite him to the State which has jurisdiction over him.

Art. 4.

Acts committed on board a private aircraft not in flight in a foreign State shall be subject to the jurisdiction of such State, and any person or persons charged with the commission of such act shall be tried and, if found guilty, punished according to the laws of such State.

BIBLIOGRAPHY

Books and other publications

ARMINJON, P., "Précis de droit international privé," Paris 1934.

BLACKSTONE, Sir W., "Commentaries on the Laws of England," Vol. II

BONAPARTE, PRINCE R., "Die Freiheit der Luft," 1914.

BOURQUIN, M., "Règles générales du droit de la paix," Rec. 35 (1931,1).

BRATSCHI, H., "Die Rechtstellung des Luftfahrtpersonals, Berne, 1951.

BUCHER, P., "Le Statut juridique du personnel navigant de l'aéronautique civile," Lausanne, 1949.

DE BUSTAMENTE Y SIRVEN, A. S., "Droit international public," Paris, 1934–39.

CALKINS, G. N., "Creation and International Recognition of title and security rights in aircraft," Journal of Air Law and Commerce, Vol. 15, No. 2 1948, p. 156.

CARABIBER, CH., "Les jurisdictions internationales de droit privé," Neufchatel, 1949.

CHARLIER, R. E., "Proposal to establish an International Court, Compte Rendu des Réunions de la Commission du CITEJA, Paris, Jan. 1946 (Doc. No. 487).

CHAUVEAU, P., "Droit Aérien," Paris, 1951.
Rapport sur la création d'une Court Internationale pour la solution des difficultés nées de l'Interprétation et de l'Application des Conventions Internationales en matière de Droit Aérien, International Law Association, Dubrovnik Conference, 1956.

CLEVERINGA, R. P., "Het Nieuwe Zeerecht," Zwolle, 1946.
Proposal to establish an International Court of Arbitration on maritime law and air law, submitted to the second Conference of the International Bar Association, The Hague, 1948.

COOPER, J. C., "The Legal Status of Aircraft," Princeton, 1949.
"The Right to Fly," New York, 1947.
"Roman Law and the Maxim of Cuius est Solum im International Air Law," Mc Gill Law Journal 23 (1952).

COQUOZ, R., "Le droit privé international aérien," Paris, 1938.

COÜANNIER, H., "De la nationalité et du domicile des aéronefs," Revue Juridique Internationale de la Locomotion Aérienne, 1910, p. 165.

DANIER, "Les voyages interplanétaires et le droit," Revue Générale de l'Air, No. 6, 1952.

DANILOVICS, P. DE, and SZONDY, V. DE, "Les infractions à la loi pénale commises à bord des aéronefs," Droit Aérien, 1930.

DAUS, E., "Die Luftschiffahrt in staats- und völkerrechtlicher Hinsicht," 1908.

DICEY, A. V., "Conflict of Laws" (6th ed., 1949, under the general editorship of J. H. C. Morris).

DRION, H., "Towards a uniform interpretation of the private air law

conventions," Journal of Air Law and Commerce, Vol. 19, Autumn 1952, No. 4, p. 426.
"The Council of ICAO as international legislator over the high seas," Estratto da "Studi in honore di Antonio Ambrosini," Varese.
FRANÇOIS, J. P. A., "Handboek voor het Volkenrecht," Zwolle, 1949.
FAUCHILLE, P., "Le domaine aérien et le régimé juridique des aérostats," Revue Générale de Droit International Public, VIII, 1901.
"La circulation aérienne et les droits des Etats en temps de paix," Revue Générale de Droit International Public, XVII, 1910.
GARNAULT, A., "L'exécution des jugements à l'étranger en droit aérien," International Law Association, Edinburgh Conference, 1954.
GIANNINI, A., "La nationalité des aéronefs," Revue aéronautique internationale No. 5, p. 318.
GIDEL, G., "La Clause Jurisdictionelle dans les Conventions d'Union notamment celles relatives à la Propriété Artistique et Litteraire, 39 Annuaire de l'Institut de Droit International (Brussels 1936) p. 248.
GOEDHUIS, D., "Handboek voor het Luchtrecht," Den Haag, 1943.
"Pacta sunt servanda," published in "Rechtskundige Opstellen aangeboden aan Professor Cleveringa," Zwolle, 1952, p. 20.
LE GOFF, M., "Traité Théorique et Pratique de Droit Aérien," Paris, 1934.
GOLDSTEIN, R., "La nouvelle législation aérienne Belge," Revue Française de Droit Aérien, avril-juin 1954, p. 115.
GOUDSMIT, J. J., "Het Internationale Ongeregelde Luchtvervoer en artikel 5 van het Verdrag van Chicago," Utrecht, 1953.
GULDIMANN, W., "Dingliche Rechte, besonders Pfandrechte an Flugzeugen," Schweizerische Juristenzeitung, 1948, p. 372.
"Le nouveau droit aérien suisse," Revue Française de Droit Aérien, No. 1. janvier-mars 1949.
HAMEL, J., "Nationalité et conflits de lois en droit aérien," Revue de droit international privé, 20 (1925).
HAZELTINE, H. D., "The Law of the Air," 1911.
HERSEY, "The International Law of Aerial Space," 6 American Journal of International Law, 1912, p. 317.
HILBERT, W. E., "Jurisdiction in High Seas Criminal Cases," Journal of Air Law and Commerce, 1951 and 1952.
HOFSTETTER, B., "L'hypothèque aérienne," Lausanne, 1950.
HONIG, J. P., "De positie van de Gezagvoerder van een Luchtvaartuig," Nederlands Juristenblad 1951, p. 317.
HOTCHKISS, H. G., "Aviation Law," 13 (2nd. ed.), 1938.
KAMMINGA, M. S., "The Aircraft Commander in Commercial Air Transportation," Leyden, 1953.
KARRER, M., "Die Einflusz der Souveränität im Luftraum auf die Abgrenzung des Privatrechts," Aarau, 1938.
VAN KLEFFENS, E. N., "Sovereignty in International Law," Recueil des Cours de l'Académie de Droit International, 1953.
KLEIN, H., "Staatsschiffe und Staatsluftfahrtzeuge in Völkerrecht."
KNAUTH, A. W., "Crime in the High Air, A Footnote to History," 25 Tulane L. Rev. 447, 460 (1950/51).
KROELL, J., "Eléments créateurs d'un droit astronautique," Revue Générale de l'Air, No. 3–4, 1953, p. 233.
KUNN, A. K., "Aerial Navigation in its Relation to International Law,"–

Proceedings of American Political Science Association, 5th Annual Meeting, 1908, p. 85.
LACOUR et RIESE, "Précis de Droit Aérien," Paris/Lausanne, 1951.
LEMOINE, M., "Traité de Droit Aérien," Paris 1947.
LITVINE, M., "Précis Elémentaire de Droit Aérien," Bruxelles, 1953.
LOAEZA, E. M., "Progress Report on the Legal Status of Aircraft," ICAO L. C. Working Draft 230, 20–12–'50.
LORTSCH, CH., "Le Statut Juridique du Passager d'Aéronef," Revue de Droit Aérien, Vol., 13, 1929, pp. 7 et seq.
LIJCKLAMA à NIJEHOLT, J., "Luchtvaart in het Volkenrecht," Leyden, 1910.
MANDL, W., "La nationalité des aéronefs n'est qu'un dénomination erronée," Droit Aérien 1931, p. 161.
MEILI, F., "Das Luftschiff im internen Recht und Völkerrecht," Zürich, 1908.
MEURER, CH., "Luftschiffahrtrecht," Zeitschrift für internationales privat und öffentliches Recht, 1909.
MEYER, A., "Crimes et délits à bord des aéronefs," Revue Générale de l'Air 1946, p. 544.
"Rechtliche Probleme des Weltraumflugs," Probleme aus der Astronautischen Grundlagenforschung (Stuttgart: Vorträge gehalten auf dem III Internationalen Astronautischen Kongress, 1952).
MILCH, W., "Die Luftfahrzeughypothek," Berlin, 1930.
MONTELLA, R. G., de "La personalité de l'aéronef et la publicité aéronautique en droit espagnol," Revue Française de Droit Aérien, 1949, p. 137.
MORPURGO, E., "Quelques considerations sur les conflits internationals de juridiction en matière pénale aéronautique à propos de la mort du banquier Loewenstein," Revue Juridique Internationale de Locomotion Aérienne, 1928, p. 397.
MC NAIR, A. D., "The Law of the Air," 1953.
NIBOYET, J. P., "Traité de droit international privé français," 6 Vol., Paris, 1947.
NIEMEIJER, V., "Crimes et délits à bord des aéronefs," Revue de Droit Aérien, 1929, p. 285.
NYS, E., "Le régime juridique des aéronefs," Institut de Droit International, Annuaire 1902.
OMTA, L. W. F. H., "Immuniteit van Staatsschepen en- ladingen en van Staatsluchtvaartuigen," Amsterdam, 1938.
OPPIKOFER, H., "Actuelle Probleme des Luftrechts," Zeitschrift für Schweizerisches Recht, 1946, p. 192.
PHOLIEN, M., "Des Crimes et Délits à bord d'aéronefs en vol," Revue de Droit Aérien, 1929, p. 289.
DE PLANTA, F., "Principes de droit international privé applicables aux actes accomplis et aux faits commis à bord d'un aéronef," Geneva, 1955.
PLANIOL, M. & RIPERT, G., "Traité Pratique de Droit Civil Français," 1943.
PRADELLE, P. DE LA, Proposal submitted to the 38th Conference of the International Law Association, Budapest 1934, Report of the Thirty-eighth Conference, pp. 294–302.
RICHARDS, E. H., "Sovereignty over the Air," Oxford, 1912.

RIESE, O., "Luftrecht," Stuttgart, 1949.

ROPER, A., "La Convention Internationale du 13 octobre 1919," Paris 1930.

ROUSSEAU, CH., "L'Indépendance de l'Etat dans l'Ordre International," Recueil des Cours de L'Académie de Droit International, 1948 11.

RIJKS, K., "Het Verdrag van Genève betreffende internationale erkenning van rechten op luchtvaartuigen," Leyden, 1952.

SAPORTA, M., "Crise de Croissance du Droit International Aérien," Revue Générale de l'Air, 1955, No. 2.

SCHACHTER, "Legal Aspects of Space Travel," Journal of the British Interplanetary Society, Jan. 1952, p. 14.

SCELLE, G., "Préface des Libertés de l'Air," Paris, 1948.

SCHREIBER, O., "Principles of a draft convention on nationality of aircraft (prepared for the Air transport Committee of the International Chamber of Commerce, 1929).

SHAWCROSS and BEAUMONT, "Air Law," London, 1950.

SMIRNOFF, M., "Le CITEJA," Paris, 1936.

SPAIGHT, J. M., "Aircraft in Peace and the Law," 1919.

STANESCO, D. N., "La Responsabilité dans la Navigation Aérienne," Paris, 1951.

STEIDLE, W. K., "Das Luftfahrzeug als Begehungsort strafbarer Handlungen," Cologne, 1934.

SUDRE, E., "Le CITEJA," Revue Générale de l'Air, 1946.

TAYLOR, T. K., "A practical Reconcialation of State and Federal Control," Journal of Air Law and Commerce, 1941.

DE VISSCHER, F., "Les Conflits de Lois en Matière de Droit Aérien," Recueil des Cours de L'Académie de Droit International à la Haye, 1934, p. 279.

VOLKMANN, K., "Crimes et délits à bord des aéronefs en droit international," Droit Aérien, 1931.

WAGNER, W., "Les Libertés de l'Air," Paris, 1948.

WILBERFORCE, R. O., "The International Recognition of Rights in Aircraft," International Law Quarterly, 1948, p. 421.

WOLFF, M., "Das Internationale Privatrecht Deutschlands," Göttingen-Heidelberg, 1949.

ZITELMANN, E., "Luftschiffahrtsrecht," Zeitschrift für internationales privat- und öffentliches Recht, Vol. 19, 1909.

ZONDAG, C. H. G. M., "Neutraliteit in de Lucht," Leyden, 1940.

Periodicals consulted

American Aviation Daily
American Journal of International Law
Annuaire de l'Institut de Droit International
Archiv für Luftrecht
McGill Law Journal
Journal of Air Law and Commerce
Journal of the British Interplanetary Society
Nederlands Juristenblad
Revue Aéronautique Internationale
Recueil des Cours de l'Académie de Droit International à la Haye

Revue de Droit Aérien
Revue Française de Droit Aérien
Revue de Droit International et de Législation Comparée
Revue de Droit International Privé
Revue Juridique Internationale de la Locomotion Aérienne
Revue Générale de Droit International et Public
Revue Générale de l'Air
Revue Générale de Droit Aérien
Schweizerische Juristen Zeitung
Zeitschrift für internationales privat- und öffentliches Recht
Zeitschrift für Luftrecht
Zeitschrift für Schweizeriches Recht

International Conventions

Paris Convention of October 13, 1919, relating to the regulation of aerial navigation.
Madrid Convention of November 1, 1926 (the Ibero-American Convention)
Havana Convention of February 10, 1928, on commercial aviation.
Chicago Convention of December 7, 1944, on international civil aviation.
Warsaw Convention of October 12, 1929, for the unification of certain rules relating to international carriage by air.
Rome Convention of May 29, 1933, for the unification of certain rules relating to the precautionary arrest of aircraft.
Brussels Convention of 1938 on assistance and salvage of aircraft at sea.
Geneva Convention of June 19, 1948, on the international recognition of rights in aircraft.
Rome Convention of October 7, 1952, on damage caused by foreign aircraft to third parties on the surface.

Documents consulted

Annuaire de l'Institut de Droit International (Institute of International Law)

Vol. 19, 1902
1906
Vol. 23, 1910
Vol. 24, 1911

Comité Juridique International de l'Aviation

Compte Rendu 1e Congrès, Paris, 1911
" " 3e " Frankfurt, 1913
" " 4e " Monaco, 1921
" " 6e " Rome, 1924
" " 9e " Budapest, 1930

International Law Association

Report of the 27th Conference, Paris, 1912
„ „ „ 28th „ Madrid, 1913
„ „ „ 29th „ Portsmouth, 1920
„ „ „ 31st „ Buenos Aires, 1922
„ „ „ 33rd „ Stockholm, 1924
„ „ „ 38th „ Budapest, 1934
„ „ „ 44th „ Copenhagen, 1950
„ „ „ 45th „ Lucerne, 1952

Conférence de la Paix, 1919–1920
Recueil des actes de la conférence, Partie VII.

Comité International Technique d'Experts Juridiques Aériens

CITEJA Doc. No. 17
„ „ „ 32
„ „ „ 37
„ „ „ 50
„ „ „ 73
„ „ „ 108
„ „ „ 128
„ „ „ 162
„ „ „ 239
„ „ „ 293
„ „ „ 298
„ „ „ 334
„ „ „ 362
„ „ „ 434
„ „ „ 468
„ „ „ 493
„ „ „ 496

International Civil Aviation Organization

ICAO Doc. 4006
„ „ 4635–LC/71, 5–9–47
„ „ 5722
„ „ 6894–AT/694, 26–8–49
„ „ 7008–AT/702, 27–6–50
„ „ 7364
„ „ 7379–LC/34

Working papers
ICAO CWP/382, 18–8–49
„ AT/WP/206, 27–2–51
„ WP/10–EC/5, 23–3–53

Working Drafts
ICAO LC Working Draft 230, 20–12–50
„ „ „ „ 395, 15–5–53

Proceedings of the Chicago Conference,
Nov. 1–Dec. 7, 1944.

INDEX

STELLINGEN

I

Artikel 3 van het Verdrag van Chicago dient te worden gewijzigd in dien zin, dat een limitatieve opsomming wordt gegeven van de luchtvaartuigen, welke als staatsluchtvaartuigen moeten worden beschouwd.

II

Het is wenselijk, dat de rechtspositie van de gezagvoerder van luchtvaartuigen in een internationaal verdrag zijn regeling vindt.

III

Indien aan eigenaren of houders van motorrijtuigen bij de wet een verplichting tot verzekering tegen schade met motorrijtuigen aan derden toegebracht, wordt opgelegd, verdient het aanbeveling in deze wet tevens op te nemen de mogelijkheid van een rechtstreekse actie van de gelaedeerde tegen de verzekeraar.

IV

In artikel 61 van de Grondwet ware aan te geven welke overeenkomsten met andere mogendheden ter stilzwijgende goedkeuring aan de Staten-Generaal kunnen worden voorgelegd en voor welke overeenkomsten goedkeuring slechts bij de wet kan worden verleend.

V

Het uitoefenen van de luchtvaart dient nimmer als een inbreuk op de eigendom van de grond, waarboven zij wordt uitgeoefend, te worden beschouwd.

VI

De wet laat toe, dat de aanleg en exploitatie van telegrafen en telefonen niet uitsluitend door of met machtiging van het Staatsbedrijf der Posterijen, Telegrafie en Telefonie, doch eveneens door overheidsdiensten geschiedt.

VII

Het verdient aanbeveling de bevoegdheid van ambtenaren met de opsporing van strafbare feiten belast te doen samenvallen met de geografische werkingsfeer van het Wetboek van Strafrecht en deze bevoegdheid niet tot bepaalde gebieden te beperken.

VIII

Het gebruik van de n.v. vorm voor overheidsinstellingen is onjuist.

IX

Kennis van de elementaire beginselen van de wiskunde heeft voor de jurist groter waarde dan algemeen wordt aangenomen.

X

Zolang burgerluchtvaart ook op andere dan commerciële basis wordt uitgeoefend, zal steun van de overheid aan luchtvaartmaatschappijen onvermijdelijk zijn.

SAMENVATTING

De bedoeling van deze studie is geweest het vraagstuk van de rechtstoestand van het luchtvaartuig in zijn geheel te bezien.

Begonnen werd met uit een te zetten hoe de souvereiniteit van de verschillende Staten over het luchtruim boven hun grondgebied van invloed is op de rechtstoestand van het zich in dat luchtruim bevindende luchtvaartuig. Het feit toch, dat de Staten deze souvereiniteit uitoefenen brengt mede, dat aan het internationale luchtverkeer beperkingen kunnen en helaas ook worden opgelegd. Onafwendbaar komt hier een verschillend optreden tegenover luchtvaartuigen uit eigen en uit andere landen uit voort. Nederland eens de verdediger van de vrije zee, is ook als voorvechter van de vrijheid in de lucht in het krijt getreden. De bestaande internationale regelingen geven het beginsel van de vrije lucht slechts een beperkte ontwikkelingsmogelijkheid. Voor onze studie van belang is, dat de Staten om het luchtverkeer met luchtvaartuigen gedomicilieerd in andere Staten te kunnen beperken, deze luchtvaartuigen gaan onderscheiden van de nationale luchtvaartuigen. Overgegaan werd zodoende tot het toekennen van een nationaliteit aan luchtvaartuigen om deze daardoor tot een bepaalde Staat in betrekking te kunnen brengen. Deze nationaliteit van het luchtvaartuig wordt tot uiting gebracht door inschrijving in het nationale luchtvaartuigregister. Een dergelijke inschrijving schept echter geen nationaliteit, maar is het bewijs ervan. Iedere Staat kan voor zich zelf uitmaken aan welke voorwaarden een luchtvaartuig moet voldoen om zijn nationaliteitskenmerken te mogen voeren.

Uitdrukkelijk vastgesteld wordt, dat luchtvaartuigen roerende goederen zijn, zij het met een eigen karakter. Dit laatste blijkt o.m uit het bestaan van privaatrechtelijke luchtvaartuigregisters in een aantal landen en de van normale roerende goederen afwijkende wijze van eigendomsverkrijging in die landen. Steeds meer Staten gaan voorts tot bekrachtiging over van de in 1948 te

Genève tot stand gekomen internationale regeling, welke de mogelijkheid tot het vestigen van hypotheek op luchtvaartuigen opent.

Een belangrijk facet van de rechtstoestand van het luchtvaartuig vormt het vraagstuk van de wetstoepassing en rechtsbevoegdheid met betrekking tot aan boord van het luchtvaartuig verrichte rechtshandelingen. In onze studie toonden we aan, dat toepassing van een enkel beginsel niet tot een oplossing kan leiden. Het in eerste instantie van toepassing zijn van de wet van de vlag op de aan boord van het luchtvaartuig plaatshebbende rechtshandelingen wordt door ons het meest rationeel geacht. Concessies aan de territoriale rechtsorde worden evenwel onvermijdelijk en noodzakelijk geacht. Wil een getroffen regeling internationaal aanvaardbaar zijn, dan zal met de belangen van de overgevlogen Staten rekening moeten worden gehouden. Deze belangen vragen bescherming door de nationale wet. Deze nationale wet zal echter slechts dan toepassing mogen vinden wanneer de betrokken rechthandeling ook inderdazd de nationale belangen raakt.

Hetzelfde vraagpunt doet zich op met betrekking tot aan boord van het luchtvaartuig gepleegde strafbare feiten. Toepassing van de wet van het land, welks vlag het luchtvaartuig voert stuit hier op nog beduidend meer souvereiniteitsgevoeligheden dan bij de bovengenoemde rechtshandelingen. Ook hier zal dus naar een compromis tussen nationaliteits- en territorialiteitsbeginsel, naar een gemengd systeem derhalve, gezocht moeten worden.

We komen tot de slotsom, dat ten aanzien van de zuiver technische regelen met betrekking tot het luchtvaartuig in belangrijke mate een internationale eenheid tot stand is gebracht. Ten aanzien van de rechtstoestand van het luchtvaartuig als zodanig blijft echter nog veel te wensen over. Door ons wordt voorgestaan de totstandkoming van een verdrag regelende de rechtstoestand van het luchtvaartuig. Het vraagstuk van de wetstoepassing en jurisdictie met betrekking tot rechtshandelingen en strafbare feiten, welke aan boord van luchtvaartuigen hebben plaats gehad zouden hierin een regeling moeten vinden. Aan deze regeling zou toepassing van de wet en jurisdictie van de Staat, welks vlag het luchtvaartuig voert in beginsel ten grondslag moeten liggen.

Batch number: 10830943

Printed by Printforce, the Netherlands